VOYAGING TO WADADLY

A Personal Journey

Virgil Demery

Demery Studios

2020

To
Aimé Césaire, and Douglas MacArthur Johnson
&
Cousin Lute, who said, when I was four years old,
"That boy can lie, he must gawn be a lawyer."

David,
I hope you enjoy
the read.

Virgil

Part One

LET THE LIGHT SHINE

1

Every day I drink. Sometimes, I almost remember how much. I also smoke weed (but only the good stuff). These heavenly drafts spottily wash my mind of time. I awake and start each day without knowing much of what has lain between evening and sunrise. I am probably not very happy with how I am living now, but I live, and I work; I earn my way. I do not accept anything from anyone. This is the creed of my colored world, though here, it does not rest on its old moral rock: "Upon this rock I will build my church." One hundred feet up from the bottom of Long Part, a serpentine cut in the backbone of a hill, I rent a perch and look out upon another hillside decked with perches just like mine. Nests butt-pegged into bitching stone, with forelegs stretching down, searching the slope for the touch of stony ground. You can plainly see; I am still tied; I have not fully left my Catholic upbringing. For I have foundered on a rock, a rock in the sea—Saint Thomas. I wish I had a woman; I think I would be happier. I am so tired of my right hand. That mute wench serves and then abandons me once it uncouples. No love, just the release and the spilled seed, clumping on silent ground.

There is no alarm clock in my room but, without fail, I will wake, put on my construction clothes and meet Edward Hart's truck at 6:35 every weekday morning. I have no will in this action, it is a duty, shackled on to my unwilling body by words from my past, "Boy, do your chores." Ten other men riding in the truck's bed are sitting on planks, nodding or covering the relevant universes with their chat. I do not understand these black men or their talk. Words beat into my ears, leaving me bloated by sound and yet stuffed with ignorance. Some want to talk of sex, but most do not; I follow this much.

Rose and Biggie bring their non-carnal interests to bear. Usually, they prevail; gambling and cricket rule the airways. I know nothing of cricket besides its name. Players, positions, actions, and strategies are all discussed in an English that baffles my ears. As the days lay enveloped in bewilderment, it finally dawns. Not one English, many types of English are being spoken. Words and Names emerge, night watch men, Sir Garfield Sobers, slip, stump, pace bowlers, spin bowlers, overs, and more. I hear that West Indian cricket rules. The former Caribbean colonies beat England, the old motherland, and all her other progeny as if they were unloved stepchildren; "Call me New Daddy!" I learn these things and more as the dimwitted do, with difficulty baked on top of public scorn. Constantly my fellow workers remark on my dullness, "Boy, you need some nooky to clear out yoh brains." I say nothing; I do my job.

But the old world, my first world, is leaching out memories of humid New Orleans, where sweat had been the master and the solvent of summer days. Alive, sentient, and above all, wise, this new place has opened its pores and is drawing in those reminiscences. Vaguely I am aware of something; my green eyes are not fully accustomed to the bright tropic light. Regardless, a dark-hued Bacchus has been stuffing my days into a conch shell full of savory excess, which is rousing my Mardi Gras appetite. I must fall, I am falling, I have fallen, face first, onto this pearly-pink horn-of-plenty. I nurse from its hard nipple; I need new strength. In the distance, the carnival entourage of unknown gods moves to the ringing sounds of steel drums. This procession, steadily stamping, is coming my way. Bacchanal will tread over me.

"bac·cha·nal n: somebody who took part in the orgiastic rites of the god Bacchus; a riotous drunken reveler (literary); a noisy drunken celebration or spree (literary) adj: relating to Bacchus or the worship of Bacchus

Bac·cha·na·lia n: ancient Roman festivities in honor of Bacchus that involved orgiastic rites (takes a singular or plural verb)

Bac·chus n: in classical mythology, the god of wine, identified with the Greek god Dionysus and the Roman god Liber. He was worshiped with orgiastic and ecstatic rites."

"Hey, I want to be your friend." I know the man as Boy Blue. He lives at the foot of Long Part. We board the truck at the same place. "Ok."

With my new friendship, I drink no less, in fact, more, and my whoring frequency does not rise. Mondays still bring eyes that burn, sanded with the grit of too little sleep and too much undigested rum. But other workers begin a running comment that finally puts Boy Blue and me in the same fraternity. "Look at their eyes. Them red!" Now, walking as brothers, we feel the land quiver.

Time and Boy Blue's help bring my ears back from the lost regions and reunite them with my understanding. The words of the sundry West Indians that have begun to ripen now open; first off, the morning ride loses its confusing jumble. Relentlessly, every morning, Biggie talks, in his stuttering Kittitian chat, of sports, and daily tells everyone of his prowess. Powerfully built and agile, his life is a living frustration. In some other place he could be giving reign to his might, flinging aside lesser men, and moving as juggernaut among them. Here, he must be content with hoisting gigantic loads of building materials and hectoring for his superiority. Kittitian Rose's plump flesh bounces as he animates his devotion to and love of chance. The cards or the dice fall as they may, but the sweetness of each downward trajectory pumps his heartbeat full of pulsing rhythms. Rose can no more stop gambling than eating, and he wins, not big, but often.

As my ears continue to open, my tongue begins to loosen. Blue and I each like to chat, but we never jostle for podium time. Boy Blue's style tends toward the lyrical. He sets his heart for the day when out of his mouth will glide words, sweetened with the rhythms of poems he remembers, that will render the listening woman helpless. So ensnared, she will bare her breasts and open her legs without regard.

I, Red-man (the second of my many names, Yankee had been the first, and, Yellow-man, the third) talk, in fits and starts, of Rimbaud, Paul Klee, and stars. Mine is a miss-timed engine, where fuel ignites but turns no gears that will remove panties. Content with this, I deserve no more because I actually say nothing. My library of words comes from Babel, where meaning had been lost amidst the din of misunderstanding. Deferring to Boy Blue when we meet women, I wait for the miracle of a singular logical-brevity to bracket-and-compress my words. "It is a beautiful thing, the destruction of words." Seeking the simplicity and rigidity of an "INGSOC" synaptic connection, I will short-speak, then the woman will want sex. In addition, personally, I would rather refrain from talk while screwing. I found this out when once I tried sex-and-talk. The vocal cords went flaccid; I became mute. This didn't bother me because I had come to my truth: why talk? What could be said with words that made fucking more real? Flesh is the sovereign; words are sycophantic courtiers (except, perhaps, the affirmation "Yes"). These notions both contradict teachings from my Catholic youth and give judgment on the sex-talk men. Now able to comprehend, I see them as pretenders.

Without pause, every day these men pound women between their mouth and tongue. They lie in this labor, until they are sure that they have reduced "woman" to its essence of caltrop-grit. Then come the slick licks about condescending, dominating sex. Only this makes bearable, to them, any contact with that gender. Too much pussy chat, they're jive. The recognition of this old cardinal sin, within the free prattle of these new men, is comforting; my eyes are blinking less.

2

Saint Thomas, The Gilded Rock, or maybe The Golden Egg, with its haunted history of sea trading and being traded, has gotten yet another identity. The island needs suitable accommodations to properly bear its new title: tourist destination. Tourist comforts are what it must provide. The eastern end of the harbor of Charlotte Amalie, Year of Our Lord 1971, has become the site of a prolonged resurrection. It is happening at a modest old hotel, whose western panorama catches the full belly of the harbor, and then sweeps out to the southwestern tip of the island. On the eastern side of the resort there will be an outside elevator, supported by a structure crusted to the land with gunite. Hotel guests will ride, from the air-conditioned heights to the warm sand-beach below, in a glass cage. In it (if they look toward the east) they can see the something or the nothing of the Caribbean waters moving toward the hidden cataract on the horizon.

"Yanki;" "Yaankii;" "Yankii;" "…;" only Boy Blue calls me by my given name. He and I meet at the bottom of Long Part each weekday. **I never miss my ride**! My altar-boy training, from my Catholic youth in New Orleans, proves its worth.

Twelve years old and serving at five AM Mass meant getting up at four. Being late was unacceptable and it brought layers of chastisement, each with its own laminate of guilt. My body learned to uncover itself and dress whether in the bone chilling damp-cold of winter or the stifling indolence of summer.

Flesh has a memory that goes past choice. I never miss my ride, but on some mornings the mass of my flesh quivers and labors, needing to hasten the decomposition of the cannabis and the alcohol into their less-menacing metabolites. Hangovers (even mere inattention) on construction projects can give a remarkably swift ride to the land of the dead.

Mornings are less difficult for Boy Blue; he never gets toasted. He drinks and he smokes, but he moderates his intake, refusing, by inclination, to be in public displaying a rattled brain. And, he lives at the lower road junction where Heart picks up his riders. I must descend from the upper road, High Road, which is joined to the lower road by four series of stairs, which give choices of alternate ways down. Generally, I use the first set at the foot of Long Path, which ends near the cul-de-sac at the head of the road. These steps are the grandest and the safest; I never tumble down. But on those nights and pre-dawns, when the climbing of the eighty-nine steps sways on sweet delirium, I must negotiate with repentance&luck to maintain an upright posture. A stout railing remains a trusted ally.

The other sets of stairs, all without railings, are less forgiving with their steep, narrow steps. On each side of every set are houses, tucked away, and approached only by narrow paths. The assumption, on the part of the builders, that everyone who uses these stairs and paths should render gravity benign, reminds me of the colored, non-white, section of the Orpheum Theater in New Orleans. *It was beautiful and frightening, a perfect mélange of segregated opposites. We, the colored patrons, bought our tickets at the side entrance and then climbed. As a small child, the windowless spiral seemed unending, but when it did open, I looked out and down upon a screen that dwarfed every other movie screen available to Negroes. On it, colored performers, shackled to the roles of buffoons and menials, were watched by their kind, in our place, which was so steeply raked, from the ceiling down to the ornate balcony railing, as to be terrifying to me (spider crawling was not uncommon going up to the highest levels), and unlawful by any sane building code. The parting, between the nappy-headed coloreds upstairs and the whites' down, was thick with coarseness.* Long Path's accommodations are far less crude.

Blue rarely comes up the hill, so Long Path belongs to Red-man. I grow comfortable in this new place, and the people of Long Path grow comfortable with seeing this young stranger who has come amongst them. My tiny room opens inside out; it becomes part of the neighborhood public.

"Ronnie, no!" heard as "Raw aw aw ni no!" is the phrase I associate with being in my room. Perversely, one weekend, I count how many times this strident, negative angelus comes from the house across the street: forty-seven.

Ronnie, no more than six years old, lives with his mother's family, his mother and her vocal discipline. There are never the sounds of blows or the boy crying, and Ronnie appears occasionally, especially when his father comes either for a visit or to take him on an outing. Despite the latter evidence, Ronnie is of a spectral quality, which contrasts strongly with his maternal kin, the Beauchamps. They are people of substance. His grandfather is a dough-man, who seems to be poised at every second to sink upon himself. His affinity with the earth carries through to his stride: a short, shuffling gait, with his feet rising no higher than the dust on the road. He drives a taxi-van. His wife, an attractive and solid woman, in her early fifties, works in an office on Main Street. The two daughters are pretty young women. The older one, Ronnie's mother, never smiles, as I can remember. The younger has a compact, generous body. She smiles at me and says hello. This has planted her in my heart, and lust falls like hard, steady rain upon that small patch of ground. I long to see her face, gentle and smiling, next to mine in my room. Then I would mount her and lose myself in the oblivion of tender kisses and genitals united. I blend my desire into this sweet dream for it is the only possible form of sex between us. She will not consider me as a real partner because she is a Frenchie, and I am not. The island's innards begin to reveal themselves.

On Saint Thomas, Louisiana Cajuns have become Frenchies, who are noted as fishermen, farmers, and for being a distinct ethnic group. In marriage, reputedly, they keep to themselves. Whatever Frenchies think concerning race escapes me. My slight interaction with them reveals only fun-loving people, many of whom are doubled-red in complexion: fair-skinned people who take in both large amounts of rum and a great deal of sun. This West Indian reality resonated softly with the Creole dynamic in New Orleans. Regardless of the origins of the word Creole, its evolution had led the term to one common, local meaning, light-skinned coloreds, with certain types of features, who had a habit of intermarriage. Some could and did "passé blanc." Lack of the following: good hair (above all), a nice nose, and not-large lips were the genetic tickets to the steeply pitched sluice from Creole to plain Negro. The South's truth is much less sweet than in the West Indies, where barriers, of all kinds, are assaulted by waves of food, rum, music, and, I suspect, loose britches—after looking in Frenchtown bars on weekends. Red-man is a very slow learner.

4

One Monday two strange men, both in non-construction-site clothes, approach me. One is a tall, thin white man; the other is a short, stocky black man. Behind the men I see activity. There are scurrying movements, and outright bolting by some workers. Wonderment causes me to stop, which allows the twosome to get within speaking distance. The boldness of their approach shows a lack of respect. They do not belong here and if they want information, I certainly am not the one to ask. I hard face them. The black man speaks roughly, "Where were you born?" A maelstrom of indignation arises. It emerged as a bellicose "New Orleans! Why?" The short man modestly says, "I thought so." Angry confusion at this clairvoyance is mounting when the white man, who has been scanning the location, said, "Hey Joe, they are heading for the bush." Both men leave and quickly move toward the hillside. Bewildered, I ask somebody "Who are those two?" The response, in a hushed, awed tone is "Immigration."

"Immigration?"

I seek out Blue, who explains. The fleeing men do not have "papers." They are in the VI illegally. Immigration's job is to collect these people and deport them. "Oh!" The world of the non-citizen suddenly emerges. After the "alien roundup," work then proceeds as normal, but during that day, there are small cluster groups where whisperings take place. At quitting time tongues are set free and the situation is discussed openly. The construction of the tourist industry on St. Thomas has amalgamated elements that hold together only provisionally. Blue and his kin and the fleeing men are elements that are from "down island." This descriptive phrase, pejorative in implication, couples with the legal synonym: alien. The people I work with everyday are of two possible types: those who can squat comfortably, or those who can sit only upon a hard, thorny cushion. I hear of a "green card" more sought after, by aliens, than green dollars. It is a reverse teleportation device. Aliens (usually black people) go nowhere; the card grounds them on US soil. The noun alien, to naïve Yankee who has gorged himself on sci-fi during his youth, always produces the picture in my brain of an odd-shaped creature. Blue, however, is my brother, born on the earth. Blue, defined legally as an alien, should not have had meaning on our common birth world. That is until Yankee remembers the hue and stamp of his own birth paper.

In my juvenile memory, the nested sets around my world are all bound to a putrid core. *The chimes rang in St. Louis Cathedral, located in Jackson Square, which was in New Orleans, Louisiana in The United States of America—my birthplace. Then the mouth of a rotund, white policeman, stationed in the French Quarter, opened, "Boy, what chew doing down here? You ain't working." Yankee turned around and caught the Feret Bus and sat behind the sign "For the seating of colored patrons only," and rode home. I fumed at the officer's mirthful intimidation, which was sanctioned by law. Near the Garden District, I got off the bus, one and a half blocks from my house. It was the same bus stop for Flint Goodrich Hospital of Dillard University. I had been born there. Doctor Coffee, a colored, female obstetrician, known for her strict manner, had delivered me, a "colored" baby. By birth document, I was certified as a costumed alien. In the words of the white politicians, "Another 'Nigra' has been added to the 'Nigra' population of the Crescent City."*

5

In contrast, the island's freewheeling tourist-trade shuttles enormous numbers of people through its narrow roads. Most come on cruise ships that usually stay for the daylight hours. In late afternoon, the boat horns begin signaling upcoming departures. As this exodus must ensue, taxi-drivers turn from small predations to school fishing. They seek to load their vans to the crammed, legal limits with the departing tourists. "Back to the ship," the standard cry of the taxi-drivers, is put on quick repeat. Its rapid uptake produces the sight of weary, sun-scorched travelers, hauling and packing themselves into the transports. The landlubbers, newly transmuted, both want and need the cool haven of their floating hotels. The enervating struggles to find the best deals, for the staple proofs-of-the-voyage: liquor, cigarettes, and t-shirts have been part of their fun. Haggling, even over a penny, was made bruising by having to bump-navigate down choked Main Street. The transients are winding down their onshore day by the time Blue and I finish work. Our socializing will not be done with these, the ones that come and go with the tide. We mingle with the large tourist-connected population that simmers in the pepper-pot heat from sunset until dawn.

Evenings on St. Thomas offer as many choices for action as there are rums to be sampled at A.H. Riise Liquor Store. Most of the rums are imported and many of the action spots have foreign flavor. Choosing? It is all a matter of tastes. But if one dislikes "anti-man" then many chic places are not options. Red-man has never heard of an exclusively gay bar. Gay people, both local and imported—one had sought directions for "a place where there was some cultured gay fun"—are just a large part of the nightlife. My feeling looking at gay men frolic is akin to watching an imagined animation drawn by the engraver Granville in his series *Un Autre Monde*, Another World indeed. Blue's issue is with decorum; he feels that a certain courtship ritual, which some "anti-man" publicly display, should be done in private surroundings. I call it the desire-of-acquisition dance. It is an unctuous, driven performance, where their longing to be penetrated is expressed to the object they crave: the coveted man who would wield his sprouted "bud" upon them as an impaling maypole. Their flesh moves them to act; it is their way. This doesn't frighten or threaten me. Gay men are constructed differently. On rare occasions, a sledgehammer alters the construction. A pas de deux begot of rum, hastily started near bar-closing time, turns lethal. An uncertain man, who had been pervaded by lust, suffered from guilt and loathing after "throwing his water." His self-deprecation is extracting the life from the body that he has been allowed to use. Crudely appropriating an old saying, I thought it came down to, "If you can't stand that fuck, then keep the prick out."

Some men, like "anti-man hater," openly preach disgust and hatred for gays, but as our fraternity explores the night, complex interactions between straights and gays seem to emerge. These are part of a larger set of relationships whose origins are both ad hoc and fundamental. Like it or not, daily life approaches a spirit akin to that of Mardi Gras. Pleasure and mirth for all, in the full human venue, is abundant enough, so that only a true "stinking ass" cannot find something or somewhere that would lead them to "cool out." Live and let live; it works.

We move among the rum shops, the whore bars, and the calypso clubs. I take to the phrase "mariposas de la noche" (night butterflies) in referring to putas because it has a beautiful sound. Then I learn the following implication: mariposa means butterfly = fairy = faggot: maricon in crude Spanish. When told this, Blue points out that regardless of its beauty, to express a fondness for anything by using the word "mariposa" could cause problems. This makes sense.

Jimbo's, a Santo Domingo bar, run by Jimbo, is a puta bar. I see profound beauty in the aging putas. Where this appreciation arises from in my sensibilities remains unknown. But the soft, generous bodies of these weighty butterflies seem sacred; I am compelled to honor them. The words I find beautiful crown their flesh. The stateside boys, who find the bimbos at Jimbo's, slake themselves upon these holy mounds. Emerging from the rank, hot cubbyholes where they fucked are changed male beings. They are, more than likely, still drunk, but they act less like asses, curbing their desire to fight. Jimbo, this service provider, is of a coarser strain than many of his clients.

One night, at Jimbo's, a dog finds its way up the steep set of stairs and enters. The bar must seem commodious, so the stray goes to the middle of the room and craps. Everyone looks. The mongrel senses the tardy but rising tide of annoyance. Harsh words are then thrown at it. In its panic flight, the mutt smooches down and smears some of its waste. The pile of slightly crushed shit sits in the middle of floor. Cries go out to Jimbo to rectify the situation. Jimbo obliges; he puts a chair over the heap and walks away. For a moment, silence, then the raised voices of patrons begin. "Nooh, Jimbo!"; "No man."; "You got to clean dat up!"; "Ah what di fuck?" Blue and I look at each other, nod toward the door, and leave.

6

"Concrete! Concrete coming, boys," shouted out, by Heart, brings everyone to attention. The concrete resurrection must rise.

The regular concrete men are from Dominica. They are noisy with their French patois, masters of this strength-task, and indefatigable. Luck and past training, in time, push me away from such spheres entirely. Yankee knows decimals, so Yankee is instructed in how to read the transit. Then the foreman, Mr. Shirl, sends me below into the piss-wafted, dank forest of the screw jacks, which supports the weight of the decking. I must ensure a level decking throughout its extent for the next pour. To achieve this balance, I sight and then direct those who turn the screw-jack adjusters and insert the shims in the T-jacks. I'm not their boss, so the relationship is always tenuous, and occasionally outright unproductive. Some of the men, sometimes, refuse either to work or to cooperate; in a way, this pleases me. It is pleasant to know that they are assholes, not white assholes; that psychic gravity is not present. But a job has to be done, and if not done, Yankee will be faulted, so I adjust the jacks myself. My relief comes from the transposed truth of a chain gang ditty. ♫♫ "They had a big white man on a big white horse. We didn't know his name, but we called him boss. Each day he came to supervise, with a great big pistol right by his side." Eventually, Heart or Mr. Shirl (the big men) come below and see the "fuckery" being done. The pistol of "you're fired," exposed merely by their presence, has no need to be cocked. The assholes go back to work, and the lazy men cannot fault Yankee, for I never say a word to anyone.

Blue inserts himself in the project by being valuable to his supervisor. The two-chambered heart of his talent lay in reliability and intelligence. His portfolio is that of the aide-de-camp, but the liability of the job means that a new boss might mean a new assistant. Blue has Mercury's winged sandals, but without securing straps. I have permanent troll-lodgings beneath every un-poured floor.

Hoppy, Blue's boss, dresses in an orange jump suit and wears a cowboy hat and "talks" like a Texan. The only baggage Blue carries is the memory of his delight of cowboy movies. Blue loves, with sincere devotion, spaghetti westerns. Their glow illuminates Hoppy.

To Yankee, Hoppy is an unknown; but his cow-boyish intimations rankle, in so many ways, that it keeps my mind darkly loaded against the man's real personality. Hostile mummery and bad taste are the central elements in the dislike. I grew up loving cowboys and westerns, both in the movies and on TV. At Christmas there could not have been grander presents than a cowboy hat and a cap shooting set of six-guns. But knowingly, these western delights all lay thickly robed in make-believe. The only people I saw wearing both guns and uniforms were the police, and among these white men there were neither noble sentiments displayed, nor heroic postures adopted. They were empowered brutes in sunglasses, avoidance of whose attention was the highest priority every colored person had.

SOBER BLACK KNOWLEDGE (circa 1963) from inside "THE MA-DRONNA LOUNGE": "Nobody ain fraid no police, but you know that they can kill you and nothing ain gon be done about it."

Hoppy resonates with a cinematic fantasy, which had been molded in flesh by the police, who believed in six shooting. "Shoot that 'black some bitch' six times; make sho."

Cowboys also are not allowed into real life, as I see it, because the dress style they sport is only for fiction. No person who ever thinks seriously about clothes would dress that way in public, at least, in public in New

Orleans. Cowboy hats are so limited in imagination and grace for proper city life; it would have been unthinkable (in the late fifties) to wear one to a dance. And only the deranged would appear wearing cowboy boots. A pair of Stacy Adams toe caps, or Florsheims or the like were the correct styles. Unorthodoxy in dress is as belittled as poor cooking. To parochial Yankee, Hoppy is also a spoof on fashion, and so again, he cannot be a real person.

7

On a memorable weekday evening, while sitting on my balcony, I see Queequeg walking down Long Part. Older now, his tall beaver hat is gone revealing grey hair; he has exchanged his harpoon for a crocus sack. Though slightly stooped, he is still tall, and black, and powerful. The pages of my vision and the pages of Melville's classic interleave, as Queequeg disappears down the set of steps next to the Beauchamps' property. Later that night, coming from the steerage of the hillside, an unchanging lament is bellowed out, for hours, by this man of the book: "Ahall di dirty mudder skunts; ahall di dirty mudder skunts…" In the morning, Mrs. Beauchamp chuckles, "Sparky put on the rum last night, boy." Queequeg's silent onyx lay shattered, and the howling of Sparky's scourged spirit turns back pages in my memory. That evening, I tell Blue of an incident.

"I never told anybody this; I was too ashamed. When I was a freshman in high school, this upperclassman looked at me and said, "You pretty lil green-eye thang, I'm gon punk you."

Wha?

He was going to rape me.

Ah what di fuck! Ah wha you do?

I stayed out of his way.

Naah man. No! No!

I was four feet eleven and ninety pounds then.

So?

I hated him, but he was twice my size.

You should have clapped his ass with a stone.

What do you mean: hit him with a stone?

Fuck yeah!

You can't just hit someone with a stone.

Him had rights for fuck you?

No!

You should have bust he in he fucking mouth. He would learn some manners then.

But to just throw a rock at someone is wrong.

Did you ever throw stones?

No.

They call stones the poor man's pistol. They got men in Antigua who knock down coconuts with stones.

Yuh lie?

Me ah tell you. You should have chopped 'e pork-hole with a rock-stone.

I don't know.

The weekend comes. Early Saturday morning, a friend of Blue's drops us up country; then we hike. By mid-morning we find a deserted beach, eat bread and cheese there, and then move upon the land as wandering cubs yielding to adventure. After swimming naked in a deserted inlet, we sit and talk. This outdoor gambol is ostensibly to "throw stones."

We play "penny loaves" by skipping stones. Each skip buys a penny-loaf of bread. Blue always has at least three penny-loaves. I fling the stones with force but without the right slant. At first, most slice into the water and I make no penny-bread; I catch on. Toward the end, by luck, I earn six penny-loaves. Then, the focus shifts. Stones with more heft are thrown at both the sea and the trees. We look around for a last target. Blue spots, about fifty feet away in the water, a small rock outcrop, which resembles an ashen face. "Look, there's the fucker over there," and he flings his rock. The throw well nicks the target's edge. Transfixed. *I can't hit someone in the face with a rock—even in my imagination!*" "Throw the stone!" Still hesitating. "Throw the stone!" Blue's stern chiding finally sinks home, Yankee unloads. The rock-stone, after leaving my hand, opens its gray-dead eye and seeks the oval-shaped goal. Their union is one of splintering impact. Amazed, then proud, then aware of the reality that no human face on the planet could have sustained that blow without significant damage. Coming from the southeast, trade winds are carrying the smell of the sea "cleaning itself," a rank bouquet born of carnage and putrescence and regeneration. Inhaling, filling my nostrils and lungs with the water's pitiless breath, my bright, pretty "pussy-eyes" are engorging themselves with lust. They are aching to see the would-be rapist's face being smashed and smashed by stone after stone flying from my hand.

"Do you see now?" Boy Blue asks quietly.

Part Two

THE BOSOM OF THE PAST

8

Early Sunday, the clappers awake in the mouths of the bells. The flat-tuned Anglican bell, the tinned-toned Dutch Reform bell, and the distant Catholic bell, each calls and soothes the faithful. But I am not one of them. In my mind the rocks still fly from an anger, (now distended) which moves to feed on a Sunday memory of The Lord's divine bread.

I went to communion only once during my summer visits to Philadelphia in the late fifties. The first experience was a watershed, unpleasant enough to make it my last. After receiving the sacrament and leaving the altar rail, my eyes followed my feet on their tentative path back to my pew. Finally having to look up, I met with unwavering stares, congregation thick. They induced a panic. I could not remember the Irish faces in my original pew. In confusion and humiliation, I chose the first open one less I would have had to circle round again, probably with no better chance of success. At Saint Michael's, my mother's adopted church, I was a visible curiosity, a Negro outsider, stared at by people turning around throughout the service. No one opted for guile, especially at the end, when the priest led the prayer "for the colored and Indian missions." This always let loose head rotations in the mass.

The consistency of this impolite behavior, by fellow Catholics, made me wonder how my northern kin related to them. Over time, I deduced the two sides of the balanced equation involved. To the white Catholics, the colored Catholics were the resident monkeys, while the colored Catholics understood the white Catholics' self-possession by their own pallid demons of self-deception.

For eleven summers, my sister and I visited our mother who lived with her sister in Philadelphia (The North), a place where prohibitions against colored/Negro did not exist, so I had been told. Since first learning to read, the word "colored" appeared in New Orleans (The South), in some exterior pronouncement, on every occasion when I left my neighborhood. I knew the word as I knew myself. From the "screens" on the bus to the dirty-looking cutouts in the walls of white bars where our kind could buy food, "colored" defined an exclusivity, "for colored patrons only," that kept the rancid order of The South's segregated world intact. The word Negro first came to me formally from the set of encyclopedias in the bookcase near the head of the stairs. "**Races of Mankind: Caucasian, Mongolian, and Negro.**" My status was that of the Y: Negro and colored person (my biological and social positions respectively), joined at the point of law. From there I proceeded down the straight and rigorous road of not being "a common Negro," whose deeds, published daily in *The Times Picayune*, led to Parish Prison or Haydel's Funeral home.

In 1955, with nine years of living impressions in my mind, I went north to visit my kin who lived outside The South. Grandma Adele, Aunt Vonnie, Uncle Rodney (dearer than my blood uncle), my sister and I, all motored up to Philadelphia. We rode in Uncle Rodney's gray Oldsmobile, Old Betsy. The car had a trunk like the backside of a large lady, big and round; the luggage had been crammed in there. Grandma had done the food; there was crispy fried chicken (never greasy), loaded sandwiches, and fruit. I sat between the window and Grandma Adele; whose lap was there for me to lay my head upon when I got sleepy. Aunt Vonnie could "drive a car like a man;" everybody felt safe no matter who drove. The delight of my days had begun.

Old Betsy was an automatic. With no shifting of the gears necessary, no distracting movements by the driver hindered focusing on the landscape, whether in a blur or frame by frame. The trees and the roadside buildings flickered past the screen on the one channel available, moving north. Somewhere, on some road, in some state, Negro lost its Siamese twin: colored patron. Racial surgery, unhygienic, impersonal, and razor-sharp, was performed by a state boundary. The unclean water fountains and the dirty bathrooms of service stations, north-vectored of that line, were the sight and reek of equality.

"Yeah, we got ah bathroom. Coast the doh don open good, I ain't fixed it jus yet. Use this here screwdriver to open it. Don let them chiren use it by themselves, they might not be able to open it from the inside."

"Thank you."

"Sho nuf."

The depressed gas pedal fed the odometer's whirl as southern became northern, and the fine rice grains of my old fare became the cratered mounds of mashed potatoes, filled with brown gravy, on seemingly every plate in every restaurant.

Philadelphia came to meet the car. Through the corridor of the nearby oil refineries, the smell—a mottle of aromatics and sour-earth scents—laid itself flat into our noses. Within minutes of passing this alley, we arrived at 7037 Greenway Avenue. After one wide-eyed glance, I knew that this was a different world.

9

The commotion of our arrival brought my kin outside. The neighbors, sitting on the screened-in porch on the other side of the duplex, waved. They were white. They opened the screen door and were introduced as the Halls; their faces were pleasant. Sights, quickly taken in, planted wonder in my eyes. Greenway Avenue was a hilly street. I had never been on a hill before, except the levee.

Aunt's Grace's house was clean and neat, though it had not occurred to me that it could be otherwise. She had a closet under the stairs, like in New Orleans, but it was diminutive and less magical. A closed door in the kitchen might have been a flat pantry, but within the first day or two, I heard the word cellar. "Like a basement?" "No, the cellar is underground." New Orleans had no underground rooms, I had been told; the city was below sea level. Neither my sister nor anyone else showed an interest in going into the earth. I was not told I could not go into the cellar, but I was not told that I could. Finally, unable to contain myself, I snuck into the kitchen and opened the door. Cool, odd-smelling air met me, and I looked down into a place where the light, from the windows at ground level, was hesitant and unsure of its duty to cast out the darkness. A set of steep stairs, bordered on the left by a wall and without a railing on the right, led below. I found the light switch and pushed it down. Three geysers of light, from unseen sources, erupted downward and came to rest in soft pools of illumination on the grey floor. I descended. The hewed walls were not smooth. They glistened slightly where the thin white plaster had cracked and dropped away, showing the mica-infused soil behind it. The huge space ran from the front to the back of the house. Small pockets of scent clung stubbornly to areas. A faint odor lingered near the furnace, and a musty dirt-scent came from an unlit room, directly below the front porch. It was a tight-gripped world, like a sepulcher (I remembered that word from The Stations of The Cross) that would part with nothing, let alone its dead air smells.

On one of my first outings, somehow, I tasted a soft pretzel with mustard. Mouth love immediately occurred, with the heavenly taste of salt guiding this passion. The sprinkled grains of coarse salt, the salty mustard, and the crusty covering on the gummy dough released northern taste from the thralldom of the bland. The "Italian" rolls were all right, but they were not French bread. They were small pretensions used to make their pretended "poh boys," whose redemption laid solely in their garnish of fried onions. I preferred to eat out rather than at my aunt's. Northern home food was too different and not to my taste. But what I understood immediately was that I could never be happy eating only northern food. Between the ubiquitous potatoes and the lack of seasoning (butter seemed to be the sole ingredient used for producing augmented taste) I would go hungry. Not technically, for I would eat, but my tastes would cringe when mealtime arrived.

"Bless us O Lord, and these Thy gifts, which we are about to receive from Thy bounty through Christ, our Lord, Amen." I had said this preamble to my meals for as long as I could remember. Prefigured by these unchanging words, memory's sweetness of a full stomach began less with a vision of Christ's bounty, than with the sounds his name rested among. The constancy of this effect flowed from the ritual words. Uncle Irving, not a Catholic in saying grace, bowed his head, and mumbled something; it was not short. Unk had become a preacher, with all at the table bound to respect his unclear sermon. This rambling outpour of free prayer was disconcerting. It seemed that a prayer, not known to anyone but the person praying, did not enfold the meal within a communal spirit. This confusion at such an improvised prelude peeled away grace from its ritual adhesion to the food and encouraged questioning on my part. Did the free prayer sound right; was it better than the standard one; how was one to join in prayer and try to pay attention to this ever-changing stream? Answering all in the negative, I began to ignore my uncle's prayer, this soon spread to my own.

The disbelief, from the unorthodoxy of northern eating habits, surpassed the sense of oddness that had formed regarding the prayer. Within days of my arrival, oranges were brought into the house. My younger cousins peeled their fruit and proceeded to eat them without sprinkling on any salt. They were in the kitchen, the shaker was on table, but they ate the oranges raw. My disbelief left me staring at them. They looked at my face and asked the problem. "How can you eat oranges without salt?" "We never put salt on oranges." "Surely then, you put salt on melons?" "No, we don't." My bewilderment, at this gastronomic heresy, took a left turn into bias. Despite everything they had, northern people were uncivilized. During the summers that followed, this became a spotty prejudice that could be dispelled by being greeted with a polite "Hello," or hardened by a bit of northern coarseness.

10

A slow-moving old horse, wearing ornamented blinders, pulls a wagon down Louisiana Avenue in New Orleans's Broadmoore district in the early nineteen fifties.

Its iron shoes: "Clip, clop, clop, clup."

Half-megaphoned by his left hand, the walking cantor sings, "Rayeed riipe waatermelon, mustard greens, collard greens, turnip greens, sweet potaatoes."

The driver's hand lifts the reins and softly down pats them on the broad rump of the horse.

"Clip, clip, clop, clup."

"Hold up." Mrs. Brown, who lives two houses away, has opened her screen door and called out. The four wheels, rimmed with iron, take their rest along with the old nag, who opens her butt and drops a load onto the street. Though as ancient as the horse, the wagon still maintains the faded dignity of a legible decal on its pale red side slats.

Large as a barrel and equally round, nimbly, Mrs. Brown steps down the three stairs from the level of her house to the ground. Her apron pocket shows the sharp contours of her pack of Pall Malls; there is a cigarette in her mouth. Her first question is the first question in the catechism of the buyer, "How much do you charge for...?" She does not take the cigarette out of her mouth. As she listens to the cantor's pricing, her mouth slightly opens. She is no longer gripping the cigarette with both lips; it does not fall. It dangles and bobs with the measured rhythms of her head nodding as the prices are given. With an intricate facility, she draws her lower lip upward and positions the Pall Mall between her two lips and takes a drag. The lit end glows red with life, subsides, and then moves down to its resting level as her lower lip relaxes. She wants to buy greens and sweet potatoes. The crier picks up a two-part scale and puts the potatoes in the galvanized metal basket. The price is given; she agrees to it. Her goods are bagged. She pulls several dollars off the little lump of bills she has taken from her apron pocket, and the exchange takes place. She walks backs to her house and mounts the three stairs to the porch.

"Giiup. Les go," as the driver downs pats the reins.

"Clip, clop, clope, clup."

The crier walks alongside the wagon and resumes his song: "Rayeed riipe waatermelon, mustard greens, collard greens, turnip greens, sweet potaatoes." Mrs. Brown "is having a "dinner" tonight. People in the area can come and buy a plate of food. Mrs. Brown "can cook." She earns her "butter and egg money" this way.

After school one Tuesday afternoon, I had walked to within a half block of my house when an unpleasant, aggressive smell, unlike any before, filled the air. It got into my nose and it would not leave. Some type of food had grown rank from the heat required for its preparation. The intensity of the stink rose, peaked at Mrs. Brown's house, and gratefully subsided by the time I entered my side door.

"Grandma, what is that smell?"

"Mrs. Brown is cooking chitterlings."

"Whas dat?"

"Hog guts."

"Do you ever cook them?"

"No! I'm not cooking that stuff in my house; they stink too much.

By some accident, I got to try, only once, the chitterlings from Mrs. Brown's pot. "Pas mal," but grandma was right.

Randazzo Seafood and Poultry, the chicken shack, was at the other end of the block at Magnolia Street. Shrimps, regular and large, fresh fish, oysters, live crabs and chickens were sold there. Mr. Randazzo, a stocky, balding white man, and his thickset wife were the owners. June, a dark-skinned colored man of twenty or so, was the help. Fish were scaled, if requested, and chickens were slaughtered, plucked, gutted, sectioned, and packaged. The oysters they sold were already shucked. The blue crabs were kept in large thin-slatted wooden baskets about five crabs deep. The place had strong smells, but they were completely inoffensive. I was sent there only to buy shrimp or to pick up a chicken that had been ordered. During these errands, the process of turning a live chicken into chicken ready for the pot became plain.

The fowls' cages were five tiers high and made of a thick wire mesh. Removable pans, underneath each tier, caught the droppings of the birds. Before the slaughter came the selection. Negro ladies, generally large, wearing aprons would make their desire known to buy a chicken. The customer and Mr. Randazzo went to the cages as two separate individuals, and as a single cloven persona: a chicken hawk. Its eyes, looking within the tiers of the caged, were those of the lady. The claw, bringing the lighting slash of death, was Mr. Randazzo's razor-augmented hand.

Candidates were examined and felt, with practiced fingers, until one, out of the many, was selected. The chosen, rudely held by its feet, was brought to a three-sided weighing cage: a front and two sides with no back. The boy never got over the dumbness of chickens. They never backed out the weighting cage and sought flight. Face forward, pecking at the wire mesh directly in front of them, they squawked and fretted while their death lay, in open site, next to the scale. At first, *You damn fool, fight; try and get away.* As my witnessing of the process increased, this bellicose fantasy faded. Mr. Randazzo pulled the oblivious birds from the scale, held them firmly with the necks extended and sliced off their heads, which were tossed away. The bodies were put into a large cardboard barrel. Out of sight, the now dead chickens scruffed and scroffed, headless, for a time. *Would people move about if their heads were cut off? The French would know; they cut off people's heads in public.*

When life's final protestations had ended, Mr. Randazzo gave the now quiet flesh to June, the plucker, who stood next to a machine with gears and belts that turned a large cylinder set on its side. Around the drum, spaced evenly, were "fingers". June pushed down a black switch, and the drum started turning. Holding the feathered-draped flesh by its feet, he dipped the headless chicken into steaming water and then held it against the rotating drum. A puttering, abrasive sound came as the feathers began to come off. Again, June would dip the bird and then put it back on the drum; more feathers would come off. He turned the bird over, and plucked the other side, and the bird looked so strange with its bare, white skin.

Mr. Randazzo, the butcher, now became the surgeon. He cut open the chicken, disemboweled it, and took out the parts that usually were asked for: the liver and the gizzard. These were wrapped in wax paper and set aside. With a cleaver and a firm, practiced hand, he sectioned and packaged the chicken. Life had been transformed into sustenance. The cook, with spice or garnish, and pot and stove, would now honor this flesh.

Buying live crabs was simple; make sure the crab was still alive. Also, broken claws devalued it. And since the claws were not on ice, they were not safe to eat. The crabs were easy to like; they always were ready to fight, each other or their captor. To handle them, a set of long tongs was used.

When I first saw fish being scaled, I found out that scales have wings; they fly everywhere, especially if one is too close to the process. Fish cleaning was uninteresting. The fish were just "beastly dead" and fish guts were more gooshy than chicken guts. The remnants of these processes were heads, feathers, scales, guts, and blood. June, now the disposer, hose-washed the blood out of the door facing Magnolia Street, over the sidewalk, and into the sewer. When leaves or dirt or trash filled the opening, the blood mixed with them and sat. The garish red pond, buzzed by flies, and broiled by the sun, reeked of metal. June would stand in the street and water blast the mixture until it conformed and went down into the sewer main. This lake of blood and stink at the corner from my house began to wear on me. Unknowingly, a dislike of the place began to form in my mind. This increased with the disparagement of June by Mrs. Randazzo. "He will always be a chicken plucker." *That is a mean thing to say. June's a nice person, and besides, Fats Domino had been a chicken plucker and he is famous.* After telling Aunt Alice, she only said that June should look for other types of work.

Momma Adele did not buy already-shucked oysters. She bought hers from Basil's on Louisiana Avenue near Claiborne Avenue, a three-block walk from the house. By the time I was old enough to be sent upon this longer run, the store across the street from Randazzo's had closed and been demolished. Mount Zion Methodist built its church on the lot.

The new church's services were quiet. Its placid wake washed over the intervening houses until the sidewalk read "CLARA." Across Clara Street corner (on the "uptown" side, going toward "back-ah-town") there were "nice" one- and two-story dwellings. All had accommodating porches with gliders or swings hanging from chains, winding arm stairs, arabesque grillwork on the screen doors, attractive framing trim, and ornate warm-air vents. In the middle of the block the houses began to turn toward an inelegant simplicity, which presaged an altered mood from attempts at swank decorative joy to something else.

The next street had come freely traveling down from "uptown" in the Garden District to Louisiana Avenue, but the sidewalk on the avenue would not let it pass. For one block up at Amelia Street, Willow had given up the accouterments of modern passage. This curious span is a narrow, sunken dirt-lane, near whose end lay a huge horse trough, half-buried and skewed from the level. On the long side of this grey, antique vessel, written within lovely tiles, was the word "WILLOW." No car or truck could pass down this peculiar block, the past full squats inside. Houses, with their fronts much too close to one another, form the gauntlet wherein the ordinary is punished by receiving blows from a time when murderous shadows prowled at night. Lafcaidio Hearns had blessed such remnants of the old life with his words as he created the decayed persona of New Orleans: a city frozen by its own past decadence. This was not without cause. If Willow had been in New York City, it would be a lost street that only a seeker of long forgotten ways could have found. On one of the corners stands a small, windowless shop. Above its door is a single, faded sign: Very Rare Books. Inside, mad Abdul Alhazred's fabled "Necronomicon" had paused, in its unending journey from unclean hand to unclean hand. This ancient volume, on the slumbering dread inside the world, is prologued in that length of WILLOW's unpaved passage. I never set my foot down in that block, nor did any of my kin.

Basil's Oysters, two houses past Willow Street, had no need of a porch or entrance flourish, its door fronted the sidewalk. The houses on both sides fell away from its wide white face. After constructing the front, of slatted cypress, carpenters cut out a rectangle shape, braced and hinged it from the inside, and made a door. With money in my pocket (regardless of it being errand-money and not mine) I entered a man's place; alcohol was served in the section near to Claiborne. Under-aged, I could not go into that section, so I never knew who drank inside, colored or white? But it could only be one or the other, no mixing for drinks. In a corner, near the entrance on the "out-front-of-town" side, there were coarse-knitted sacks full of oysters. Sliver/black grit came through the knitting. Next to them, a long, high oyster bar stood with a big-faced, balding white man behind it. He seemed huge, though I never saw him full, just from his chest up.

"Wha cha wont, bawh?

"Two dozen of oysters, sir."

"You wait right deh."

"Yes sir."

The oysterman bent forward; his shoulders and body movement and downward directed gaze showed purpose. Unlike at Randazzo's, I could not watch the process, so I opened up to everything else. The same space housed Basil's restaurant. The presence of the kitchen lay heavy in the nose with the oily crisp of frying thick in the air. Plastic, red and white-checkered tablecloths covered the tables, each with a bottle of "Louisiana Hot Sauce". Sound, music, talk, laughter, the clink of things, neon tubes glowing with the names of Falstaff, Regal, Dixie 45, and Jax beer: this was life, not the slaughterhouse.

"Heer yah go bawh; das two dollars."

"Heer yah go sir."

One Friday, the man said,

"Bawh, yah ever eat a raw oyster?"

"No sir."

The man handed down to me an oyster on the half shell.

"Heer, they good for you, bawh."

"Thank you, sir."

I picked up the oyster with my fingers and put the silver-grey/white mass into my mouth. I chewed it for a moment then the probable occurred. The oyster took to the smooth descendancy of its flesh. It went down like slippery okra.

"Yah like it, bawh?"

I did, but it could have tasted like shit, and I would have said I liked it. It was man food.

"Yes, sir."

I sped home and looked into the mirror to see if the tiny hairs on my upper lip had darkened.

11

As a threesome, dressed in good clothes and starched with proper manners, we waited for the #11 trolley at the stop directly in front of St. Michael's church. I had heard of the subway, but it took me unaware. Like the streetcar in New Orleans, the tram rode on tracks and it had a connection to an electric wire overhead. The windows could be raised or lowered but there were bars preventing head, hands or anything from sticking out. While not ugly, its green and tan coloration could not match the attractiveness of streetcars in New Orleans. There were no screens; colored people did not have to sit behind white people. I quickly got used to this. Moreover, I could not embarrass my mother as I had done in New Orleans.

During one of her Christmas visits, my mother and I were returning from downtown on the Feret Bus. Mom put the "screen", the ordinal marker of the society (whites first, colored patrons behind) into the slots in the seat in front of us. The form had been adhered to; the seating was legal; we could not be ousted from the seat. *The Feret route ended in the predominately white Garden District. Somewhere along the route a white couple, of no particular description, except that they were not young, got on the bus. The section in front of the "screen" was filled. Standing was the only legal option for them. They approached our seat and asked us to get up and give them the seat. My mother ignored them. I tried to ignore them as my mother did, but she was next to the window and I was next to the aisle where the two stood. Seeing the initial request, to my mother, ignored and the fixity of her face in not yielding, they upped the stakes: they got belligerent. Both the woman and the man, talking loudly, had the same theme: "We give up our seats to you people when this happens; you people are so ungrateful; you should get up." The bus driver said nothing, and the volume of the couple's discontent rose. Finally, the man's voice disappeared, only the woman's shriek prevailed. It seemed to be approaching an apoplectic climax. The woman's voice had crossed the uncertain ground from ordinary to the unknown. Her screeching rage, at her white privilege denied, was so unexpected and absolute that it made my mother's deliberated non-response impossible for me. Above my head, unceasing in its venting down, was something that I had no experience in dealing with. Never having been around either the insane or anyone who showed anger of such a height, my secular understanding collapsed; only my religion provided reason. The nuns had warned us of this terror. Conjured in hell, this must be the noise the dammed or the possessed made. A primal fear of taint from proximity to the fallen and the demon-inhabited had been ingrained in me. In terror, I fled to the back of the bus; my mother followed. The bullies took possession of the seats. Mom did not scold me; I did that to myself. The backs of the couple's heads gave me focus, I feared and hated the two white people; I wished damnable evil upon them.*

On the subway, in The North, it was different. The funny little coins, called tokens, used in place of real money carried the same weight, whether they were held in a white hand or a colored hand. "Stand and deliver" became "Fare is fair." The ride downtown, to city hall, became a clattering, squeaking, jolting, swerving carnival fun ride. An anxiety of joy racked me. The movement of the car was glorious. I fell in love, not just with the subway, but also with the entire journey. Around 50th Street, the bright fronts of the buildings being passed turned more toward the stately and less gaudy.

A wrenching, tugging sensation, felt as the trolley moved around a tight curve, alerted me, letting me get a quick glimpse into the new direction. It showed a large, unlit opening. Lights came on inside the car, and a small downward pitch was felt. When on the level again, the #11 crept forward slowly. Along the entered-tunnel's walls were pipes, and lights in metal cages like the "trouble light" grandfather had hanging in the shed back home. The trolley became a glow-bug in the night. It groped forward and then halted. A red stop light on the wall went to orange-yellow, then to green. The trolley left the holding point and picked up speed. Speed went to more speed. The streetcars in New Orleans never bolted so. The close-confining walls of the tunnel kept this lawful pandemonium from prying eyes. The spaced lights outside became one, rapidly blinking fixture. The tunnel's breath was cool with hints of long-aged tile, old-gouged mortar, scraped-metal girder, crumbly-moldy insulation, and thwarted-rust patinas. There was a dank, earthy bind of these elements but suffused with a gritty-dirt motif, moved forward by tired air, spiked with electric discharge. The finish was short, with half notes of stale urine when the train stopped. The point rating was 100 on the scale of novel odors. The squealing of a multitude of pigs came from the car's undercarriage as it turned and braked at the 44th street stop. When six years old, I had seen *Superman and the Mole Men.* Now, for the first time, I saw underground life. Its reality held me fixedly to the subway car's window. A platform, level with the trolley, had people, white and colored, moving about. Some were waiting in the exact place where the car stopped. Others moved quickly to the two doors. It was ordinary, just like the stops in New Orleans, only here, columns held up the new sky. The first stop caught me unaware; I prepared myself for the next. The bleak-walled tunnel gave way to the dingy tile of the station, whose name, in contrasting tile, was written over and over as the car traveled to the end of the station. In stop after stop, until the end of the line (11th and Market: City Hall) the multitude of faces renewed itself. I had been on a moving carnival truck (for whites only in New Orleans) watching faces. The North was so different.

My mother, Mom, took my sister and me to places in Philadelphia that were remembered from books and television. Independence Hall and The Liberty Bell were national sights, but the eagle at Wanamaker's Department Store was magical. *In the middle of the first floor, poised on a plinth, a monumental bird of prey, with fierce eyes and burnished-gold talons, waited. The Roc, come from the land of Sinbad, had been frozen into bronze silence by a jinni or someone like Mandrake the Magician, who had "gestured hypnotically."*

Every day the wizard did this in the four-panel comic in the newspaper, which I read and reread, with unabashed wonder and joy. The power of Mandrake's gesture and incantation could subdue all, even the Roc. But the spell that kept the bird's heart quiet could never be fully trusted. One day, inevitably, a headline would read: The Eagle at Wanamaker's Awoke. I could envision no further, for it would be too frightful to imagine the remainder of that day. I loved seeing it, but terror and awe always kept my feet ready to flee, for it could carry away an elephant. During the summer, I learned that an often-used Philadelphia expression for a convenient meeting destination was "Meet me under the eagle at Wanamaker's." Regardless, I still believed. Once, after staring at the bird for long minutes, with certainty, its left eye twitched.

12

"The Original Brown Derby"
"Est. 1932"

This proclamation of authenticity, and a drawing of a brown derby sat seven feet up the light-brown wall on the Feret Street side of the bar and restaurant. Next to the sign was a large window about three feet square. The words The Original Brown Derby were painted on it. Around the corner next to the bar was a door to an attached pool hall. The Avenue Social and Pleasure Club was written, in painted script, over the single, shuttered opening. Both establishments were across the street (Louisiana Avenue) from Flint Goodrich Hospital; this was a good placing for all concerned. Cut and patch were but a "nutra ground" width across from each other.

I had passed The Derby thousands of times; it was one and a half blocks from my house and in straight line with both school and church. And hundreds of times, I had waited by it for the Feret bus. The high, broad wall, of this imposing monument to coarse, colored behavior, had buffered us, from wind, rain, and cold. Through the genteel white guts of the Garden District, then through the moderate-price, colored-catering stores of Dryades Street, to the high-price white-clientele stores of Canal Street, rode the Feret. The Derby was the sophisticated nadir of the vulgar contact, with colored, that was required by fashionable uptown whites, who traveled by public bus. The Saint Charles Streetcar bypassed colored neighborhoods, but it also missed the two-lobed intellectual heart of the Garden District: Loyola University and Tulane University, which were at the end of the Feret line.

Encounters with The Derby's façade, via bus rides, generally yielded nothing but the occasional detachment of the runners from the electric power wires above. The white driver would then have to get out and pull the cables of the spring-tensioned poles and realign the runners on the overhead wires. After power had been restored, the bus would proceed toward downtown. For those who had the gift of high luck, the detritus of an incident might be glimpsed. What would mark the most common sort of luck (for traveling whites) to view this segregated world, while the bus waited for the light to change, would be colored men and hard-looking colored women going into and coming out of The Derby. To those who lived in the neighborhood, luck gave way to the ordinary flow of life and death around the bar.

The Derby and the pool hall were popular. Usually a visible crowd was playing pool, laughing, and socializing. I never saw a fight inside the pool hall or any spill out into the street from the bar, but of course they happened. The neighborhood got the first notice of an incident, sent out into the air, by the loud buzz of "news" traveling. Then eyes, hungry for a look, and ears, straining for the full story, converged on The Derby. The official presence of the white police and the ambulance meant that the occurrence would enter history.

The Times Picayune police reports would notify of minor colored deeds, but a full article would be given to a major colored performance. Neighborhood news was made to live by word of mouth, and it was just as well. The daily fret of "proper" colored folk was summed up in, "I hope a colored person didn't do it." Or, the question, "Was he colored?"

Within the walls of The Derby, this hope was dashed, and the questions need not be asked. What was known, to proper behaving Negroes, needing only details to be filled in, was that colored behavior had occurred that was more common than common, but all too common among the common.

"Hell no! That ain't the way it was!"

"Yes, it is!"

"Yall both wrong, it was"

"Nigger, who ass you?"

"Stay the fuck outta other peoples' business!" Two men and two knives let loose the blood of the intruding man. The bartender looked up, and in doing so, he halted his service to a customer.

"Man, fuck them niggers! Gimme my drink."

But The Derby did not have top ranking as a place of sudden, murderous passion. At the corner from our house, next to the white-owned store, was The Mighty Earl. It was a tiny bar where death visited a bit too frequently for the authorities liking: they closed it down.

Men from this same hardened stock gathered and wept in public. Unable to help, they watched flames engulf and incinerate the apartment on the second floor of the building next to The Derby; three young children were trapped inside. The tenant screamed and tore her hair as she ran back and forth in front of her flaming charnel house. She had left her children and her sister's child upstairs while she went down to get a drink. Most people felt, that more than likely, the uncommon wrath, soon to be vented upon the woman by her sister, would also become history.

13

A chili hot dog, and an ice cream float, from Kress's Five and Dime Store, became the standard highlight of a downtown trip to Canal Street. Only Kress served colored. Segregation, in New Orleans, permitted forms of stilted commerce between whites and coloreds. Two Canal-Street stores, Maison Blanche and D.H. Homes, were my favorite. Both were run for white people, but they would accept full-price money from coloreds, as long as the latter could do without any accommodations. For example, clothes could not be tried on. However, one could try on shoes at Maison Blanche while wearing socks, which, seemingly, were sufficient protection from colored race-germ contamination. My aunt's proper dress and looks rested well with the white ladies who were the shoe clerks. They remembered me: the one with the "pretty eyes." An awkward acceptance of these words occurred, and then the task of choosing a style—acceptable to my aunt—was completed, with as much speed as I could find a pair and say, "Yes, they fit."

The one shoe-buying time without embarrassment, in fact, to me, the highlight of all my previous shopping trips happened with my grandfather. Daddy George took me downtown to get a pair of shoes. No Maison Blanche, no white women mooning over my "pretty eyes," just two males confined within the errand's masculine time. The huge width of stately Canal Street had visceral tether-streets, feeding and relieving it. The uptown side had its radiations: the wide streets of Baronne, Corondolet, and St. Charles accommodated streetcars, buses, and hard-moving automobiles. The downtown side's narrow streets: Chartres, Royal, Bourbon, were the province of bars, restaurants, music places, and the striptease clubs, with their "b" drinking, and solicitations for prostitution. Streets, where, not for my colored kind, gumbo, hot sausage, and truffles & pâté de foie gras stoked the tongue. Bookstands, with "nature magazines" posting bare breasts and pubic hair, gave anatomy lessons, when caught with eyes twisted in hook. I was not allowed to go into the quarter, but its emanations were radioactive. The contamination was dark, febrile and alive. Daddy George bought his shoes at Schumacher, a half block off Canal down Royal Street. It was a small place, where Jim Crow's prohibitions had been lost within the flow of money. With unfeigned courtesy, the white clerk said:

"How may I help you sir?"

I forced myself to choose, from the many, my first pair of man-shoes. Pointing, "Daddy George, can I try those on?"

"Yeah, they alright."

"That boy got some big feet," said the clerk. Proudly, I, the diminutive man-boy put on my choice: black, toecap, Florsheims with white sole stitching.

This first, shoe-buying-trip euphoria had its climax in the almost stroke-inducing fit it produced in Aunt Alice. She exploded.

"Those are hoodlum shoes!

He cannot wear them!

He has to take them back!"

"I bought the boy those shoes; he can wear them."

Aunt Alice, whose brown skin was now under-toned with apoplectic red blush, became silent. Daddy George, patriarch to both of us, was Daddy George. "Proper" colored attire had yielded in this skirmish.

The lack of signs saying "For Colored Only" lost its notice, as the giant of Philadelphia stood like Gulliver, oblivious to flyspeck directions made into law by my birth-city of Lilliput buildings. The tallest building in New Orleans was the WDSU TV transmission studio, atop the Hibernia Bank Building. It was a graceful, colonnaded structure, where the largess of television was flung out and over the grateful, squat city. No hills, no valleys, just tamped-down river land, belching up manhole covers after a hard rain. New Orleans' note was a bass downbeat, bubbling, percolating through thick delta mud.

The city had only one monument to the sky: Lee Circle on St. Charles Avenue. It was an enormous fluted, white marble column, squared off by high stairs, garlanded by sumptuous zinnias and lit, at night, by grandiose lights. Atop stood a gigantic statue of Robert E. Lee, a bearded white man in army dress; the garb, and he, gone to weathered bronze green. With his arms folded resolutely across his chest, he controlled the view. *He was a general for the South in the Civil War. He signed the peace treaty at Appomattox. He was the greatest southern general. He left his northern connections and went south to defend his homeland. He was great. He was… He was…* All this was trivial to me. Robert E. Lee, on high, was still the defender, blocking (even the sight of the entry point to) the wide, beautiful road (St Charles Avenue) that led into white land: an irrelevant place for a colored Yankee. Clattering, in making its sharp curtsy around the staunch defender's memory, the Saint Charles streetcar went halfway around the wide circle, and continued down into the world tangential to my world. A quarter way around the circle, the Feret Bus peeled off from the end of the common ground of the two routes. It began its snake trail of paths through the colored section. Flung away, at a right angle, by the general's still-living world, Lee's tower was as reduced in my mind, as were the rest of white peoples' things.

In contrast to New Orleans, Philadelphia rose high. City Hall was the most impressive building I had ever seen. It was huge, and its façade overflowed with splendor. It was so tall that it hurt my neck in looking at the top. There, when I had a clear view, was William Penn. However, I thought that it was a statue of Benjamin Franklin. There was no martial pose; he had a lightning rod attached to his Quaker-looking hat. *Benjamin Franklin discovered the nature of lightning. He was a founding father, he invented bifocals, he wrote "Poor Richard's Almanac." He was from England. He helped write "The Declaration of Independence." He was a swimmer of great renown, He did… He was a great man. His picture is on money.*

Later, from Uncle Irving—who intensely disliked white people—I learned that Franklin's genius did not bridge the gap between his rational mind and his human comforts. In his later years, Franklin came to argue against slavery, but Peter, his personal valet, remained a bondsman. "The City of Brotherly Love" was still great, but it seemed that even in its greatest citizen's mind, there was to be reserved seating at the communal love banquet.

14

"We're going to New York." My sister took our mother's words with glee.
"Whom will we stay with?"
"Cousin Bertha."
"Y'all go head on." Grandma Adele wasn't going. Such accommodations

did not please her; she was related to Bertha only by her daughter's marriage.

We caught the train (my first time on one) to New York at Philadelphia's 30th Street Station. The building rhymed with my idea of a Greek Temple: huge columns outside and inside a ceiling that went up, and up. There was a statue of an angel, holding up a wounded or dead soldier, with words engraved on the pedestal. It was all immediate and joyous. The jumble of whites with coloreds was becoming less odd. I bounded into the first seat that let me sit by the window. The ride was short and without magic.

Julius, cousin Bertha's husband, met us. Calling him by his first name was unacceptable. I created the title of Cousin-Julius. Cousin Bertha's house was on 126th Street and Saint Nicholas Terrace. Directly across the street there was a large park. Where this was located in New York City was unimportant because my sister and I were not allowed to go outside, except on the stoop, and only there when semi-monitored. The word dangerous was never used, we simply were not allowed outside unless accompanied by an adult. We were both content with this stricture because we had found our seats in the theater. Kneeling on the sofa, resting our chins on top of its back, we stared through the window, reveling at the show outside.

We had done this in New Orleans also. From my sister's room upstairs, we could look directly into Fifth African Baptist Church. At least once a month, on Sundays, we had watched colored people worship in ways that seemed unfathomable to us as Catholics. The mirth of ignorance gave both fascination and incredulity. We listened to the passionate, complex rhythmic syncopations of the preacher and smirked at the ecstatic outburst of women writhing about in pew, and on floor. In New York, this seasoned, observational practice allowed detailed watching and communal judgments. The street was always crowded, and stickball always seemed to be going on. How this enormous number of young people did this feat was not solved. The game or games just never ended. There were unpredictable tides of sounds that rose and fell. We assumed that sometime during the night, the play ended, though this was not known for sure. What was demonstrated was the command the players had over the street. Once a garbage truck came to the head of the road. It must have used its horn, but, inside, we heard nothing. The truck advanced to the head of the street and into the space vacated by some players. It halted. It could not move further without running into a part of the swarm. The truck driver, maybe to save face, for the initial impossibility of proceeding was evident upon its arrival, waited a half hour or so. Then it backed up the quarter of a block it has been allowed to traverse. The game never seemed to pause. Our humorous disbelief, in possession by "the spirit" of those in Fifth African who fell to the floor shaking and screaming, went to open astonishment at the actions of young people forcing a city vehicle to back up and leave. Never in our timid minds did we imagine such power wielded by young people. That both black and white would do this together, and not to have it reported to the police registered strongly. In New Orleans, the leeway given by the law to colored misbehavior, and the armor given by the law for protection of its Nigra citizens were one and the same: a skin-tight, fragile shell. This was easily shattered by a knock, from the inside, made by a free moving colored or from the outside, by a baton, from a freewheeling enforcer. My grandfather called the latter "dagos." I never dwelt upon the word, nor even pronounced it, (its sound was unpleasant), but its meaning was clear: mean white people. The streets of New York were a different type of ground to walk upon; there were whites that were less mean. Terror firma was not the bedrock in The North.

The colored people that my sister and I got to observe close up were those who sat on the stoop next door. Stoop sitting was new. In New Orleans, most of our neighbors had porches, usually with swings and gliders, and chairs to sit in. We had seen stoop sitting in Philadelphia, but our cousins sat on the porch, not the stairs. However, in New York, there were no porches, and many, from the building, came outside and sat on the steps. Most were just getting out of the apartment "for some air," but our observing twosome agreed that "business" was conducted there also. People would come and give money to sitters or the opposite would happen.

One person stood out: a dark skin, young man, whose stature we never could determine for he never stood up all the while we sneaked peeks at him (no staring at anyone was the rule, even though we were inside: it still seemed rude). We bestowed on him the name "Gift." His actions made it seem that he felt that he was God's gift to women. He liked the color red; he wore it a great deal. Sitting in languid postures, looking, for all the world, as if he were bored with sitting, yet he sat. Gift gave the impression, while speaking to women, of looking at them through a telescope: he was near; they were distant. And with slow deliberation, most of the time, he ran his fingers through the waves and curls of his "do." Our gawking twosome thought that not even Shirley Temple's hair received such caressing. But with Gift, there was more of a focus on the "kitchens" than probably would have been given to that same part of the white child's hair, if indeed white people had "kitchens."

The immensity of downtown New York was incomprehensible. Of course, after having seen *King Kong*, the Empire State Building with its spire was a mandatory sight. But it was impossible; the surrounding skyscrapers were too tall. The ride, up the rapid elevator, to the first scenic level of the building, pressured my ears and surrounded my hearing with an aural fog that muffled the world. The sensations were unpleasant. The doors opened onto a terrace surrounded by a chest-high protective wall with a wide ledge. Embedded in the wall were gleaming pinions that secured a thick, crosshatched screen, at least as tall as my sister. The hatchings were so open that after a short time of looking through them, they disappeared. For the first time, I experienced great height. Everything on the street below had become tiny and moved slowly; ant-buses crept, and speck-pedestrians inched. *"Look, up in the sky. It's a bird, it's a plane, it's Superman,"* my favorite introduction to my favorite would-be-persona sank. In my innards, from stomach to genitals, radiated queer energy. Its initial effect rendered movement difficult. That quickly refined itself: movement toward the screen was conducive to the paralysis. My testicles, for the first time, tingled. An unbearable discomfort had been induced from looking down and assessing the drop or realizing the height, which was the same. I had not felt this on the approach to the ledge or looking straight out nor even looking down, only linked with understanding was this, this… The word dropped through the gray and white matter of my brains, and into the red marrow of my bones: fear. Once named, structure formed that yielded immediate understanding: I was terrified of heights.

My sister joined several others in sitting on the ledge. I railed at her, constructing ad hoc arguments concerning her safety. The screen might give way; impossible I knew. A wind might lift her over the screen; this was more implausible than the first reason. She might have enjoyed me radiating fear, but it seemed that she genuinely liked the view. I was bereft of the adult words needed: "Go to hell, bitch", so I sulked and stayed well back from the screen. The highest scenic level made us both equal. A room with flush, thick glass, about two feet high, took away her prowess. Still wishing for voice, "Now bitch, you can't show off." I silently disliked her all the way to the pavement (she could easily beat me). Megalith New York was not as nice as Philadelphia.

However, ground-level Manhattan, where the bus-worms sped by and the pedestrian-specks walked rapidly, captured me. We went to 42nd Street, and ate Chinese food, a first for me. Egg rolls were better than any sweet, except for heavenly hash or pralines or brownies. The street was filled with movie theaters; mom picked one out. There were two movies, a cartoon, the news, and a serial: *Commando Cody, Sky Marshall of the Universe*. I left the theater less disheartened. With Commando Cody's flying suit there would be no fear of heights. A new figure had entered my pantheon of super-folk. Commando Cody had made space for himself by agency. I was certain that the rocket pack could be made; it was possible because it was of science. One day I would build one and then...

Grant's Tomb, and The United Nations, were part of seeing New York. The Statue of Liberty was a sight and a boat ride and vindication of my prowess. Being enclosed, there was no sense of height, only spiral stairs to be climbed without showing fatigue. At the top, the glass around the crown, was similar to the glass lookout in the Empire State Building. I was told that, at one time, visitors had been allowed to walk out, through the arm, to the torch. Believing the story, a packet of sudden symptoms formed quickly. Just in case a sudden unexpected access to the torch might be announced, these ills would give justification to my inability to proceed through the arm for my mother and sister would jump at such a chance. When we were ready to leave, my mother had the standard souvenir photograph taken.

Before the end of our New York stay, we went to the Bronx and visited Melissa, whose husband had been damaged in the war. The house was in a sparsely populated area, somewhere near 262nd Street. My sister and I were not allowed out; we were told that bears were about. Othar, wheelchair bound, living near to a veterans' hospital, in his neat house in the woods, needed precise care from his devoted Melissa. It was a fragile, isolated world of bygone valor and perpetual tenderness.

By the time we returned to Philadelphia, Uncle Rodney and Aunt Vonnie had left for New Orleans in Old Betsy. Momma Adele, my sister, and I would go back home on the train: *The Southerner*. It would be a day and a half ride.

16

Unlike the trip to New York, this was a true departure. Given this significant event, suitable rhythms and protocols shaped themselves. My family was never late, whether as a group or as individuals, save my sister and my first cousin Barbara, whose perpetual tardiness evinced itself, many times, during that summer. Both Barbara and my sister were made to conform, on this occasion, to the family norm. Food, for the journey, was prepared and packaged so that it would be unnoticeable; wax paper covered everything. We carried enough food so that we would need to buy only dinner on the train.

I had the freedom in dress of short pants and a comfortable shirt, impeccably clean and pressed, of course. Also, my shoes were clean and polished. Grandma Adele and my sister had, what seemed to me, the burden of dress associated with women: starched frocks. My grandmother's was simple, but my sister had embellishments on her dress that I called "frivils." Both grandmother and sister would have to sit all day in the seat, and then sleep in those clothes. In my mind, there was too much fuss made over clothes by the ladies in my family.

We arrived at 30th Street Station with such time to spare that I wandered about and got lost. Fortunately, after realizing that I was lost, and before panic set in, I was able to spot my family using frantic searching. By then I had seen lots more of the station. When the announcement was made that the train would soon be arriving, passengers were granted access to the platform. *The Southerner's* route was from New York City to New Orleans. Philadelphia was only a stop, so the train was not staying long.

Within the loading cavern of the station came *The Southerner's* engine sporting its high-cheek metal face. It flew by the spot where we were standing. The squealing of stopping, with the snorting out of steam from the under-carriage, pushed out the smell of its diesel-oil sweat. These living traits and the implacable power it had, fused with its domestication (or tolerance of humans), made the notion of possibility for animate, mechanical creatures seem natural and inevitable. One day, the train's future kin would leave the rails and point their nose-beacons to the black space beyond the blue sky. This was a prophecy laid down by *Lord Science and Tommy Tomorrow*. A nickel *DC* comic book, which, along with the cartoon serial *Buck Rogers*, told the story of the forthcoming evolution of human transportation.

The necessary, but inherently theatrical quality of departures by train seemed the politest method for the rupture of physical presence that could be imagined. The wonderful scrambling, of those outside, to locate the window next to the seat where the departing would sit, brought in the feeling of a hunt. When found, the rapid, last goodbye-waves and attempts at lip reading the well-wishes, through the darkened windows, gave enough excitement, so that the calming walk, back to life without the visitors, brought back the heartbeat of the ordinary. We had experienced this when my mother went back to Philadelphia. Now, we would see it from the other side.

We found our seats and a porter helped put the luggage onto the rack overhead. The darkened windows were not as difficult to see out of as to see into, but reduced light subdued the entire car, despite the bustle of it being loaded with people. I took a window seat. Its comfort snared me for a second or two, and then I looked out the window trying to find my kin. I saw them and waved and mouthed "goodbye." Having not slept much the night before, the pitching and swaying of the train rocked me. Pulling back from the window and sinking into the patterned seat, I fell asleep.

When I awoke the train had only two modes: that of being at a designated stop or moving with open throttle. Its resonant horn flung out warning to all ears, Beware, *The Southerner* was coming, and it was laying claim to its road. It was dark outside. The tracks cut through places where streetlights or any type of light was sparse or far away. Stations, in small towns, were speed-rubbed from the eye before any real notice of them could take place. Despite the monochrome sparseness of this kinetic canvas, looking outside was not boring. The ride was alive and stinging with vitality. A fracturing and synthesis of the world was occurring. Countless bits of sensation had, unwittingly, fallen into place and made for an ecstatic harmony. The light in points, in jots, in blurs, in streaks, objects caught by pinpoint light, or partly seen with the remainder swept by the smear of slow sight, fell into the black background. Sleepy Hollow's station might have come and gone. Or within a pitch-black frame, suddenly, two distant, yellow-green lights appeared. White-skin Leviathan, upon hearing the noisy passage, opened its two glowing eyes, and began searching. Hunger?

Grumbling, the imperious master had awakened. But this time, he would be appeased within the dining car, four coaches to the rear, as the Nautilus increased its southern descent.

17

Momma Adele produced the washcloths. One by one we went to the tiny closet bathroom at the end of the coach. I had only to wash my face and hands. My hair, cut to scalp height, did not need combing; my sister returned with her hair primped. Northern understandings remained in mind; the single bathroom in the car was unmarked as to white or colored and I took no notice of the lack of it.

After the novelty of going through four cars, we met a small line of passenger waiting for seating in the diner. *The Southerner, even here,* still had The North inside it: white and colored stood intermingled. As the line decreased, a view of the inside of the dining car became possible. The person directing traffic was a tall white man, in black livery with a white shirt and a black tie. He looked like the man from Basil's. He had the same way of talking and his manner was similarly out-front.

"Y'all just hold on a minute and that there table," he nodded toward it, "will be ready, just presently."

The waiters, who were also in livery, were colored. The linen was snow white, and the serving platters, and the serving pitchers, both for water and coffee, were silver. The carrying of heavy, laden, ornate metal trays was made graceful and stylish. Random motions from the rails were given a preternatural response by the staff: nothing fell. Weaving in and out and around the car and the customers and each other seemed as fine an arabesque-of-purpose as could be imagined. The blaze of the full lights in the diner inspired the polished silver to shine almost wantonly.

"Hah many y'all got?"

"Three."

"Step this way folks."

One place setting was removed, and we were each given a menu. *The soft leather covers were pretty.*

"If them children are under twelve, you can get child's portion for them. It's half the price."

"Both are under twelve."

Inside the menu were more choices than we knew how to accommodate. I could read the entrees, but they were meaningless to me. The French words were pulled long in my obstinate, ignorant attempt at the language. "H's" were no longer forbidden, and those "e's," cast by fate, either in awkward clusters, or at the caboose of words, were relieved of their child's status of being seen and not heard. What emerged was, Grandma, can I get some chicken?"

The child's portion (more than half a serving) was, by no means, as much as I would have liked, but it was more than I expected. It was tasty, too. The walk back to our seats allowed for more boldness in staring, but only at the backs of passengers' heads. Everything was an induction to inaction: the hour, the soothing motion, post-meal torpor, and increasing boredom. The fraternal *Southerner* had removed, or suspended, for a day and a half, the taboo of "proper" colored folk regarding sleeping just after eating. Though some read, most yielded, as we did, without a care. When we arrived in New Orleans, we took a Morrison Cab. The colored-only taxi smoothly carried us back into our world.

18

"New Orleans was nothing, just a lot of two mule carts," Momma Adele, my maternal grandmother, had said. In 1910, at fifteen, she came to New Orleans from the "country." Daddy George (three years older) also came from the country, but from a different parish. In 1915, he proposed marriage to Adele, and she accepted: "He was so kind and nice." They were married and settled in the Belmont. They had seven children: three boys, and four girls, two of whom were twins. The firstborn, John, died from pneumonia when he was five years old. Joseph, the next-oldest boy, died in 1945 on Okinawa. His sister, Alice, said that the day had been gray and rainy. The doorbell rang. A soldier handed the telegram to her. "We regret to inform you that your son Joseph…" The story, as I understood it, was that Uncle Joseph was trying to put out a fire at an ammunition dump and was horribly burned. He died several days later from infection. George and Adele were man and wife until the summer of 1960. On a humid evening, my grandfather, sitting down in his chair, arthritis had made kneeling impossible, was saying the nightly rosary. He toppled over unseen, while everyone's eyes were closed in prayer, and died. "And the dead went where?" dropped in and out of my dreams like the soft pinch that jolts but leaves no bruise.

"No man can be exactly six feet tall, because Christ was six feet tall." A truth from Daddy George.

At the funeral, Momma Adele's face, wreathed in sorrow, had no tears and her breathing rhythm was strange and frightening. "Grandma?" "My grief is too heavy; it won't let me cry." I heard these words, but the emotional meaning lay beyond me. About two months later, leaving church with my grandmother, she began to weep. "My grief has finally let me cry." With a handkerchief wiping her eyes, she wept heavily for the full six-block walk home.

The "camelback" house on Louisiana Avenue, built by my grandfather and his kin, was the most splendid on the block and for blocks. But within the backyard, tucked away from front view, was a garden of sugarcane, a fig tree, a parsley patch, pineapples, tomatoes, okra, and strawberries. The front view was of a lawn of thick St. Augustine grass, a sidewalk with a lowered runoff cutout, two porches with gliders and chairs, and stairs with wrought iron banisters, and two ornate flowerpots with plants. These were all for me to keep clean and in order as parts of my daily chores.

Years before, the yard had been smaller, by the size of a triangular "shotgun" house that sat between Mr. Moore's and our house. One morning, before leaving for school, I had to pick up the remains of crabs and shrimps thrown over the fence. An early sun had prodded the stink of the refuse to rise. Several days later as my sister and I entered our yard we saw the large lady, who lived in the house, leaning on the fence. The smooth brown of her face showed a blankness set within the pleasure of the savory as she ate and spit and tossed bits of crab shell over the fence.

"Ma'am, you should not throw your garbage into our yard."

Drawn outside her reverie, the woman looked down at my sister in a curious manner, all the while tongue-rubbing her bottom-front teeth to loosen a piece of food. She soft-spat this over the fence. Then gold in her mouth sun flashed as her lip curled and in effortless contempt: "Lil nigger, you better shut the fuck up, foh I come over deh and kick yoh fucking ass." There was nothing to say to her. We both knew that she was not bluffing. Her manner and her evident size confirmed this. She would come into our yard and try to hurt us. We would run into the house. Daddy George or Momma Adele would have to try to protect us. We went inside and told Daddy George of the incident. He told us not to worry. He was in the process of buying the house; she would have to move. He would then tear down the eyesore. Before she left, a vindication of the woman's prowess occurred that was both sudden and convincing.

I was outside sweeping the sidewalk when I heard the tap-tap-tap of swiftly moving feet. I traced the sound to the walkway between the fence and the shotgun just as the passageway's spring-closed gate flew open. Out ran a small man. Not looking back, he turned left toward Claiborne Avenue with his feet still making a machine gun's rapid staccato: tat-tat-tat-tat-tat-tat. The gate flew open again. Our large neighbor appeared with a good-sized butcher knife in her hand. She looked both ways to see where the meat-to-be-gored had run. Too late, halfway up the block, almost at the corner (near to the "chicken shack") the man-cow ran free. She snorted and panted, and I slunk back toward my gate; she was a fearsome, brown bulla, in a rage to impale with her dagger in hand.

When the triangular shotgun house was purchased, and about to be torn down, I got my first look at this peculiar style of house and how it sheltered its people. With all the furniture gone, its odd shape stood out. The continual press of the living space toward the vertex found its bizarre conclusion in the commode point: the front of the toilet seat. Without space to put one's knees, the big lady would have to sit as though mounted for a damsel's side-saddled canter, albeit with this riding form strongly compacted. The converging walls, covered by torn layers of wallpaper, also moved toward a fundament, however here unseen, and made from plaster-covered wood lath. The wallpapers' visible patterns alternated between sickly anemic colors and dizzyingly full designs. Floorboards had been torn up exposing some joists, but there were places where, within the undisturbed boards, there were holes. In two rooms, some linoleum remained. The carpet decals motifs had been scrubbed down, over time, and had lost their sharpness. The high ceilings and closed windows guarded the smell of the exposed soil that joined with the reek of old, sour-mopped, stubborn wood. The dwelling had been an ark for the poor, gentle or coarse as they might be. It had rendered service, and now it had sunk. Not a trace of it would remain in the green grass, the peach tree, the pear tree, and the gorgeous azaleas that were coming.

19

Four houses down, toward Magnolia Street, was the fourplex: a duplex on top of a duplex. It was mainly rented, I had heard, to people coming from the country. It always seemed to have different people living in it. If I did see someone, I never spoke to them nor did they to me, and I wanted to avert my eyes when passing the building. The place was ugly, run down, and dirty. It was the luck of the draw that put, next to our house, the disposable shotgun, rather than the large, hideous fourplex that could not be easily purchased or demolished. Despite living in the area for sixty years, and knowing everyone else in the block, no one in my family ever knew anyone living in the fourplex. Its annex, in spirit, was the new Magnolia Project, built in 1950. It stretched from Magnolia Street to Claiborne Avenue, between Toledano Street and Washington Ave. The renovation project razed most of the Belmont section, and grew a boil in its stead.

Misshapen, possibly maliciously simplistic, drafting pens made a multiplex horror, three stories high, and squared blocks wide. The designers had carefully considered those building elements that incorporated harmony and dignity, in my aesthetic, and dismissed all of them. The new project put the fourplex into high fidelity and turned up the volume.

When I walked down Toledano toward Claiborne, and looked into the place, with its replicated sameness on its barren ground, too much sight was allowed; life was too exposed. Nothing seemed personal. It was like a huge public building without doors for privacy. In every building that one could see, the central doors made of metal with a glass lookout panel, though they appeared sturdy, were partway broken or totally broken or torn away. The barn with stalls comparison could not be avoided. The unattractive porches were always in need of paint, and either a rummage sale or trash bins. Grass, where there was some, was communal; the commune trod it down. The huge security lights, which were no doubt required, did not permit night, only more observation time. This new housing community's ethos was that of a lit menagerie. And the new residents, along with their ways, found shelter and purpose inside. Casual deconstruction was always in progress, and it seemed reasonable that it should be so. The place, reputedly, was made for poor people from the country and poor people from the city. And from the poverty of this invention by the planners, there were those in the city who lived with disquiet, as the earned reputation of the new section's inhabitants spread.

The open border between the new section and the original part of the project was Magnolia Street. My passport had been issued for and from the old section. I took no liberties by walking on foreign soil; I normally kept to the old-project side of Magnolia when walking the four blocks between my house and Washington Ave. The undiplomatic sovereignty of the new section was a cutout within my world. Outside this artificial nation, whose only internal law, for non-citizens, was: "Stay Out Under Pain of Probable Loss," I moved with prudence, but not fear.

Some of the streets that had been eliminated in creating the Old Magnolia were refashioned into block-long green corridors, where there were benches, and buildings fronting both sides of these visible green ribbons. In other areas, there were courtyards, with benches, trees, and grass. The narrow backyards could be fenced off, if desired. The project was large and, at times made eerie, by not seeing anyone in a communal area. I respected these silent places, when I met them, by not disturbing them, but I was never afraid. The Old Magnolia was as attractive as the bits I could see of the white project, just off Canal Street on the downtown side.

Education was part of the Old Magnolia, as it was nestled around Tom Lafon School. My aunt once taught there and had said that it was a "good" school (though its nickname, to my friends, was Tom LaFunky). The old, barn-like school building was finally torn down and a new school, with design elements, in clear rhyme with the New Magnolia, was constructed. And in time, as the new project's inhabitants' children settled into it, both casual and willful deconstruction of the school commenced.

The uptown-riverfront cube, of the old project's volume, held Flint Goodrich Hospital, the only hospital where colored doctors could practice. It was one block square. Its brown sand-colored façade was taken for granted, but the art deco design and the semicircular walkway, bordered on both sides by two-feet high trimmed hedges, were beautiful. The hospital was of human scale, I could see the top floor when standing in front of it.

Violence must have occurred inside the Old Magnolia, but I never saw any, save for one fight. Standing on John Petan's porch a crowd came from the Feret St. side into the long grass lane that went to Magnolia Street. The elevation of the porch gave a good view of the two young women who were surrounded by the group. Between the two, there were loud words and accusatory gestures, but the crowd was supportive of combat. When egged on, to the precise pressure needed for fusion, they flew at each other. It was a cockfight with spurs, re-gendered to a hen fight with claws. Four hands, nails at the ready, groped and raked with such rapidity, that in a few moments, blood was drawn, undergarments were torn, and a white bra appeared, which went quickly to a brown breast exposed. As its owner struck out at her foe, it heaved and fell back to itself, Jell-O-like, but suppler, more made for the touch. The jut of the dark nipple was unfathomable, save that it seemed like a type of treasure: something rich, crafted for the suck of the lips. Of course, no one paid attention to me, but if they had, they would have heard me gasp and seen my mouth drop open. No thought, but the longing was there to see the other breast appear. Those nearest to the combatants quickly parted the two, and a garment was produced to cover the exposed flesh. It made no sense, and maybe everyone didn't want the fight to end, but enough did. Then the crowd fell apart and was absorbed into the neighborhood. But the image of the breast remained, unsullied by the circumstances of its exposure. My erotic mind focused and became aware of itself for the first time: the form and movement of breasts were wondrous to behold. This, my first visible axiom for the construction of impure thoughts, had been given to me by accident. In this same operation, all the females in my family were rendered women without the portfolio of allure.

20

Clocking around the perimeter of my dark world, the passage of days and the respective rites to be performed on them brought harmony and order to my colored time. My house defined the two most precious periods in my life: those of nourishment and safe repose. The inclusion of the prayers before meals and the evening rosary brought minutes of the day within God's time. 6PM, the rosary commenced, fifteen minutes of kill-time. The incantations, for the supplication to the deity and his host, had become wearisome. No longer able to focus on their purpose, the fifteen minutes went by in nine hundred numbered seconds.

The travel of the day, going from my house to Holy Ghost School, was also fifteen minutes. But these minutes, when timed by my internal clock, were of the duration of a tick, not even with an ending tock. I opened my gate and in one seeming step, I was at the school's door. No physics was needed to convince me of the Lorentz contraction: length contracted in the direction of motion (to school, especially when assignments were not done, even if my velocity was snail-like). The reverse was also true. When an ill report was to be carried home, length shrinking again occurred. Overall, school was enjoyable, but outside school was more so, except at lunchtime and when movies were shown.

School lunches were always palatable except for the normally, tepid-to-almost warm, gross-tasting milk. The half pints cartons sat in the malice of palate-neglect. It was not hot milk (an impossibility) but it was not cold milk, not even cool milk. Somewhere in the movement of the cases, from refrigerated storage to the lunch tables, the milk cartons paused, sat, and became, to me, the opprobrium in the temperature scale that Jesus had admonished on. "Be thou hot or cold, for if thou are lukewarm, I will vomit thee out of my mouth." This lack of concern, as to drinkability, could have been responded to by not drinking the milk or throwing it away. But the nuns brought the asceticism of their vocation to the lunch hour. No food, regardless of its fitness to please the taste, could be wasted. "There were starving people in China" was garmented over by their minds, and somehow prestidigitated (perhaps by a molded prayer) into not throwing away scraps in New Orleans. Any person discovered throwing away solid food was made to retrieve it and then eat it. Students who brought lunch from home were forced to eat the dried-out crusts or the disliked lunchmeat enclosed in mayonnaise-limp bread. Part of the torment, in the expiation for the sin, was having to eat the refuse where it was found. The large brick incinerator in the schoolyard, belying its oven shape, was the scene of many deft moves of food disposal, some successful, some not. If not, then the nuns (one or two with great zeal) would enforce this edict. The incinerator's smell of sour milk, ash, things not fully burned, grimy dirt, and garbage was repulsive. Tightly twisted paper bags were always to be found in trashcans. They were seemingly empty, nothing but brown paper (thus escaping detection), but if picked up, by some sleuthing sister, they often proved to contain highly torqued sandwich remains. Occasionally a student would balk, refusing to "eat out of the garbage." They endured time consuming punishments as a result. No one learned any lessons from this full-consumption regimen, except to be cautious, and that the nuns were strange women, at times slightly ridiculous, with some tending to be mean.

The week wore on like comfortable shoes: home and school, pray and play, eat and sleep, night and day. Occasionally on Fridays we were shown a movie. The school would assemble in the cafeteria; everyone was fidgety but behaving properly. A nun would thread the black and white film and project 400 hundred colored children into a color-drained world of flickering joy.

Fridays also meant the weekend had arrived. Social functions, both sacred and profane, required the pomp of being well groomed. Hair was the first step and the highest rung to climb to leave the base ground of the kinky for the aesthetics of the straight. Nappy-headed coloreds needed the rituals of renewal; barbers and beauticians and unlicensed hands could know no rest.

"Boy, cut that shit off yoh head!"

Knowing that the laws of beauty lay outside "au naturel" sight, mechanical help was used to forge synthetic harmonies. The time of the hot comb, or the clippers, or the "conk," slather and douche with the runny-lye goop, had come for most of the pickaninny-heads of the Nigra population. Mr. Ralph's Barber Shop, around the corner on South Robinson (directly in front of Fifth African Baptist Church) was crowded on Friday afternoon. Early Saturday morning, I brought my "b-b shot" hair, my twenty-five cents and my longing to be outside into Mr. Ralph's shop. I waited my turn by looking first at the same, old, worn magazines: *Jet, Ebony, Tan,* and *Bronze Thrills,* that all grew staler each week. When the magazine-scan was done, the fidget began. If the men were in conversation, I would listen; sometimes, it was interesting. Once the talk turned to sex. An old, big-belly man, wearing suspenders, and whose pants' button was not and could not fastened, started a gravelly prologue about "anudder problem with dem women." "Wait, wait," Mr. Ralph said to him, and to me: "Go outside, the talk is getting too strong." Mr. Ralph was fulfilling his charge. My grandmother had taken me there the first time, and said: "Take care of him, Mr. Ralph." "Yes, Mrs. Fassitt."

Before this, I had gone to Mr. Charlie's Barber Shop around on Magnolia at Amelia. One Saturday, in a near empty shop, Mr. Charlie's breath, as always, was bellowing down and breaking its path upon my head. But the bullying smell from his last cigar had lost its place to the stubborn reek of alcohol. And his occasional words stretched long in his mouth, like pulled putty. Aunt Alice used the word slurred when she heard the story. On the next haircutting day, Grandma Adele took me to Mr. Ralph's. Mercifully, Mr. Ralph would allow me to go outside the front door of the barbershop and amuse myself, just nearby of course. I had not been allowed to go outside Mr. Charlie's.

Mr. Ralph, a short, powerfully built, dark-brown skin man had wavy, thick hair. He sported a thin black moustache on a calm, but serious-looking face that was dignified and religious to a preacher's mien. As a young man, during the depression, he had worked in a "CC" camp, where there were some men who were jealous of him, because he "had pretty hair." He showed me a picture taken of him in his camp clothes. What was striking was the fullness of his uniform due to his bulging muscles. Mr. Ralph added, "I was strong."

The clippers moved quickly over my head, cutting away my small coils of kink, until a suitable length was reached. Then with a slight wrinkling about the mouth, as his concentration pulled tightly about itself, Mr. Ralph would use the straight razor to shape the sideburns. Smelling of bay rum and feeling the alcohol cool from it, on my scalp, my day of hair maintenance had ended; "bad hair" laid low on the floor.

For the women and the girls, the process was more elaborate. First, there was the internal beauty shop conversion from the kinky "bad hair" to the faux "good hair." Second, there was the external job of preventing, before the end of the weekend, the dreaded reversion of "going back" to natural kink. The most effective and frightening agent for this undoing was water; a dousing could bring tears and rage. The hot comb seared the straight world into and on to their colored heads. My female kin went to Mrs. Olivia Beauty Parlor on the uptown-riverfront side of Louisiana Avenue and LaSalle Street. From Friday morning to Saturday evening, hair was cooking; it was the corner pong. The heated metal comb passed through each grease-prepared section of hair, which then obeyed, cowed by the sizzle, and cowled occasionally by smoke and always by the smell. Pressed into obedience by skilled hands, deftly working the hot iron of correction, hair and the beauty shop existed as a closed world that held no interest for me. My intrusion into it was passing by and hearing occasionally the involuntary "Ouch!" made by a young female's voice. Then an older woman's voice would quickly scold, "Sit still child." Constant, hot retraining, from the natural "bad" to the provisional faux "good", was the Negro-females' burden of hair.

Sitting in the colored section of the bus meant sitting behind white people. I came to see that all white people did not have "good hair." The worst was the hair of many directions. Some white men had hair as straight as the bristles in a scrub brush, only thinner. The effect reminded me of my aunt's pincushion when it was full round with pins. Others had lank hair, without twist or bend. It lay upon their heads, wanting vigor, fatigued. When I heard the word flop, its intonation matched.

21

After having taken the vows of poverty, chastity, and obedience, the mandate of the Sisters of the Blessed Sacrament was to serve among the "Colored and the Indian races." The founder, Katharine Drexel, who came from old moneyed stock, was destined to become a woman-island, floating in the country's boiling crock of racial stink. Eighteen Ninety-One, black necks popped, by Mr. White Cain, who on boring nights, freely burned blacks to black crackling, and from screams took laughter, while chorusing the Lord's name in a blasphemous vein. "God Damn! Look at dat black summumbitch cook." Again, you murdered your brother! You are dumb, Cain. And you drank your hot toddy Major deSpain, with God's love soil-washed by your whiskey-distain.

Mother Katharine: Black-gowned Bride of Christ; myopic monolith for a disparate humanity; long-visioned monument; avatar of training black, back for their own. From her fecund, untouched womb came grammar schools, high schools, and Xavier University: un-tethered responses to cutting dumb cane. My mother, her twin, and my sister flew long into purpose and high upon excellence, praising the lift from her black gossamer wings.

I had great respect for the nuns, but the gender-effacing garments of their religious vocation countered any feelings of warmth toward them. It was natural for the students to comment on who was ugly and who was pretty. Both types were present. Unsexed by the religious habit, the face became vignetted by the wimple. An attractive face, thus displayed, was even more noticeable. Sister Gerald's face was remarkably pretty. It was well proportioned and ovular, with an occasional pink blush, most noticeable when she was flustered. She had a small sensuous mouth that had full lips, and she had doe eyes and her nose was well shaped. Most of the class agreed that she was the best looking of the nuns.

The crucifix they wore on the chest, a chaste reminder of salvation, obeyed the laws of physics. It could not sink into their dugs but lay flat on top of them. Thus, its pitch brought into notice the dimensions of what it lay upon. The ostentation to conquer pressures of gender, by wearing recognizable mummery, ironically accentuated the face and ranked the sizes of their bosoms. Their garments' most potent aspect of de-sexing was its smell. A musty odor, the spirit of sackcloth and ashes, came from the gowns they wore.

A punishment detail brought me inside the convent. It was sparse, and an odd exposition existed inside. The beds, one to a room, were almost as high as the top bunk in bunk beds, but nothing was stored under them. Such a volume of emptiness turned my mind around. The bed seemed to be a mere cover on a block of space. Being in punishment made my reasoning ugly. *They want to make sure no man was hiding under their bed.* Within their rooms, to ensure the mental ease of freedom from the taint-of-comfort, the beds had been rendered sterile platforms resting upon gaunt legs. By obedience to their law, chastity in repose had been wedded to the poverty of sight. When finished with the punishment chores, the several of us were in the garden preparing to leave. We were told that we had better run out of the yard because "Lady" a huge, black Doberman, which normally ran free, would be released when the nun reached its doghouse in the rear of the grounds. Everyone ran. John Petain even leapt over the fence. True to her word, the nun released the dog. It tore after us, but all were safe.

The nun's behavior was mean, but meanness was not gathered up only in the black folds of habits. Miss Kone, brown, round-rumped and full-chested, taught third grade with a stinging tongue. She liked green clothes, but not green-eyed Negroes. Teedi and I both knew the whimsy of her mouth's fury. The eyes of the cat seemed to have meant her ill: maybe a tryst, and then an un-promise of wedding bells.

"You green-eyed alley cat."

"Sit down, you green-eyed rat."

"You green-eyed cat from Saint James Street."

"You cat-eyed thing, you."

Unable to respond to what I did not know, or what I had not done, my mind shrugged in hurt wonder. But in the private wound from her public malice, I wished for thoughts, which I could not conceive nor express, but which should have been, for justice sake. *Yeah, and I got something too for yoh big booty.* However, even if I could have formed this counter, being in third grade, perhaps, I would have not fared well in the inescapably heated jousting.

22

The travail of firmly disciplining the students fell to Mother Calista. In her office, yardsticks were smacked upon the palms, with the count matching the severity of the offense. She rarely missed, except when the hands were withdrawn, flinching from the memory of the burning sting or the soreness building up, clap after clap. The ways of inducing discipline and showing displeasure varied with each female teacher, lay or religious.

Mrs. Charles, in second grade, had tailored hers to the class and to her person. Being enormously heavy, with a wonderful smiling face, she would counsel, with enough frequency to merit attention from young children, "You all better behave, or I'll sit on you and make you a grease spot." Everyone smiled at this nonsense, but....

Miss Wright, the fifth-grade teacher, and the last of my four lay teachers was tall and angular and projected a look of strength. She reminded me of the lady who came each week to collect the insurance premiums. But that lady was friendly; Miss Wright was not so cordial. On the first day of her class she addressed discipline and her principles. With a stern face, she overlooked the class, "Just because some of you won a contest last year, don't expect any easy grades in this class." The broad base of her remark went to all the students, but it sloped down to personally address me (I had won the contest). Puzzled as to why she chose me as the example, for I expected nothing. Ever since kindergarten, everybody knew that Lydia and Marlene were the two smartest people in the class. During the year, I did my work, caused no problems, and never thought of Miss Wright except when looking at her in class. Like a branch of a rose bush, without the roses, just avoid it.

Sister Immaculata Marie, tall and witch-like, at least, in apprehension, once, became incensed at me for a joke, with her as the butt. For an infraction, I had been made to stand at the front of the class. With her at her desk and me slightly behind, I faced the class: my audience. Looking down upon her and spiraling my index finger about my temple, the sign of being loco, I then cast a glance at her. The joke got a few smirks, and I thought that I was free and clear, but no. Though delayed, my poor joke's recoil finally reached me. Turning her head, Sister Immaculata grabbed my chin. With her large face magnified by her headgear, she excoriated me. My straightforward defense: I was making a joke; no, I did not think that she was crazy. My ad lib routine had been topped by Rafael, who told the nun about the joke.

I was not angry with Rafael, because Rafael was who he was: an embryonic campy entertainer. Everybody understood this, not in words, but in the knowledge that needs no words (these would come later, as our store of coarse conceits increased). The tattletale, the mêlée stirrer, the gossip sluice, all flowed naturally out of him. Not just because he wanted to curry favor but wanting to be in the spotlight possessed him. A kinetic dervish sat inside and pressed its dictates upon him. He would be a lively cheerleader. And with age, he would have loved for the chance to be dressed up in an oriental costume, with a feather in the turban, doing a shimmy dance on a huge stage in Vegas.

Rafael's sister's thighs touched an appreciative faculty in me, but through what agency I had not a clue. Some called her legs "fat fine." When Rebecca was in eighth grade and I was in sixth grade, her quadriceps induced the second imprinting on my mind for the construction of impure thoughts. Breasts now levitated over thighs in this evolving Frankenstein monster, whose completion promised repetitive confessions, long prayers of penance, and perdition, if death overtook before a sincere Bless me Father, for I have sinned. This invocation, in an inchoate fashion, I began unknowingly, to keep at the ready. If upon death's cut from life, one could truly repent in the speedy passing, then all of one's hell-crimes were made into something less. The normal cleansing route was not under such dramatic conditions, but it was still harrowing.

The walk to the church from my house for Saturday confession passed through a corridor of distress. There was no bustle about the church at that hour. In the twilit light, the doors' small cutouts, of translucent stained glass, were opaque to both color and sin. They appeared as dull slate, keloided by the lead joints. Inside, for the ritual of the sacrament, the lights had been quarter struck. Scattered about the darkened church were the penitents, totally self-absorbed, not sitting, but kneeling within the pews. Heads were bowed or uplifted in supplication, with hands clasped around the promise of forgiveness. It was quiet, only the breathing of the church could be heard. In the tapered shadows of each other's sins, they silently moved past one another within the two minor aisles leading to the confessionals. The queues were never long, they accommodated themselves to moderation. They would dwindle, and then by one, two, or three, their size would be increased again. Inside the confessional priests were men of power. Their ears were portals, and their hands and words, making signs and utterances into the clear air, breached into the past, and drew out the warm, red drops from the wet ground beneath the cross on Calvary. Golgotha, The Place of the Skull, drowned all men's sins upon its mound.

"Bless me Father, for I have sinned…" burned my mouth like dry ice. Frozen fast upon young lips, my private shames were to be torn away in whispered hisses and dropped into the ear of the priest. The venial wrongs, the ones easy to recount, came first. It was the murky and religiously damnable ones that shamed me. They would have risen unbidden, and perhaps prolonged themselves within my mind. When the full measure of these spites to God had been transferred, the priest gestured, and brought the undeserved magic of "I absolve you from your sins, in the name of the Father, and of the Son, and of the Holy Spirit." The drama was profound in its conjuring. Still wrapped tightly in the concupiscence of mortal flesh, my clean soul heard, through my human ear, "Go and sin no more."

The prayers of penance: the slight rendering due for the miracle given, were cool to the tongue. Kneeling upon the stone step below the altar rail and resting my forearms on top of the polished marble barrier, I faced the altar, the warm heart of mercy. In the devotional alcove of The Virgin Mary, there were burning offertory candles. Their dripping beeswax had made clotted trails of pale gold on the black, iron candleholder. I would inhale deeply. Now, the scent had the fragrance of the long promise of eternal union with God the Father: the abundant infinity of forgiveness.

We adore Thee, Oh Christ, and we bless Thee, because by Thy holy cross,

Thou has redeemed the world," *and rescued mankind from Your Father's lawful judgment. But why, Oh Lord, did you make us from slime: to ape the slug? to leave behind our line? Must we be senseless to know your way; to find salvation?"* "Bless me Father, for I have sinned." Thought crime was deadly, for it sought to climb into a perilously opened mind.

The black-gown troika: Sister Andrea Marie, Sister Gerald, and Sister Antoine, guided sixth, seventh, and eighth grade respectively into the willing and mostly obedient minds of the students. Andrea Marie fractured, but did not shatter, my imagined mold of how women were made. First, to the eye, she was unattractive. A small fleshy growth, like a bump that sought notice, was on her upper cheek. It did not disfigure her; it only brought more attention to her face. Her mouth was always set, and her eyes were black lanterns focusing dark fury. She was short, but this was only noticed from afar. Up close, everything drove vision to her face. Her curtness faced forward with a slight coldness that put me off thinking of her as a physical woman. She was the most learned teacher I had encountered. Her competence and knowledge were like the wringers in the old washing machine. If the lever was up, there was space between the two cylinders. But if nonsense was with your cloth, the lever was pushed down, and the sloshing excess was squeezed out. She read everything we wrote, "…and their destiny was manifest and made known…" tucked away in a line of an essay, and felt clever by the word "manifest", was spotted. "What is this? The two words mean the same thing. Don't use a word if you don't know its meaning." The censure, done in hot-heat timbre, without any meanness, was impressive. I never forgot the lesson of being pushed away from ignorance. Of course, I had no affection toward her, but respect for her abilities formed. She was a woman/nun, made with a new type of clay, not that from which Eve descended. *Eve would not have had to be a nun.*

Tall Sister Gerald was virgin incarnate, as though she had been plucked from the womb and put into habit. She turned red when in temper or when lost in dealing with unaccustomed situations. Given her obvious beauty, she would have been perfect as a caricature in a deliberately offensive, sexual parody of nuns. But there was no artifice in her; she was the pearl grown inside the never-opened oyster. One could wonder if she bathed clothed, or not troubled by her body, took to her cleansing touch, with nerves cut-dead at innocence's behest.

"Gottfrey got a hard-on," whispered Scrappy as Gottfrey walked to the front of the class. Echoed, more loudly, by me who was ignorant of its meaning. Gottfrey heard and trumpet flared. "That's not true, you nasty thing, you," fixing his angry retort upon me. Sister Gerald asked Gottfrey what the problem was. Gottfrey with a vocal bitchiness, almost campy: "That nasty thing said I had a hard-on." Sister Gerald's face, now as puzzled as mine, turned quickly to restoration. "What is that?" Gottfrey fumed but offered no explanation. "Nasty," indicative and provocative, brought a natural response from her ignorance: "Go wait outside the classroom!" Exiting, I heard Rafael attempt to explain to the nun: "When a man sees a woman something happens."

"Huh?" she said.

Outside the classroom door, in the quiet of the corridor, reckonings commenced inside my brain. Gravity, more gravity, then strong compression promised itself upon me. All of this within a nimbus of ignorance: what was a "hard-on" and why did Gottfrey get so offended? The corridor had a dead end where unused desks were stored along both of its sides. A large door was in the wall, and its swing carried it into the area of storage. The first desk, on the left side of the aisle, prevented the door from going more than a half full swing, so it fully shielded that side of the corridor from sight. One could sit in the first desk and be unobserved. My judgment rapidly led me to this meditation place. At the end of the class, Sister Gerald would go to Mother Calista, who would be told. More than likely she would understand the full import of the situation. Also, since "nasty" was the nature of the offense, her judgment would be severe. Once, when told of a "nasty" act by a malefactor, she declared that she would use three yardsticks to punish him, rather than the usual one. Rafael's "explanation," because of his natural entertainment skills, would add emotional intensity to Sister Gerald's understanding or dread. All of this was not good. And I had done nothing wrong, so I felt. Adjudicating myself innocent, I saw no reason to subject myself to punishment. So, after half an hour, having obeyed the words "to wait," I left.

Upon arriving home, my grandmother said she had received a frantic call from the school: Was he there? No, he was not. I told Mamma Adele the truncated truth. I had waited, and they must have missed me by not looking behind the door. She thought this reasonable. The following day, the nuns' anger had gone flat. My disappearance had so unnerved them that my reappearance was heaven sent, especially, since they had erred in not looking in an almost obvious place. The original incident was incinerated by their joy.

Both Rafael and Gottfrey were homosexual. Rafael enjoyed being flighty; Gottfrey's way was different. It was dangerous to confuse their dissimilar dispositions. Gottfrey was both "cock strong," and had a volatile temper, but face on he would front someone. Rafael, on the other hand, might conceal a knife, and slit the threat's throat.

Sister Antoine (the last of the three) was of an old-sagged matron's build. She was reputed to be the best, and the most formidable teacher in the school. Her class was known to be a treat and a challenge, and she was aware of this. Seventh Graders knew that they had to face her. Hers was the final grooming class before high school. She took her wisdom seriously. Many a young mind owed much to this wrinkled, old white woman. I found her no more knowledgeable than Sister Andrea Marie, but more forgiving, more akin to my grandmother rather than my aunt. But my grandmother had nothing to prove; Sister Antoine had long been laurelled for her prowess. She was truly admirable, but unfortunately, instead of the pith of wisdom she would, at times, insert the embellishment of story. Her days of handling smart, adolescent students were closing. Soon, she would be a mock of herself; her career's end should be more dignified. Sitting in a comfortable chair with an open book in her lap, but peacefully nodding in a mild mid-afternoon sun, was her due. She had given me the wisdom that great pleasure could reside in learning. I would learn, in the years to come, that great distress could also come from knowledge.

For almost a decade, my class and I had come and gone together, thousands of times, through the same doors, at school and in Church. I could see their faces with blind eyes, but except for four, I had never visited any of them in their houses. We fell from each other at the end of the school day like seeds dropped from an unzipped pod. Each, in our own way, burst and sprouted the school day, in the not-school time, in front of unknown hearths. But embers, from inside some of them, popped and sparked, and told of the dark spite, masked by the faux bright.

"Come outta there, yall know yall ain white!"

With a growing blush, Catherine and her sister looked about to see who might have heard these words. The park, the beautiful park on Napoleon and South Liberty, should have been open to them. Their blue eyes and golden hair solidly fixed with the trapping of ivory skin gave them the right. Paul, Saul and John "loud capped" their wrong.

After Louisiana Ave was widened, a white motorcycle policeman occasionally hid behind the large live oak in front of our house. The officer's whistle was the shrill notching of tickets being given from the legal ambush. As my sister and I walked through our gate wearing impeccable school uniforms, the policeman, less than ten feet away, would turn his head toward us, and freeze the instance with the gravity of his being. Initial attempts at greeting an officer were pressed into oblivion by his Gorgon-closed faces: grim contempt and lethal authority. No officer ever wavered from this bearing in all the years the trap lay open. My x-ray eyes saw Duo Glide centaurs: rude, coarse beasts, whose foraging brought them into my beloved neighborhood. I wished that THE LAW would stay away. *Let them go back to the all-white areas where they lived.* Jesus had said, "In My Father's house there are many mansions." Negroes would live in some, and Creoles in others, and whites in the rest.

23

The nuns and the priests told us that earthly delights were but a shadow of what awaited us in heaven. This made sense only without thought. Divine fragrances could be admitted, but I would never reject the earthly scent. Being co-opted in heaven did not appeal to me, but infinitely less was the roasting smell of hell for all eternity. Always, always, perdition lurked. It courted and waited. Upon its heated, smoking doors, the mathematics of damnation was graven. Leibniz's and Newton's calculus taming of infinity held no sway inside those gates. "Let a thousand million-million years pass; not a second has gone by in infinity. This awaits the damned. If every second were a million years and you counted till the end of time (and time would end on the day of judgment), infinity would not have begun." For adults who dislike the numbers, fatigue and acquiescence promised safety, as per the panicked reasoning attributed to Pascal: suppose Hell does exists, and you have acted like it did not. To a child, unschooled in this logic, the numeration offered a numbing, non-countable infinity of terror.

Lent, the time of abjuration, not Christmas, was the moral core of the year: Jesus was born that he might die. Every Friday, during Lent, the school went to the church for Stations of the Cross: fourteen tableaus that recalled mankind's rescue from deserved infinite torment. "We adore Thee O Christ and we bless Thee, because by Thy holy cross Thou hast redeemed the world." Finally, giving God his adieu, with the last genuflection and leaving the pew, the counting to infinity became, "one, two, and many." It was getting hot; summer was coming. This meant Boy Scout Jamborees at

Indian Village were approaching, three days away from home having fun in the woods. To me, the four seasons of the year were Mardi Gras, Lent, summer, and Christmas/New Year. They moved from the profane, to the sacred, to the profane, to the sacred, then back round again.

24

In lieu of spring, where renewal, slyly, in its own time, puts new buds on dormant stalks, the coursing energy of arousal came to the city by calendar fiat and without guile. Mardi Gras was the erection that greets the morning, which arises not from conscious desire, but from the arousal of life proclaiming its existence. During the two weeks to Ash Wednesday, the pores of New Orleans would open, and the sweat of carousing would lave the brows, readying them for the painless stigmata of ashes. The grey/black smudge would acknowledge that there would be death, decay, and the scattering by wind of the precious human flesh, which was both borne and adored. But before the onset of Lent's forty-day meditation, the corpulent honoring (the time for the fatted ox) set the city on fire. And, it blazed for Catholic and non-Catholic alike. No one who resided in the city could escape this impending crescendo. The young floated on top of the delirium; they would sink into its thickness, as they grew heavier with age.

Of course, the festival was split by race. The nexus for coloreds and whites formed itself in the streets, now made common by the parades' cry: "Hey Mister, throw me something." But the centripetal Cajun cry: "Laissez les bon temps rouler!" did not mix colored faces with the whites' way. The French Quarter, The Vieux Carre, The Old Quarter, kept to the old ways. The only permission passes for coloreds were still the required uniforms of janitor, maid, busboy, delivery person, and minstrel. The krewes: Bacchus, Comus, Proteus, Rex, et al, sported their royalty in *The Times Picayune*, and *The States-Item*. Old white kings, young white queens, and retinues of age-mixed whites daily unmasked themselves for society's applause. My eyes, made crass by segregated distance, took the photos to memory as I did with most white people's faces: fleeting looks at indistinguishable Caucasian-featured humans.

The Louisiana Weekly, (the colored newspaper) whose motto: "A Voteless People is a Hopeless People," told of colored carnival affairs: the dances, the balls, the restaurant parties, and the route of the Zulus (the only colored parade). During those two weeks, the greatly lengthened police report in the white newspapers gave Grandma Adele so much more to read. It seemed to me that it was more of the same, except that drunkenness, prostitution, "b" drinking, and crimes against nature had promiscuously increased in The Quarter; most of the men named were not from New Orleans. No doubt, sometimes, carnival behavior required a great deal of explanation.

An in-the-stomach frying riff on a snare drum with a tinny-tingle grate from cymbals played out the day of the season's first night-parade. This was the jitter-and-quiver prologue to the curtain of night dropping; then, the performance would commence. Uncle Rodney, "Crump" to his adult friends, took my sister and me to the night parades in the late forties and early fifties. Tall and thin, and uncle by marriage, he worked in the postal system as a clerk: one of the few careers open to coloreds. Because of his job, he knew the streets flawlessly. (Mail was hand sorted and each street had to be known.) He parked "Old Betsy" on an off street that would not encounter traffic and all of us walked to our spot. Most folk had a favorite spot to watch the parade. It might have been a good luck spot where they caught many "favors" or chosen for ease of watching or for its proximity to their house.

Wherever there was depth of space there was a crowd. No part of the parade's route was without a sea of intermixed white and colored. None took notice, it seemed. Uncle Rodney hawk-watched us. Far from home, in a large crowd, tiny me kept one eye near to my uncle in addition. Peanuts, fresh parched, were the food of the parades. They were sold everywhere, and in the crunch of the shells, between the tips of my fingers, a reassuring feeling asserted itself. The crowd waited for the moving spectacle; to be late meant a waste of time. Behind the curb, because of the crush, movement through the crowd took serpentine forms: slither and dart. Before the start, the stratagems of viewing came into play. There were no crowd-barriers; only common sense would separate parade from onlookers.

Those whose temperament suited orderly behavior, with a pension to be legal and correct, stood on the sidewalk at the curb. The view from here was technically the best, and their position legal. The ones, with temperaments given to a love of risks and a slightly selfish strain, stood in the street. These two groups warred at every parade. Normally, it was not physical, but oil and water are of different types. The traveling buzz through the crowd ("Here it comes") preceded, by scant moments, the wail of sirens. The police car or cars making the noise spurred the clash of the groups. Those waiting in the road had to fit somewhere. The official cars, which moved slowly in the center of the street, could be avoided, but then, with a side canter, huge horses, topped with helmeted white police, rump-drove the street people onto the curb. Occasionally, when the mounts paused, tumbling out their asses, mounds of horseshit would fall. The police never looked down; the understanding was manifest: **Heed the equine line!** *Oh, how large the hooves are, and the frightening clacks they make.*

The curb waiters never seemed to grasp this dynamic: anger, always, was in some of their faces. Once, in the shuffle back to the curb, a split occurred. A small, old colored woman (she had not put her false teeth in, so her mouth sagged) had an open knife with a four-inch blade in her hand. She held the weapon of righteousness directly in front of her; it was visible even in the darkness made by the crowd blocking the small light. Not loud, especially given the clamor of the moment, but somehow unmistakable in its power to instruct: "Just stand in front me! Go-head on. Ah deh ya. You gaun get this here naaf." She held her spot. The disorderly curb-moving wave split and smoothly flowed around this small, gritty rock and found place behind her.

The streetlights were not generous with light, so, for proper show, the parades carried and burned their own flambeaux. Smoke and a bizarre pinkish/red illumination came forward as though up from the mouth of an LSD-high, moving forge. The flat haze of the smoke broke when curls of it were drilled upward only for these to end as frolicking wafts, rising into the dense blackness overhead. The source, when it could be fully seen, was lit flares in holders mounted on eight-foot high sticks. A crisp smell came along with the burning embers dropping from the lights. The mounted police were right; the street was not safe. Carrying the flambeaux were goggle-eyed colored men, spaced out in a motley grid, four or five abreast and five rows deep. Each one hooded in a thick, one-piece, dingy white gown that reached to their knees. Darkness was the color that came from inside the peaked, hooded hollow where even the fused light could not breach. The poles rested in an inverted codpiece lashed around their waist. This opening tableau moved as a lattice held together by weak springs. Each point, though joined to the form, moved to the funk in singular feet: jigging jiggaboos. Not a torch was bound by gravity; they could not fall. Only spewing of the spent fuel felt the need to touch ground. After the pink lights, with sufficient space (to prevent panic), came four giant workhorses pulling the first float. Led by firm-handed, colored grooms, blinkered-horses, whose clacking hoofs made a rhythm of restraint, moved the fifteen-foot high, half-street wide moving-stage. And the noise of the crowd was so loud and sweet from appreciation: squeals, hoops, applause, whistles, and hollers. Reciprocity had begun. The river flowed, but its banks defined it.

The king and queen floats passed. They were barks for royalty, with surmounted thrones that rocked to the waddle of iron wheels rolling the huge constructions down the road. Hot-pink combustion, from the flares, had deadened the royals' vision in front, and the cupolas, they sat in, limited sight to the sides. Waving and waving only to a dark, screaming undulation, light-blinded rulers ruled over their night dominion until they reached the streets of bright lights. The little pages studding the front and the sides of the royal floats did not wear masks. They served by standing and waving, with one hand inside the loop of the safety rod next to them. These gaudily dressed pages, proclaimed innocent by wearing no masks, did not throw favors. The King and Queen never threw favors; royalty's gift was accepting acclaim.

After the horses, white faces decked around with band uniforms went by. The sounds of the bands never ceased; they grew louder upon approach, softer as they receded with the lost volume supplied by the next band. They came from all over white land. The slides of trombones were swung from side to side as the marching feet stamped out the time between them and things of interest. The words were hurled upward in half the loop that bound the frolic: "Hey Mister, throw me something!" The circle came round as favors flew down and out. The merriment was now one thing; segregated parts had been fused in a pitch barrel of funk. Everyone sweated inside the frenzy.

Sequins, brocade, and silk were all stitched together with gaudy flair in the krewes' costumes, which extinguished the stars and even mocked the moon. All the revelers were masked. The salmon-pink, full-faced coverings hid them from the crowd. And the uncertain and moving light distorted the crowd's faces below. Now the fusse' has been exchanged for kerosene flambeaux, which were heavy and demanded more robust carriers. The eight-foot high poles remained, but on top was a cylinder of fuel with a line of jets on each side and a foot-high aluminum reflector behind. The crotch pouch was strongly made leather. Strong Negroes, in full white gowns, were carrying torches that looked like Latin crosses with flaming arms. These lit the way for the white revelers; each wearing masks fitted with archaic smiles. The torch men danced, and the on-high whites jigged. Each invoked the gods of levity. Gravitas would have been an affront. The colored men put balance in the soul of the torches. These were twirled and handled without hands, and their bearers bent and contorted both to the applause of the crowd, and the chink of coins thrown in appreciation. A torch falling or burning kerosene lighting something could only be in answer to a prayer to the god of foul tidings. All would wish that that deity be undone (for this night).

Leaping upward and screaming forward, the energetic in the crowd, try to create notice by their large motions. The largess of the Mister, caught by supplicants, vindicated their method. Beads, finely wrought in Czechoslovakia, were the staple. A knotted loop of stout-woven twine joined thin, two inch, colored, glass cylinders traveling its round. The colors were as bright and gaudy as the krewes costumes. This exchange token was as durable as the fete. They broke, but not without effort. Two sets of hands grabbing for the same favor, need not come to Solomon's fair bisection. Often, they went to the hand with the firmer tug. But the beads were only one type of favor. Small, nice things were given as favors also. In the better parades, well-decorated clickers were flung out: ladybugs or green–eyed beetles or some other cunningly wrought metal, shaped and painted. All were fitted underneath with the flat, metal, click-tongue that allowed these metallic crickets to live within the sweet, surrounding din. They were prized; their utility could live wherever revelry desired sound.

Other favors, lighter upon the air, sailed out. Colored rattan strips, woven into finger-cuffs, were pitched out, to let them fall (but not heavily) down. Seemingly, without bite, they did catch. Index fingers easily inserted into the open ends of the five-inch plaited tubes could be removed only if the plaits were not under tension. In the frantic pulse of the living-parade moment, some who tried out the favor did not relax immediately. Two hands, unable to separate, were raised and linked waving, in the almost involuntary spasm of: Hey Mister, throw me something. Catching something would have been difficult and falling down would have been easy. As soon as they stopped pulling the trap opened and out came the two fingers. This favor was safeguarded. The first victim wanted a second victim, but this one they themselves would catch. People with fat fingers were best advised to leave the thing alone.

Tan and white giraffes, green alligators, brown hippos, and such, all about two inches long and made with plastic skin and plaster of Paris innards, also dropped from the sky. The scrambling for favors was wild, athletic, and full of head-butting potential if the trinkets landed on the ground. Sometimes it was ugly, but usually ire lasted but an instant. The bands marched, the torches bobbed, the gorgeous floats and their bright riders flowed by. The crowd's life lit the night as did the torches, and, as more than likely, alcohol did for some of the people on the floats. Strong probabilities and certainties were evident. One day a torch might fall. But before that, one of the float riders would not have their hand in the safety loop atop the safety rod, and too near the edge they would do a jolly kick-step, and they would slip and tumble down, un-favored that night by fate. And they would be mortally hurt. The moving train stoked the fire of frenzy until the last float. Then it was done.

Street cleaning crews followed immediately. The peanut shells, the waste food, the remnants of burnings, paper, cups, bottles, and all other undesired strewn things were put into collectors. The noise of a beehive in dispersing disarray, after the queen has died, covered the area. Walking with Uncle Rodney back to the car, pockets full, the single thought formed and stayed in my mind: tomorrow night was another parade; hopefully, we could go.

In one carnival, in the early fifties, instead of horses pulling the first float, a tractor appeared. Without hesitation, my eyes opened wide in amazement. Immediately afterwards, my gaping mouth joined the rest of my face in a look of revulsion. The tractor was irremediably ugly in these surroundings. Sight, sound, smell, and taste were all affronted in less than two seconds. The visible exhaust carried the oily diesel smell of a poorly running engine. The movement of the thing pushed the odor upward and outward. Outward was into the crowd, where only tiny gaps allowed it to dissipate further. The active palate was assaulted with the vile taste of fuel-oil fumes settling in the mouth. No clack of hoofs, no whinnies, no sounds of life, just a grinding monotony as the thing revved and tugged by using its large rubber tires made for the sod. A slouching white man, who seemed wearied by the task, played, without any sense of style, upon the thing's throttle. The bland machine went by pulling the float. Another came and did the same. Modernity had crashed into Mardi Gras. This cracked it, for me. As yearly-upgrades were hitched to the tractor evolution, the breach widened, and my enthusiasm for the fete grew less and less.

25

Es war verboten! My segregated eyes could never see the public carnality in the Quarter, where carnival-inspired raunch was reputedly unfettered. But, "Everybody from New Orleans can really do that thing," sang Louis

Armstrong in 1925, while playing with The Hot Five. That will "to do" would find its place. During one carnival season: A colored man entered the telephone booth located on the neutra ground of Louisiana Ave. and LaSalle St. on the river-front side. The booth made of clear glass had thin aluminum struts separating the glass sections. The man picked up the receiver, put a coin in a slot, dialed a number, and began to talk. A colored woman, both large in height and size, waited for him. On the uptown side next to the booth was a utility pole. The woman, within touching distance of the nude tree, moved slightly forward and pressed her front against it. Lifting her right leg, she wrapped it halfway around the brown cylindrical pole and put her arm softly on the post where it met her embrace. She worked her pelvis directly upon the possibly splintery pole. She was absorbed totally with two foci: looking at the back of the man's head in the booth (who paid no attention to her) and her grinding hips. I walked on and wondered: *Did the white women in the Quarter worship dick so boldly?*

Mardi Gras, the entire day, was fat. Only this one day remained to ingest the full measure of carnival's sensual gluttony, so that on the following day, Ash Wednesday, there would be no lack of actions to repent.

Citywide mummery was in effect with masks being allowed until sundown. Praise of costumes rose with the skill and the wit shown in the designs. My aunts were all accomplished seamstresses and orthodox. They made me conform to the dictums of the day in a simple, elegant way by making an outfit, for me, crossed between a bullfighter, a gypsy, and a gaucho. It had bright colors, a vest, a sash, pants with no cuffs, and a head tie. I wore my Mardi Gras outfit for several years to the sound of my one-day name, Toreador. My sister's, without intimations of masculine tasks, had only the wit of the gypsy in her costume.

The Zulus, Colored men in black face, stepping off a river barge, early Mardi Gras morning, signaled the start of the day. I never saw them, though for several years I saw their expectancy: in front of The Might Earl bar, at the corner from my house, a three-step high wooden platform was built for a toast on route. Drinks would be passed up to the Zulus. Many colored establishments had these stairs; too many it seemed. The story was that people on the floats got drunk and were unable to finish the route. An ad hoc path was then taken, with non-Zulus riding on the floats. Year after year there was this same story. What was tangible were the gold painted ZULU labeled coconuts my aunts brought home each year from their dance.

Abra Cadabra: The Indians just appeared. In the neighborhood, word spread without wind, The Indians. Louisiana Avenue, wide, with a large neutral ground, and lying within colored lands, was a grand stage.

"Heeee, Heeee, Hayyyyy, Hayyyyy!"

"Whyyyyyy, Eheeeeeee!"

Cries of greeting, cries of war, cries of masculine prowess went back and forth in the tongues of lost languages. Prepared by the "Indian Talk" in Western movies, all ears understood.

"Highhhhh, Highhhhh!"

Pride, going to aggression, danced in the air with these no words, along with decorated hatchets or makeshift tomahawks in hand. In the whole of carnival, without exception, their costumes were unrivaled. More than simply good costumes, many broached genius in craft. If one, plus one, plus one, and on, and on were the steps in putting beads and feathers together for these costumes, then time both slowed and stretched. Three hundred and sixty-five days were not sufficient to make them. Masters in guilds would have balked at the task and demanded large sums for the work. And then, the masters would have increased the number working in their studios. For one day, The Indians pranced and danced and, became wandering shows as strongly done as the mighty floats.

A tambourine is being struck and a refrain, from a lost time, is being chanted: "Two-way-pock-away, I-nine-ni-nu-nay, two-way-pock-away." But these were colored men, wild colored men, chiefs with their squaws, and their tribes, all properly outfitted for this solitary day of show and yell.

"Haaaaaa, Haaaaa!"

"Yuhhhhhhh, Huhuuuuu!"

They were separate nations. One clan saw another, from afar, and the presentations began. My colored eyes watched these strange people, who, related by law (in-laws), kept the dark purity of carnival alive. Their feet struck the ground, and their long, feathered trains sync-moved to the hot pulse of each heart. On occasion, the tribes warred with each another. Dislike, or respect adjudged not sufficient, or jealousy (some costumes were better than others) could strike tinder. Sharp edges would move, and stain themselves with another tribe's blood.

"HIgheeee, HOoooo, HEEEEeeh!"

As I grew older, The Indians kept the spirit of Mardi Gras, not the parades.

REX: King, Monarch of the Day bent the pageantry so that carnival's acclaim was forced to bow to him. His floats, if not the grandest, were somehow the most noble. Daylight brought bright, full sight; no skulking night-blooms rode with them. His intermixed train of retinues was the longest. And his trailing dross of never-to-be-noble "trucks-krewes" grew with the years, as epiphytic moss clinging to the body of a giant "live oak."

REX wore a three-tiered crown. The day was his. The sun rose and gave to him its gold on high: The Sun King. Till nightfall, he was lord. His float's wit peaked into a moving throne, which rocked, in movement, as though he was borne on the high litter of kingship. The krewe's crown defined his personal reign: one season in time. Then he lived in memory where the splendor of his day would be compared to others past and those to come. When the horses left, and the tractors pulled, Rex lost all that was colored in joy: the parade became precise and clinical enjoyment.

REX is coming! Clear the road! The mounted police, then those on motorcycles took to their tasks with eye-blinding shining boots and gleaming chrome bikes. The pinpoint sun bounced off every reflective surface: the metal of the stirrups, the rims, the jackets of the cartridges, flanks of Harleys, and from the dead eyes of the law in sunglasses. Five-year old me knew, without being told, that this gleaming display of road scouring law was for show only. The police would never protect either my kin or me. They were not there for that. It didn't matter though; I would never encounter them. They were as distant, in mind, as the rodeo groups who were from Texas. Both were circus-foreign, yet, now, being so close to cowboys allowed for great admiration of both costume and ability in maneuvering their mounts. (The colored seating in the circus was never close to the center of the ring.)

There were women riders who held flags on poles. There were young white children who were skilled enough to keep in orderly ranks with the white adults. And the costumes they wore were not cowboy outfits. Black and white television never intimated, with enough reality, the blaze of these suits. "Abundant in generosity," The Sun King threw his rays upon his mounted retinue whose sparkling garnish from faux jewels bounced into the eyes. Patterns of rhinestones and metal studs jittered to the bounce of the horses. They all wore Sunday-best's best. The dust and grime of trails, and outposts, and Indian fighting stayed inside the movie theater.

Bands that played for the King were huge; no diminutive groups were ever there. They all rode in from my out-world. Outfitted in bright uniforms with tassels, and epaulets, and assortments of hats ranging from soft tams to helmets, they were crisp in appearance and in vigor from youth. They played the tunes of marching that gave stamp(ing) plap-plap-plap to their step and brought applause from the crowd. As they passed, sometimes someone would holler out the name of a state or a university and give a rapidly forgotten origin to the scores of young white men and women who moved with precision, for everyone's pleasure. Their notes, rising to the sun, flew past the dark ribald forms of moving Negro feet. No "second line" could or would dance with them.

Within REX were themes that validated the continuity of his rule. A genial old white man, who ran the parade's full route, had on his T-shirt: Life begins at 65. The next year he had 66. After he reached 70, I no longer saw him in the parade. Milling in the crowds, on this day of fantasy, were costumes that lent their wit to REX's day. A favorite theme was white men, covered in pitch-black grease under dirty hides, with Spanish Moss as hair, all holding large bones. They would make caveman gestures. They were looked at, judged, and then applauded (if warranted). They also were given a wide berth; nobody wanted to accidentally touch them.

The floats, when seen in daylight, took on mythic scale. Cantilever effects had portrayals protruding out and bobbing from the motion of the float. Everything sparkled. The favors were consistently of the highest sort. REX was king because of quality, daylight, and its upkeep of tradition.

After REX, came the trucks-krewes. Riding on large flatbeds trucks and pulled by cabs, with loud-braying horns, each krew decorated its false-floats as best it could, with some done much better than others. The riders wore costumes based on a theme e.g. *The Voyage of Sinbad* might have them all: white men, women, and children, dressed in oriental outfits. None were elaborate. The truck had a facelift made of skirts of cloth or painted card-board, and some type of structure on the flatbed rhyming with Sinbadness. A few riders were masked, most were not. The favors they threw varied in quality, mostly they were poor. Being close to the ground, one could see plainly their white faces enjoying themselves immensely. A certain sum had allowed their participation in Mardi Gras, but they had no magic. Their wonderful tomfoolery was boring, and their favors missed my interests. Once, someone, in the crowd, managed to lift a covering on a slow-moving truck and snatch a large sack of favors. The man was so pleased with his action. But the sack was useless and the action stupid. Mardi Gras was the give and the get: Hey mister, and then the prize. Maybe the favors could be sold, but this would have no pleasure for me. It was like taking one of my grandmother's prized fruitcakes and trying to eat it all at once. Even if one could, it would spoil the enjoyment, because pleasure of something so rich came in measured doses. So I was raised; so I believed. The white truck-people had some means, but they were of poor pedigree. Canal Street, the major shopping district, for whites, in the city, had the same type of mix. There were stores of high standard: Adler, Gochauxs, Gus Mayer's, Maison Blanche, and D.H. Homes, and then those at the base of Olympus. So too with the parade: there was REX above, and the flatbeds below. In later years, as the number of truck-krewes grew and grew, my kin and I left well before the end of this disjointed, ill-bred motley.

Comus, the final parade of the season, ruled Mardi Gras night. Despite the engorgement from the day, there would be a last flambé treat given by this pre-midnight show. I welcomed it as the sentence looks forward to the period. The fete was not done until it should be done. Two clock hands together, pointing to heaven, and having been apart since noon, told mortal ears the moments of pleasure's death. From the fattened ox, to the picked-clean skull of man, in the sounding of the twelve sobering chimes of midnight:

Bong,
Bong,
Bong,
Bong,
Bong,
Bong,
Bong,
Bong,
Bong,
Bong,
Bong,
Bong.
ASH WEDNESDAY; LENT…
"Ashes to ashes and dust to dust."
"We adore thee, O Christ, and we bless Thee, because by Thy holy cross Thou has redeemed the world."

26

Uncle Rodney's father was Uncle Bo, a jovial man with dark brown skin that had a red under-sheen. He liked to eat bread with bread pudding, which struck me as amusing. He also trapped and cooked both possum and raccoon. The few times I ate them, I liked them. Strictly speaking, this was not an enlargement of my taste sensibilities. It was more akin to capacity for engulfment: the new meats went down well. By that logic, possum and coon were delights.

Uncle Rodney's mother, Mrs. Thomas, was a tall, light-skinned woman with friendly face, but the reservation it held put off any levity one might have tended toward. Her kindness was palpable, and it settled me. It flowed in a slow undulation from her look, to her words, to her movement. Maternal grace, in any form, made for reverence in my mind. It was akin to the sacred comfort of a full stomach.

One visit, Cousin Henry (Uncle Rodney's brother) talked about something called a television. It was like a movie, but in a person's house. Nothing more was said except that the man across the street at the corner had one. I went outside and saw four or five people peeping in at the man's window. Its low height allowed me to peer inside also, and because I was small the crowd let me move right to the ledge. It took a second or two to adjust to the dim light inside from the high sunshine outside. When my eyes did accommodate, perplexity, wonder, and love all hit me at the same time. From a 9" porthole, sitting inside a "box," I saw cowboys riding horses. They were not in "color" but in black and white, like most movies. There was no projector or film present, which would be my only way of explaining this thing. There was sound, but this was minor; the horses galloped from one side of the screen to the other. It was evident: science magic was at work. Someone else must bear witness to this. Racing back to Uncle Bo's and standing over my sleeping sister, I called her name and shook her. Of course, she did not awake. Time was important; the set might be turned off. She was petulant when roused, even if sleep itself had moved on to another person. I hit her and stepped back. She was larger, but there would be a fight if she did not come with me. She glared as she sought to make sense of my assault. "They shrunk people and put them in a box." Breathless and belligerent, I would have my witness to this magic thing.

"Huh?"

"They shrunk people and put them in a box. Come and see."

"Where?"

"Across the street. Come on."

She yielded. Putting on outside clothes, she and I both went to see the "cathode-ray tube miracle."

The freedom to venture around Uncle Bo's neighborhood carried with it an assumption of common sense. At times, as a youth, this had to be learned by the lash, either from a switch or a tongue. "Hey boy," came through the screen door. I hesitated in my walk, and my head turned toward the darkness on the other side of the screen. I saw nothing. "Hey boy, yeah you. Come here." The voice was an adult's, but now sounding white and singular.

"Who me?"

"Yeah, come here." A preemptory summons from an unseen adult—a white adult—was without precedent. My feet moved in a slow shuffle. The voice was not belligerent, and it sang in the drawling manner of country white people. This was a white man. I turned my head to the levee, then back to the stairs, and then I walked up them. The porch was unfurnished and bleak looking. The clapboard house needed work and a painting. I looked inside. A white man was sitting in a chair facing the door. "Come in." Now curiosity pushed me slightly. The man was not close to the door. The door opened outward (*the screen needed cleaning*). Inside was a pudgy, youngish looking man, slouched back in a fabric chair, which had empty beer bottles next to it. I went no further than the door, keeping it open.

"Yah wanna make a quarter?" I notched my ears at this offer of such a large sum.

"How?"

"Pull me off."

"Wha?"

"Pull me off."

"Whas dat?"

Exposing himself, the man shook his penis and said, "Pull this off."

Not knowing what the man meant but knowing that it was "dirty" I ran from the porch and went back to Uncle Bo's house and told Uncle Rodney.

Uncle Rodney's response was not sympathetic. He did not denounce the white man's criminal behavior (which would have served no purpose). Instead, he strongly rebuked me for breaking a rule that I should have understood, and never violated.

"Who told you to go in there?"

Who had told me to go in there?

Nobody.

27

"Troop 130 is dirty." "Troop 256 is full of dick." Holy Ghost and Blessed

Sacrament scouts were bonded by common schools and years of friendship. An easy back and forth ribbing between the two Boy Scout Troops was always part of summer jamborees held at Indian Village. For the three days there would be no females present. Therefore, the respect, necessarily accorded them, was not needed. During this free float, the scouts revealed to each other the extent to which the gravity of domestic living pulled upon them. Some saw no value in either order or cleanliness; they were pigs whose hearts lay in the sty. Most, though, including me, were reasonable. The camp was near the Pearl River where it south-east bounded both Louisiana and Mississippi. That river, known to have drowned the traces of foul deeds, had its muddy bank vouchsafe a stage for the arcane rites of the Choctaw, the Natchez, and the Ofo. Once, from afar, I witnessed "La Danse des Serpents" that was in progress upon the moist dance floor. Shaded from the sun of a broiling noon, the many who attended the ball writhed upon and around and under each other with tellingly sinuous grace. This wonder, for several moments, let my eyes hold in check the primal terror in my heart, from going to my feet.

Colored troops from all over the state, joined in law at birth and in compact by Baden-Powell, lived the life of woodsmen's groups. Contests were held to see who had the greatest skill in aspects of frontier life. In the rope tying contests, Buck, our troop's "expert" had a gifted hand. His fingers touched the rope and a slipknot was formed in a movement hard to follow with the eyes. Achievement awards were given for the best communal deed performed by a troop. One year, my troop won; it cleaned out a storeroom. The huge room had hundreds of mattresses and scores of rats, large rats. Over the years, generations of them had rendered the bottom of the piles unusable and the room foul smelling. The rats that were unable to escape were hunted with tent poles, whose ending metal pegs made wonderful bludgeoning weapons. Tenderfoot scouts pulled out the smelly palettes, and the higher ranked scouts got to chase and terrify, and then smash the vermin. When all were dead, they were burned in a large fire. On the last night, a full gathering was held where skits were performed, the best winning an award.

The final act, for each troop, before breaking camp was the disciplinary tool of the belt line: a gauntlet of scouts armed with belts. Any person, who, by common consensus, had brought disorder to the festival, was made to run down the line with belts lashing them. I understood the need for correction, but I had no heart for being one its agents. In my last jamboree, I witnessed a fundamental unfairness that set me against this type of communal justice. A new scout, Paul Garcon, came to the gathering. Paul had a reputation, earned or not, of giving up "booty." I was unsure of what this fully entailed, but whatever, it was not in accord with a good reputation for a male.

Late, on the last night, a thrashing about in a nearby tent awoke me. Going to see what could be causing the commotion, I peeped in and saw Paul sitting on his pallet and flailing at several scouts from troop 256 who were trying to overpower him. Paul drove them away. It was odd. Later that night someone poked their head into our tent and whispered: "Paul giving away booty." Two of the scouts in my tent, in a silent flow, went out. I followed. There was a short line outside Paul's tent. In time it was my turn to enter. Inside, lying face down with his head away from the entrance, Paul could hardly be seen. He had been straddled and was being ridden. Finally, the scout dismounted. Paul's ass was brown, and hairy. He raised it and lowered his back, saddle-readying for the next rider. It was my turn. Unfathomable ignorance in my mind as to what was expected of me moved quickly to an overall feeling of the aberrant. What enjoyment lay in this, both for the rider and the ridden, and it was obvious that both parties liked it, was beyond my threshold. I had seen, now I knew something, though I was not quite sure what. I slapped Paul hard on his ass, rose and turned to leave the tent, puzzled. The next scout, behind me, started sliding the notching pin in his belt to loosen it. My eyes saw the faint star glow outside the tent. From within, my ears heard a grunt of satisfaction. What sat in my mind was not the strangeness of Paul's actions, but the follow through. The scouts did not respect him, yet they did this with him who accepted their disrespect; this was beyond belief. Of course, he was chosen for the belt line. Some of those who had ridden him were swinging their scourge with gleeful enthusiasm. In later years, Paul, after going to the other colored, Catholic high school, became a "big time morphfahdie" a local categorization of the male homosexual that was profound in both loathing and contempt. Paul's flesh had remained straight unto itself. But it was still being partaken of by orthodox men who felt moved to dally upon an unorthodox hump.

Nature burst its summer belly onto the land. Its humming spawn, indifferent to violent slaps, squirt cans of killing spray, and pyrethrum coils, owned the season. The itching goads of the mosquitoes carried the sweaty lessons of the days. But until the end of summer, outside, only the "mosquito hawks" were steadfast allies against the hordes.

The tussock caterpillars came in the early summer. From the branches of the live oaks and crepe myrtles, they dropped down and hung, as living pendulums-bobs, on their own-spun fibers. They fell onto heads or clothes or whatever as they sought to reach ground. Only an inch or so long, and covered round with long, colored bristles, which made me think of needles, they exuded a pungent stink. There had too much runny-green stuff inside them to kill with the hands. Brushing them away was the common sanitary procedure for ridding oneself of them. Even walking on them was avoided, if possible. Moving on the sidewalks, where they abounded in their season, gave a hop-step bounce to strides.

One summer, new transients appeared on the mailbox at the corner of Feret St. and Louisiana Ave. The short walk there had lulled me into inattention. As my hand reached for the hinged flap, the normal, dull-green color was different and there was movement as if this new-color skin pulsated and flexed. Focus came back to my vision. Spiders, not large in size, but huge in number, covered the mailbox in a thickness. A crawling in my skin matched the crawling in front of my eyes. I refused to put my hand on the flap and walked several blocks to another location to drop the letters. The large roach and the fire ant and the unclean fly knew no season; they bedded down with man and his would-be land. All three were natural; all three were hated; all three were indestructible.

28

My summers in The North repeatedly showed Nature's disregard of the parochial.

"Make sure you close the lid properly." Aunt Grace sent me outside with a limp bag of refuse to be put into the garbage can. In Philadelphia, as opposed to New Orleans, the can was always kept outside. On nearing it, I noticed its high, but not revolting odor. Philadelphia's summer smells and sights were novel, my education was continuing. On the handle were flies. Green flies were bizarre, but they were less disgusting than New Orleans flies: grey/black hairy things, with a vile, two lobed head. Its eye in one lobe urged it to land and loiter upon shit. When done, it rose on transparent, black-veined wings, as its other eye had it try to wing its way to someone's plate. Philadelphia flies appeared armored with their green iridescent skin, shimmering like a gaudy painted shell. I kicked the can; they moved, and then I opened the lid. Buzzing around the can, they were as impotent bees incapable of protecting their now-disturbed home. For an instant, the scale of nasty balanced: an unclean cover in one hand, and in the other, a bag of garbage. The small sack of enclosed potato peels, and the skins of other vegetables, and the rejected flesh of animals went into the opening. A summary gaze, to align the cover, made me look inside (something which I disliked). In this quick glance, I saw movement, and I thought, I heard something. In New Orleans, roaches may have proved clever enough to get inside, but they would shuttle themselves out of the light by darting under the refuse. This was nothing like that. A whitish mass, articulated by small, white worms, without legs, moved within the garbage can. My eyes froze and a look of disgust must have come to my face; I felt the look.

In one sighting, this living cover contradicted so many of my aesthetic norms relating to food, sight, and propriety, the natural occurred: I wanted to vomit. Only bizarre curiosities tamped down my stomach, and not for long. These things lived in the garbage, not outside as the ant or the roach or the dog or the cat or the pig. They never got up from the table! They were unrepentant gluttons, which to me was a distressing trait (a cardinal sin, in fact). Also, they made a sound; it was faint, but it was there. A continual squishing came from the soft, viscous bodies meeting, touching, adhering, and then breaking apart the slime adhesion. Without limbs, the contact with each other was too intimate; the foulness of the can was the common body rub they gave each other. Their mouths and their anuses, in this movement, mated both to both. The softness of their bodies allowed too much influence on them from the mass they made with their small weights combined. The narrator of *The War of the Worlds* described these garbage things with his description of the Martians when he first saw them emerge from their cylinder: "Unspeakably nasty."

"Aunt Grace, there are white things in the garbage can."

"Someone didn't close the lid properly."

"What are they?"

"Maggots. Remember now, you have to shut the lid tightly, so the flies don't get inside."

"We don't have those things in New Orleans."

"Well, uh, we have them here."

"Uncle Irving, those maggots come from flies?"

"Yeah, flies lay eggs in the garbage, and they hatch."

"But, Unk, we got flies in New Orleans, and I have never seen those things."

"To get a fly, you got to have a maggot."

"Flies don't even look that nasty."

"Tyger! Tyger! burning bright
In the forest of the night,
What immortal hand or eye
Could frame thy fearful symmetry?"

After the fleeing deer has fallen, and when its doom's bright is both dark and cold, "the tender Maggot, emblem of immortality," finds succor inside each of them.

That night, in Uncle Irving's yard, a small yellowish light moved erratically about the fence next to Mrs. Hall's house. It was not a constant light; someone was playing with the switch: Off-on, off-on. The glow seemed warm, like a tiny beating heart. It did a pixie dance around a blossomed rose, and then straightway made a dart, to another who liked its art. Following its movement to thick bushes where the other glow rested, I could see its shape, slightly, when the two pulsing sources were near each other. A bug, but a magic bug, I might collect them in a jar and…

"A lightning bug," was the answer to my question. "They stink if you smash them." When I finally got up close to one, my spirit made obeisance to the wonder of it. The small abdomen, with its mix of noisome fluids, softly pulsed its presence, and hoped that one of its conjugate-kind would answer. I caught them, collected some, and damaged a few while trying to corral them. I looked less to the stars when the peopling of the night air by "Photuris pennsylvanica" became heavy. A new firmament, below the high sky, danced, and whirled with its desires told in blinking amber lights. Color, pushed out from the gut and set off by the gloaming, seeded richness into my two-tinted world.

During my first summer in Philadelphia I saw Maria. She walked with a regal slowness down Greenway Avenue toward 71st street. She had black hair, café au lait colored skin, and a distant look on her face. Her head moved neither to the right nor the left in her processional glide. She never noticed or spoke to me neither that summer nor any other summer. Hardened concrete would have flowed easier than words from my mouth if I sought to speak to her. Why she should have noticed me and spoken was not considered. She knew my cousin and by politeness she might have spoken. Maria in the summer (I never thought of her when in New Orleans) gave me my first phallic ache. Finally, this grown-weary longing for her was pushed into and contained inside an evening game of "spin the (empty) bottle."

The liberating game was played on the steps and on the sidewalk of the Parkers' and the Nights' row house. On summer nights, when boredom and the heat were high enough to drive everyone outside, the stoop teemed. The Parkers, (all ten of them, plus oft visiting kin) could themselves have almost filled the space. But there were many others, from the neighborhood, whose friendly ties made for a gathering of the young that was both open and hot. Robbie Flair, Earl's younger brother, was the caller. He and Earl, each tall and lean, had lascivious personas that oozed. Earl let flow his flux with smooth rhetoric, horn rim glasses, intelligence, and extraordinary dancing ability. Robbie, still uncouth, maybe destined to be so always, had a satyr's pulsing energy. And he sought to encourage, as his powers would allow, the rushing of the blood to the head and below in others. At least twenty people were sitting on the stoop, a fun-filled number. The larger the number, the more contestants there were to cross mix. A soda bottle, the pointer, was placed on the sidewalk in front of the stoop. The caller spun the bottle on its side. The person pointed to by the bottle was "it." Some did not desire to be chosen, especially if they were shy or wary (by knowing the mindset of the caller). The caller gave a command to be performed or a penalty action if the command was refused. Robbie, with eyes gleaming when he became the caller, usually took one of two paths. He would tell a person to kiss someone who, by intuition or knowledge, he knew would want the contact. (And, that the contact would be welcomed.) Or, he would ask two to kiss, when he knew that at least one would not want the contact. In the latter, the defusing of the induced negative energy was often amusing. Amanda Parker, Minda, became "it." Robbie told her that she had to kiss me until he said, "stop." I had known her since my first summer visit; she was pretty. Frozen within the social cohesion of the game, I watched Amanda's smiling face come toward me. She was more than pretty. The streetlight played upon her face and it glowed warm and sweet like sun-bright honey. My agape mouth lurched, and her smiling mouth lunged. Our teeth banged together; nothing cracked, but we hardly noticed. Because of prescient Robbie's directive, the two flesh became one. But this one flesh now knew that it had missed the contact with its other self. Our mouths strained to reacquaint. We lashed tongues, we swallowed each other's saliva, we licked and sucked each other's lips; we rejoined the sundered cosmos. Stopping was more a matter of fatigue than Robbie's say so. When we did, the game dully continued, while looks of wonder linked our two eyes. Robbie commanded Sandra, Minda's sister, to kiss Jimmy Night, or do some foolish penalty. She chose the penalty. Before the evening ended, Minda and I were put together again. We were still famished, but now we knew our food. My heart understood that I loved her. My Catholic unity (body, mind, and soul) sluggish and heaven bound, watched this with suspicion.

Sandra came by two days later: "Minda wants to play spin the bottle again." I also wanted to play, but I also didn't. It was improper and impure, and more. I was afraid. Had I fallen into the sweets of Minda, I would not have cared to rise to the dictates of any on-high law; I would have stayed near her, whatever I had to do to make it happen.

I never stopped having feelings for her.

29

Minda's parents, The Parkers, were a couple whose imagining abraded the inflamed quick of people who hated miscegenation. The wonderful irony of the Parkers' relationship was that it seemed as if Jack Johnson had been domesticated. His tallied affection for white women, now confined to only one, showed each bearing season: another remarkably fine-looking child. It was a poster family for KKK recruitment. But the enshrouded, cone and cross wearers would not have wanted confrontation, or if so, only with large numbers on their side. Mr. Parker was black iron. A wandering duppy, with a playful turn of mind, made a man mold, and then it ladled liquid iron into the form. Internally, it never fully cooled, but it was animated, and it left the mold and took the name Mr. Parker.

He worked at Peetrick Piston Rings, a factory not too far down and off Woodland Ave. The sight of Mr. Parker stepping up Greenway Avenue was martial and metal at the same time. His brimless hat let his strong face lead his inclined form. His feet were almost fully iron-shod in his foundry shoes: Right, Left, Right, Left, right up the hill.

"Good Day, Mr. Parker."

A nod with a smile came back. The Parkers did not get along with the O'Malleys (whose yard bordered Uncle Irving's). Mr. O'Malley, a red Irishman, and Mrs. O'Malley, a very breast-and-butt black woman, had six children together. She would stand in her back yard and list down her off-premises brood, calling them to roost. If they were within a block or so they could hear her. If any had wandered further, they would be out of her range; upon their late return, she would discipline them with audible vigor.

Whatever the origin of the disagreement between the two families, there was a settled state of affairs. This included the license for a free-handed beating of a single rival by a combined force of the other side. On one occasion, several of the O'Malleys thrashed a Parker child. Mr. Parker, in response, beat the entire O'Malley family: man, woman, and children. The rules of familial engagement stated: Hand was to be given back to all who had given hand, and sympathetic, non-physical hand counted also in this reckoning. By such methods, détente in the neighborhood was established, for those who like warfare.

The Potts, a large family who fought as a clan, were rumored to be severely unusual. Ping and Sazzy, if typical, were beyond anything my imagination could conjure. Heavy-faced Ping sometimes would walk slowly down Greenway with an odd shuffle. I never thought anything about this until one evening Frankie and Richie and some others were harmonizing on the corner. Fars spied Ping and laughed: "Ping's carrying a load." All looked, all laughed. Ping trudged on by, turned and went up toward Yokum Street. Staring at Ping's backside, as he went up 71st Street, showed the seat of his pants did seem to have a low bulge. Sazzy, one of his sisters, reputedly, had seven children from seven men. Two of the infants had died by falling out of windows, or so I had heard. Sazzy was thin, dark, coarse, and electric: the white bark torn off a bolt of lightning.

From one of the harmonizers, Mark Anthony, I heard for the first time the chant of the "mother fucker." After every three words came "mother fucker". The rhythm and roll of the expression were amazing in their variations. Mark was rigorous with this speech pattern. Though not said loudly, the sheer number of "mother fuckers" I heard staggered me. Listening to the "boom", "boom", "boom" of "mother fucker" without respite, beat my brain as with a cudgel, for the phrase never lost its purpose. "Mother fucker," for me, was a lightning zap of verbal heat, and not a choral refrain for daily speech. But the discovery of a less literal, more elemental, coarseness lay two blocks up 71st Street.

The Marble Bar and Grill on 71st and Woodland lit the slime-fueled lamp of wasted behavior. A coupe pulled up to the 71st Street steps of The Grill. Out jumped a young man dressed in jitterbug style: stingy brim hat, high water pants, and high-top comforts shoes. He faced a man sitting on the steps and said:

"Hey man, les go, we got some pussy on the line."

A woman got out of the car. The man on the steps looked at her. She was both old and drunk. Her clothes were disheveled and spottily stained.

76

Her large lips looked swollen and bruised, as if they had been knocked, possibly from her having fallen. Her hair was not groomed. And her face, as to it being pretty or not, it was impossible to tell.

"I ain't fucking nat!"

The woman, repulsive to most (possibly even to herself), refused to take the slight. Out of her mouth flowed, in the slurred cadence of an offended drunk: "Well if you don't wanna fuck me, nigger, fuck you, yah mother fucker"

The man turned his head away and pursed his lips in disgust. The free-booty pimp, seeing the woman's mood rapidly slipping into anger and away from giving gratis sex, placated her quickly.

"Hey baby, don't worry about him, com awn, get in the car, les go."

His words of desire brought back, to her, the mood of wanting to be used. This also buffered her against the dig of the man refusing what she was freely offering. The car's rear door on the street side was opened, and by a light touching of her elbow, she was escorted into the back seat. It was filled from side to side with men. The car started, and then it sped across Woodland Avenue going toward Overbrook, with its rump-shaped rear becoming more and more distant.

The men lounging on the Grill's steps adjusted their positions to the sun's movements. In the afternoon, the Woodland steps were the more accommodating. Alighting from the #11 trolley somewhere after 4PM, I started walking down 71st toward Greenway. Suddenly, a car flew down Woodland Avenue going toward the Parkway. Another car, speeding behind it, tried to ram the first car. The fleeing car made an evasive move. (I wanted to see the ramming attempt again, to make sure that what had been seen had been real.) A white man was driving and the white woman in the passenger seat screamed out in warbling terror: "HELP! They're trying to kill us, call the police!" The pursued car made a sharp left-hand turn, up 71st Street. The pursuing car had missed and had to turn around. In the middle of the street, it did. Two unshaven, grim-faced, white men were its occupants; both seemed huge. They sped after the soon-to-be-harmed. That was the storm clap in the white Atlantic. The dark Pacific did not stir, not even a raised voice was heard concerning the death drama unfolding. "Hmmm, I guess he's fucking with the man's woman." And the lounging continued, seemingly, without additional comment on the matter.

These men of the neighborhood were all tidally bound to Paschal: the small knurl of oneness that defined the area. But it was not a community. The jitterbugs and the churchgoers lived lives in plain sight of each other, but they met only at the zero points. Greetings, nods, acceptance, acquiescence brought the intra-tranquility that defined Paschal. The families I came to know, in my pre-college summers, were steeped in the wisdom of understanding. The Grill was the inevitable canker that must exist because life exists. Greenway Avenue, between 71st and 72nd streets, was not the damaged rose that endured or surmounted this public sore two blocks away. This block was as sturdy as a live oak and as tranquil as a forest road. On both sides of the block, trees shaded the sidewalk, the parking lane, and a good bit of the street. The contrast of coming from an open block to one where less sun shone gave it the quiet of the respite. There were no stoops, only porches with low stairs. The block looked less dense; no hints of warrens existed. The houses were not fancy, but they were kept in the fashion of respecting the grace of one other. In this strongly colored lane, spanning only one block, an evening surrey drive would have found its setting, though out of its own time.

30

Paschal, but a dot on a map of Philadelphia, was a terra incognita to me when I first visited it in the early 1950's. As the summers filled in its features, I saw northern grime match southern dirt. Sepia Night (Tuesday) at the skating rink warded off white interference in colored enjoyment.

"Tonight, is not Sepia Night. None of your friends will be here. You won't enjoy yourself," whined the young white man at the door.

"I have no friends, I've come to make some," countered my mother with my sister and me in tow.

Or reversing, non-sepia nights (Wednesday, Thursday, Friday, Saturday, and Sunday) persuaded coloreds that blanching was too bizarre to consider.

"You went there? But it wasn't Sepia Night," said my cousin when I told her about the doorman's attempts to discourage us.

This sharing without mingling was not universal. Some public facilities belonged, in a fundamental way, to its immediate citizens. The terror incognita of these places was based on mental cartograms I had to master. For example: Dick's Swimming Pool, a reasonable walk from my cousins, was only used by "Paddy Boys." (I learned this phrase from my best Philadelphia buddy, Clarence Jones. I had been in the Catherine Playground, when repeatedly: "Hey, nigger," came from an overarching walkway above me. I turned in curiosity and saw a young white man who looked down at me and smiled somewhat, and repeated: "Hey, nigger." Never having been called that before by a white person, I looked in perplexity at him, and said, without guile: "That's not my name." The boy returned the same look and walked away. I told Clarence. He said: "It was a Paddy Boy." "A Paddy Boy?" "Yeah, a white boy." "Oh.")

My mother was insistent on us going to a pool to continue swimming as we had done in New Orleans; Dick's was the most convenient. After hearing about the place, I wasn't sure that I wanted to go, however the decision to go was not mine to make. On girl's day, my mother took my sister and Barbara to the pool. When they returned, Barbara said that they were the only coloreds there. And as far as she could make out, everybody else had continually stared at them. The next day was boy's day. Mom asked Earl Flair to come with us to the pool. He was older than me, much taller, and macaroni thin. We three walked to the pool, though I kept to the rear as my mother and Earl talked. While approaching this unknown sea, my contained apprehension was resting inside a small, crammed-tight dinghy. When we rounded the last obscuring corner, the full expanse of the recreational complex opened to sight. It was an enormous communal space. There were baseball playing fields and basketball courts, complemented by benches and grass.

The pool itself could not be seen; only a large concrete façade, with a long line at an entrance, was visible. My mother veered off and went around the front toward the benches that faced the long axis of the pool. She would be able to see us through the wire fence. I had managed to keep my vision tight; its sole focus had been my mother and Earl. There was a crowd, and I refused to segregate it into faces; a diffuse, but noisy, background drew my notice. When my mother left, I now focused solely on Earl and our conversation, but this narrowing of attention was difficult to sustain. Saying that sight has no feel or physical force is belied by the phrase "a touching sight". So many eyes were touching me, I started to feel unclean. Every glance away from Earl's face showed white faces looking directly at us. Mainly the expressions were like the stares and grins given to the animals at the zoo. The line moved slowly. Bzzzz, bzzzzz, bzzzzz droned. Not conversation, but a pocket hum of "news" was being buzzed-passed through the crowd. Sniggles and giggles were all about. The line led inside the building to a counter. Two adult white men stood behind it. Their function was to give each person in line a numbered basket for their clothes, and a large safety pin with a metal tag with the same number. The man who gave me the basket looked down at me and smirked, curled his mouth and snorted slightly. He turned his eyes upward and bared his teeth in the fashion of ugly glee. The other worker, who waited on Earl, was no better than the first. He was simply less offensive; he kept his dour look.

The changing location was a huge room with a high ceiling. It was packed full except within a circle of several feet centered on Earl and me. We set our baskets down on the bench. A quiet came over the scores of boys in the room. A muscular young white boy, wearing green trunks, walked up to us and said in a low, firm, clear voice, "We don't want no niggers here." Balking because of my notion of my supposed northern rights: "They can't stop us from swimming." The quiet continued. The young white boy put his thumbs inside the elastic of his trunk's waistband and thumb-tugged it ever so slightly. He then tilted his head, as a deliberately patient gesture. Slowly and calmly, putting ice edging on every word, he said again: "We don't want no niggers **here**."

My heart wasn't afraid, because lacking complete understanding, I had not yet attempted to breathe in my fully swamped position. Earl, well understanding the situation, said, "Come on, let's go." We left. In leaving, what we saw was that almost no one was outside; most were inside. Now, as I walked away, I allowed myself a glance at the few remaining white boys near the exit. My mother, who was sitting on the bench in front of the pool, looked up as we walked toward her.

"What happened?"

"They won't let us swim," Earl said.

"**Who** won't let you swim?"

Earl related the story. My mother's face, in an instant, became a montage of expressions. She said nothing; she began to walk toward the exit of the park. We were going back home. As it dawned on me what I had just escaped from, it was a good place to go. And as for swimming, I did not care to make a fuss. I did not want to be around those white boys. I did not like them. Some of them had splotches on their skin, and many looked dirty. Besides, they were mean, which meant that they were dagos. Greenway Avenue was just the perfect place to be. My mother walked so fast that Earl and I had difficulty keeping up with her. At Woodland Avenue she turned right; we were not going home. When she got to Woodland and 68th Street, she left the sidewalk and went to the entrance of the police station. She pushed the door with the force of a swiftly moving piston in pneumatic abandon. The door shot open. All the police inside quickly looked up. She was now in the middle of the small central room. The totally startled groupings of police stared at her, wide-eyed. With a manner akin to the prophets of old, who called inequity by its true name, she hurled her words of truth.

"They won't let my son swim, and I pay **TAXES**!"

Her blast awoke them. A bewildered officer came over to her. "Yes Ma'am, what's the problem?" He was told the problem. The next day, five police cars were at the pool and around the complex. Barbara and my sister, having had no trouble initially, had the same non-event. The following day would be the test. Again, police were everywhere. They watched from their cars; they surrounded the pool; they protected the taxpayer's rights.

The same two adults were behind the counter, but there was a difference. The mobile face of the smirking turd had shifted to one of the sycophant. "Good Morning," la-la-la-ed out of his mouth with a freshness that could not be mistaken for irony. A dry, automatic, "Good Morning" came from me. The other man at the counter, true to his unchanging feelings, said nothing, greeting or otherwise. He dispensed the basket to Earl and turned to get another for the next person.

On my first visit I had not looked closely at the pool. Looking at it full on from the dressing room's door, I judged that it was not as large as either the one in New Orleans in Shakespeare's park, or at the scouts' camp. In addition, the pool was not nearly as crowded as on the previous boy's day, but the space was nearly full. The white boys looked and stared, but Earl and I were not pressed tightly, we were being given the distance of dislike.

Boy's days followed boy's days, and despite the heat of the late summer's sun, the water's chill grew deeper, each visit. The now sparsely used pool was not enjoyable. The smaller white boys began to increase the cannon-balling of each other, and their constantly inaccurate strikes, invariably, landed near my friends and me. I could not swim nor hold my breath for long; care had to be taken that one of the whites would not land just as I was arising. I learned this prudent tact by getting a hard choke from a well-timed cannon ball. No white ever spoke.

At the end of the summer, Juby Akins and other young colored hoodlums began to come. Before, they had been afraid. Though the police presence had dwindled to one car, it was sufficient. Juby's group had no desire to swim; they longed solely to have some protected fun at the "Paddy boys" expense. Using the same weapons, they mercilessly cannonballed the whites.

Summer ended and I went back to New Orleans. In subsequent years I heard that through Negro disuse, the pool returned to its Irish roots, without violence, without uproar.

Each summer, Philadelphia and The North gave me incremental knowledge of my world. It was a field trip that shifted me between two words: Nigra and nigger. Confusion was the inevitable result. I could never be unglued from New Orleans; nor could I accept the malicious cold I saw in The North. But the odious necessity, in The South, to have Negro life toady to white whims was not sustainable. And though The North's "malice toward all niggers" was written across ethnic fault lines, it was not codified by statute. Riding the whirligig of Nigra/nigger, I found a natural calming-center: fantasy. I dream-stepped through the world.

31

"In the beginning was Benaat, who was all thought; she reasoned, I am lonely: I will make myself a tongue. And her tongue let flow sounds into the silence..."

Before learning the rosary and the other prayers, and before the Bible, (and when my ears were young) the blind radio had impressed words above my sight. In a softly lit room in the evening, my family heard, each in their own way, the worlds coming from the little box, whose insides were too hot to touch. *Inner Sanctum, The Mercury Theater on The Air, The Shadow, Stella Dallas, Gunsmoke, Gangbusters, Amos & Andy*, and their like were my first story-makers. As I listened, I saw nothing: no kibitzing cranial images formed. Traveling into narrative, the sounds entered me as carnally as food. They arrived at my place of dark sense, where the words of myths touched ground. In the beginning was the world, and the stories about it were good. My upcoming faith would tellingly declare the opposite. Its dogma's origin was not the world made into words, but **"In the beginning was the Word, and the Word was with God, and the Word was God."** And God's Word did not speak well of this world. When my faith's mountain of stories became part of me, a skillfully sung new terror had been joined to the old earthly ones. The verb "to fall," the genetic bane of dense flightless animals, opened its declined limbs: I fall, you fall, we will fall, and they have fallen (**for all eternity**). This infinite declension of dread covered the mute earth of the grave with an air of unending moans. My faith, resting on the axiom of silence-from-the-world, gave me stubby wings. But no graceful soaring into the bright, ethereal heart of goodness came to me. The hard flight of the heavy bee, which lived so close to the earth, was my lot. I dreamt of soaring and of flying over meadows and rivers, launching myself from the spired towers of castles and skyscrapers. My cast down eyes saw more danger below than glory above. To fall was death; to rise was to mount on smoke and chant. I fell in love with the smells of ritual and the sounds of singing made by cloistered monks. No high registers could come from the dry throats of these buried priests. Earth tones—browns, and grays, and blacks—moved against the bare and thick walls of their tombs. I reveled in joy when these songs carried me into the unlit-bliss of no-place.

Both God in heaven, and the devil in hell seemed further away in Philadelphia. Though my mother remained steadfast in her faith, she never pressed me in my church duties. I was grateful to her for this leniency because entrance to my Sunday worship, in Philadelphia, was always unpleasant. The comfort from the sound of prayer at Sunday Mass at Saint Michael's, when surrounded by the Irish Catholics, was not automatic. The suckle from Mother Church now left grit in my mouth, like tiny stones not sifted out from beans. To spit would have been the appropriate response.

I would mime the ritual correctly, but I closed off from the sacrament and began speaking only to my own mind. The thicket of speculation grew. Thoughts about prayer itself came and went, as I spent my time of confinement among the Irish. The catechism gave me just enough answers to twist around my simple logic into mental heresies, all predicated on the infinite attributes of God.

God surely was not deaf, and He heard all prayer. Then why must we keep repeating them? Perhaps a certain number was required for Him to respond, in the sense of paying dues before entry. But one could never know whether the prayer was to be answered or not. So, one might be wasting time by praying for something God will not give. Then perhaps this prayer was the worship God expected without giving anything. But prayers were part of the covenant where prayers were to be answered. Each trial answer pruned the former answer, with the newest speculation growing wildly, for a time. There was no unambiguous, or even sensible way out of this copse of infinite unknowns, and the service would have finally ended. The grind of these musings scoured me clean from the pestilential touch of the blue irises. A blackened worm always bored into my chagrin and let ooze my thick bile: *Why don't you mind your own fucking business by worshiping and stop minding me!*

Where was The Lord God in all of this? I saw a glow as I tried to understand the mysteries, but from what direction? Up or down?

The summers in Philadelphia had the eroding force of wind-driven sand against limestone. Fantastic new shapes were hewn out of my Catholic, educated, southern, segregated, colored upbringing. I would carry these forms back to New Orleans (as would be legally allowed) when my whirligig spun back round to Nigra. Prayer now sat in my mind as part of the ritual incantation to open the door: "Open Sesame", but not to a cave, but to the supernatural. Prayers from the laity were a mock; the priests had the true power of sound and gesture, because only with them was there consistency. Reliably, every time they performed a different ritual, some aspect of the divine entered the world of men. Something supernatural occurred when the priest blessed people. Just what occurred was unclear, for I felt nothing after it. "I bless you in the name of the Father and of the Son and of the Holy Ghost," and "Mandrake the Magician gestured hypnotically," grew closer together in effect.

But the efficacy of Mandrake's visual signs and mental powers were seen every day in the comic section of the daily newspaper, which I quickly scanned and then reread several times. When they were particularly good and the day lent itself to it, Mandrake and "The Phantom" became cud. Sunday's comic section was mine. No one else in the family needed it; I did. The color and extended length of my daily favorites sat as sweetly in my head as my grandmother's Sunday biscuits did in my stomach. Once a week feasting augured for more. Somewhere I saw a wasted comic book torn and rolled with its cover gone, it might have been a fly swatter. Its stories were without interest to me, but the format engulfed me. Thirty pages of visuals were thirty pages of hard sight. Not like in schoolbooks and not like in *Snow White* or *Little Black Sambo* books, but narrative made entirely by pictures. The dialog and story were part of the drawing. These easily damaged delights became gospel to my eyes. I sought them out.

32

LaSalle Pharmacy, on the downtown-riverfront side of LaSalle, was between Louisiana and Toledano, across from Flint Goodrich Hospital. Prescriptions, salves, hair preparations, hot combs, skin-bleaching creams, greeting cards, ointments, beauty supplies, wound dressings, et al. were in this small business, two blocks from my house. The owners were two colored pharmacists, Mr. Julian and Mr. Ott. Mr. Julian, a tall, light skin man, spoke huskily, while always having friendly expressions on his face. Mr. Ott, short and dark-brown skin, had a round stomach, not yet fat, but poised to join the potbelly droops. A slight nasal tone to his frog-croak voice gave his speech a timbre of impatience. He would look at me and want to complain. I never gave him a reason to carry this out. LaSalle Pharmacy was a sacred place; it had comic books: my book of hours.

Settling myself upright on my bed, I surrounded myself with my favorites. This mosaic of colored, magic oblongs peeled away, layer-by-layer, human complexity, and devolved the world into the days of myth. Powers and terrors moved through the pages with consummate contempt for the laws of the ordinary.

But the words and the ingestion associated with "powers and abilities far beyond those of mortal men." were not fully the heart of my devotion. Some artwork alone, especially on covers, justified the selection. The story might falter, lapsing into the trite endings of it-had-to-end-some-kind-of-way, but the transport of the drawing or drawings made the exchange: my dime for that comic, a reasonable deal. *Superman* became the first flame whose glow shrank in brilliance, until its flat drawings, and wearisome stories warmed me with the tepid heat of wearied kindling. This taught me frugal behavior, of sorts. In rut, to spend the dime, I undressed each possible candidate with an eye to find something that would excite me. With grim effort, I chose. But when they lay on the bed on my blanket of transport, the magic from the uninspired books sputtered. These were put back into the box, as would be the garment that remains in the closet, unworn, an enigma both to its utility, and to the desire that spawned the waste of money.

Tales from the Crypt always had strong covers. The stories had a two-sided terror theme. The innocent door-to-door salesman, spirited away into a hell of murderous fiends, frightened the traveler. The bestial door-to-door salesman, who slaughtered the innocent family, terrified the resident. The glitzy gore issues had the two themes intertwining. The energized haint met the ax murdering family. The battle sequences, drawn frame by frame, were wonderful and sometimes scary. But only the weapons flew, and participants usually sank into the uninviting grave. What might lie beneath the surfaces of Mars or Venus was far more refreshing, be it angel or demon or monstrous machine. And the transport to these places: a rocket ship, teleportation or an inter-dimensional doorway seemed less eerie than a bogle's jalopy, which might contain a box of eyeballs a fiend had plucked out. *Tales from the Crypt* and Tales about Hell were not far removed from one another.

Grandma Adele believed in both types of bad: the natural bad and the supernatural bad. Her superstitions were the cautious face she put toward an uncertain world. For the real bad, she told her own crypt story. In the early 1900's there were men—dressed in black gowns—who silently moved about at night. She called them "The Black Veil Men." At one with the dark lanes and the poorly lit streets, they were merchants who hunted, and brought the shroud of death to the weak, and the unaware. The cadavers they made were sold to medical schools, she said. Both the devil and these, his future wards, lay in waiting in the places of no light. **Grandmother Adele's wisdom: Where the light is uncertain, beware.** She disliked going to restaurants, but she deemed it folly to go at night. "They could be unclean, and I wouldn't know. Besides, it is too dark in them. I'm not sure of what they are serving me." Her overarching protective, which safeguarded her fundamental belief in this natural understanding, rooted itself in the intractability of certain types of change. Knowing the ways of light meant not trying to find ways of turning it on in others, who were irrevocably benighted. "Never argue with a fool, because then there are two fools arguing."

33

During her Christmas visit to New Orleans in 1956, my mother gave us a permitted slice of the whites' segregated world. She took my sister and me to the Orpheum Theater to see *Fantasia*.

The movie, in Superscope and in stereo, was glorious. The Sorcerer Apprentice's cautionary message of magical dabbling sat as prologue to the main jolt. *The Night on Bald Mountain* locked an animated fabrication into the reality of my Catholic faith's admonitions. Edison and Bell (electric sight and sound) both got the revival spirit. Inside the tent was Disney: the part angel, the impresario, the producer, and the creator of a new electric ethos. What was seen and heard, though obviously artificial, resonated as literal, visceral intimation; it clung to reality as an epidermal film. A demon's substance had been changed into an equally fearsome celluloid proxy.

The nuns had insisted on a fundamental understanding, Archangel Lucifer, the most powerful and resplendent of all creatures, fell because he thought himself equal to God; he would not bow. Pride, eternal, unyielding, and damnable was his core. His wants were all one, to drag the world to his lair. There he would flay it eternally; his barbed lash reaping a bounty of tears with each stroke.

Disney's demon, Chernabog, disrobing out of the stony peak of Bald Mountain, revealed himself as monarch of the darkness on Walpurgis Nacht. His power, enthroned by night, raised the damned dead, who were now to be mocked on the puppet master's dark stage. Mussorgsky's music spoke of black ascendancy. Its motive force did not pull the hands to pray; it pushed the frame toward undulating frenzy. The marionettes, having risen from the graves, lived again. And again, they lived their same fate. Cajoled, by the copulative joy of the master's lure, their unwise joining to the world lasted but a single night. Dancing and writhing (inspired by Eros), they gave of their best, on their lord's night of nights. Then with casual spite, he flung them back into the burning pit.

"Lord of Darkness, where are you now? My anguish is unbearable, relieve me of this plight."

"I Am, Who Am the hatred of God. He, Who made you, to know, love and serve Him."

"But the wine of the earth was so sweet."

"And bitter will be your burnt soul in its eternal longing for Him that made it."

The rendering of the fabricated demon's self-intoxication with its power and malice was stunning. Likewise, his palpable cowering from God's dawn was a triumph. Chernabog retreated into hell. With reins of sound, Disney's morning church bell pulled the tiny animated faithful along a forest path toward divine worship. This cinematic vision was conjuring of the highest order. The two realities: Disney's modernity and Catholic imprinting conjoined in a natural free-flowing way. This well-wrought movie moved and copied itself, virus like, into the structures of belief inside my brain. I was without immunity from it.

After the movie, the walk down the long spiral stairs from the coloreds' height to the side entrance of the theater seemed short. Outside, my mother gripped both my sister's hand and mine. She would let neither of us stray and get lost in the mixed flux of the amazed faces. This segregated magic-box show had caught the moviegoers by surprise. Most had been unprepared for the performance.

"Step right up folks, look what we have in here."

The barkers were two blocks down Canal Street in front of The Monkey Bar: a tawdry venue of strutting white, female flesh. But the Orpheum's silent and gaudy movie marquee, and its ad posters of Mickey Mouse had not set the correct cast of mind. The costumed, smiling rodent had been playfully drawn with a magic wand in its hand. When the fierce, black Chernabog stepped onto the stage, in power and glory, true fright-of-the-devil appeared in the audience's Christian brains. He was vanquished, but the contact had been unnerving in its immediacy. Chasten pride feathered out into social accommodations. A communion, impossible in their separated churches, was shown by the singular politeness of all in the fracturing crowd.

"Excuse me;" "Pardon me;" "Go ahead, by all means;" "You were ahead;" blew through the dispersal like cotton fluff driven by heavy-breathing winds. "Humanity was putting shoes on its huge child Progress."

The reverse irony of an animated film seeming more real, than one with human actors, did not register with me. However, from then on, I believed what I saw on the screen, its actuality, or its potential. But it took only one colored actor in a film to spoil these delightful fictions. With overwhelming frequency, "the Negro role" would be done incorrectly. This produced an unconscious, mood-destroying winching. Too much colored foolishness, or too deep a-love-of-whites were the two untenable assumptions Negro characters bore. Nothing in my life gave me reasons to understand these character designs. The movie was thrown out of joint, as if its back were broken and twisted around, leaving it to walk forward, while it was looking toward the rear.

I could "see" white pharaohs in Egypt, or white cowboys and red Indians or Commando Cody flying. In fact, I had no doubt that these depictions were true. But a rolling-eyes Negro, or a "Yah, sir" drawling colored seemed unfathomable. To be stupid was unfortunate, but to aspire to comic ignorance around white people remained unthinkable. Such behavior would have been met with the harsh look that denotes the witnessing of licentious insanity. No one, in my colored world, displayed any sympathy for mental incapacity.

Excessive devotion of colored servants to their white employers was unnatural, illicit love. I knew no white person (the priests and the nuns did not figure in this reckoning) toward whom the emotion of love could be directed. **None!** Seeing this emoted in a film made it knowingly inauthentic and distressing and embarrassing. Always the desire came to leave the movie. With a segregated plot, I could enjoy the show without the disruption of perverse integration. Brandon de Wilde's line "Come back, Shane" brought tears to my eyes. While the monster in *Frankenstein's Revenge* so terrified me, I spent most of the movie with my head in my mother's lap.

"Jungle" movies, at first, put me into limbo. There were coloreds present, but patently, to me, my world was not of the jungle; so, the realism or lack of it in the films was uncertain. The "nature" magazines on the white newsstands drove this point home. The sagging breasted, semi-clothed African women on the covers were not my people.

"Hey Tuck, Polio said you can talk African."

"Yeah, it's easy. Ooogabugajuga, Whoooo, jougajuga."

"What das supposed to mean?"

"Das jungle talk, it mean I like yoh momma."

"Fuck you, Winki."

"Whooo, the shit done gone to the kitchen."

"Polio, you got some nerve to talk, with that nappy-headed bitch you got at home that nobody wont."

The greatest jungle movie, *King Kong*, had incredible action sequences and I even felt for Kong as he fought at the end, but something wasn't right. The beauty and the beast theme needed a foil. I soured on the choice the screenwriters made. My friends raved about *Mighty Joe Young*, but I didn't go. Co-mingled black and white could never avoid burrs.

I had heard tales of white people (Cajuns) living in the bayous, where life was primitive, and alligators and snakes were staples. Cajun Pete came on the radio every day with his humorous voice hawking Doctor Tichenor's Antiseptic. I never visualized him, but the notion of a hairy, semi-civilized white man cocooned Pete's persona. Familiarity plus ignorance could breed contempt.

Every day, the bipolar realism of New Orleans's newspapers pulled Jim Crow's publicity wagon through the streets. By early morning, its uneven load of white-grace and Nigra-soil had been deposited on the doorsteps of the city.

"WHITES RULE WITH THOUGHT, AND CIVILITY, AND CULTURE: THEY KEEP THE CITY FUN. BUT THE WHITE POLICE MUST NEVER FORGET THEIR GUNS."
FOR THERE ARE WILD NIGRAS,
WITH UNKEMPT HAIR, AND WITH EYES AS DEAD AS STONE,
WHO ROB, AND RAPE, AND MURDER, ALL DAY LONG."

This constant renewal of hardening reagents to white supremacy co-opted *The Daily Mirror*. "The Daily Dose" was more in line with the effect. All who regularly bought the paper felt the subtle addiction to the pungent ink of the black on white comparisons. To read and believe was both to exalt, and to cringe from the same dime. With a faulty memory for white faces and a total disinterest in politics, society, race, and crime, only the comics held sway. The artwork and stories of the segregated world of the funny papers were my daily charge. Mandrake, despite the African Lothar, was my favorite. Though dressing like an "African" (in a fancy loincloth and wearing a fez and an Alley Oop tank top), Lothar, an exotic that fit, was the only person of color who did so. Had Mandrake been animated or made into a movie, no doubt, disaffection would have occurred. It did with The Phantom, even without him coming to life. I loved the comic, but my excitement for it had faded, long before high school's noggin-clanging reveille. Nothing in the integrated world seemed comfortable. In it, *Heart of Darkness*, which I was yet to explore, had been infused with white spines. Embracing this mixed thistle, given Momma Adele's tender, black heart, would not have been sane. My grandmother's broad injunction remained, "Boy, don't let'em hurt you."

34

The South's citadels of advanced wisdom, though reputedly gem-like, were blind to color: no colored allowed. My mother and her twin in seeking graduate degrees had to travel to The North. After NYU, my aunt returned to the land of the cotton gin, while my mother, with her Drexel degree and her large sack of ambition, journeyed first to the deeper South: South Carolina and Georgia, then to the land of anthracite coal. She went to Philadelphia, following her sister, Grace, who had married a northern Negro, Uncle Irving.

The twins had supported each other in their marathon journey from childhood to maturity. But as women of color, in New Orleans, their stock of societal currencies was unbalanced. One was high: they were both highly intelligent. Another was low: they lacked the high-worth coins of Creole features. Without having the © of the high-pretty Creole, they accustomed themselves to creating the beautiful through mastery of the domestic arts.

"Hay que bailar al son que les tocan."

Wearing belles-of-the-ball gowns, which their hands had crafted, they waited their turn to dance and whirl, as they competed at the marriage fairs, with the fair for the eye of the conjugate fair. But the pained mirrors they looked in, every day, would have had less fractures if they could have seen the sovereigns of "good" hair, or light skin. Fully escaping, "mirror, mirror on the wall" would have been to fully reinvent the world. To un-believe in walls, still would not have freed their world from kinks. Orthodoxy, the only reputable landmark in their maze, had laid its firm, heavy, guiding hand upon them. Catherine Drexel's Xavier University capped their struggle.

But Drexel's and NYU's approbations seemed frozen; they led nowhere. For the twins both remained teachers in their respective cities, with no advancement possibilities offered. My mother, however, learned the ways of solitude in the cold, un-segregated land. She lived in a small room in her sister's house for sixteen years. Teaching in both day school and night school, she kept her pennies close for the day when her large-bunioned feet would walk over her own doorsill.

Heat flagged; New Orleans schools closed earlier than those in Philadelphia. I had my first look at a "mixed" school when my mother took my sister and me, for one day, to her school in North Philadelphia. The building was huge and full of students and noise that never seemed to fully die down. I saw mainly colored. No one was small like me; my eyes always looked up. My mother introduced me to the office staff. The principal, Mr. Pointdexter, looked white; my mother said that he was not. I went to my mother's homeroom and wandered around it, reading posters and looking at things, finally sitting in the back as the students filled the room. Occasionally, they turned about and looked at me until the end of homeroom. When lunchtime came, my mother, having lunchroom duty, called a student:

"Charles, would you come here please?"

"Yes, Ma'am."

"Charles would you watch my son for me? You understand?"

"Yes Ma'am, ain't nobody gonna bother him." Charles was three times my size with a rotund build.

"Stay by me now," he said. He loped when he walked, and his mass went slightly up and down with strong elastic tugs. He was a brown bear sporting an ivy-league hairstyle and wearing low cut sneakers. No one called him Charles.

"Hey, Fat Daddy."

"Yeah, whas going on?"

"Everything awe right."

"Awe right, baby."

In the crowded halls, the students' eyes that faced the twosome sometimes went first to Charles, sometimes first to me, and then they would switch to watch the other. To the curious, Charles' responses were dual in meaning. I was described and circumscribed: Charles was my protector, and by every acknowledgement, Charles was viewed as a formidable person. Fleeting looks of scorn toward me rearranged themselves into blank looks after they gazed at Fat Daddy's face or heard his words. After the lunch period, my mother thanked Charles with a politeness that was formal and gracious and heartfelt.

"I told, you, I wasn't gonna let nobody bother him."

I had been given a brother by my mother, if only for an hour. I wanted to wear my brother's shoes. I knew that Aunt Alice, in New Orleans, would never let me get tennis shoes; I had asked. She thought they were common, and besides, they could not be shined.

"Mommie, can I get some sneakers? I'm just scuffing up my good shoes. I can save them for school next year. I will wash the sneakers each week, so they won't smell." How she took this plea: full truth or admixed with something else, I didn't know. But she allowed me to get a pair: my first pair. They were as near to my brother's style as possible. I tried to "stroll" when I had them on. But I could neither walk as Charles did nor move with the rhythms of strolling. I knew I looked foolish. Settling for just wearing them, I felt less diminutive.

My thoughts went to Lawrence, a classmate at Holy Ghost. I felt such shame in being afraid of telling on him. In malignant delight, Lawrence, whose dark eyes twinkled when he did mean things, had snatched my new hat off my head and tossed it over the fence in the schoolyard. The dogs on the other side tore it apart. *I liked the hat. My ears hurt when they got cold. The earmuffs kept them warm.* I told my grandmother a story about the hat. She got me another; it wasn't as nice. *But if my brother had been there, I would have told him what happened. And Charles would have pitched Lawrence about.* The low-cut sneakers were not sturdy. By the time I was ready to go back to New Orleans the treads on the poorly made shoes had started to become bare. My feet were like my mother's: large and flat.

Despite Joan of Arc, bravery was male, I figured. In the second summer visit to Philadelphia, this assumption began to fray, badly. I was in my mother's homeroom, just waiting. Looking into her cabinet, there were envelopes with names on them and things in them: knives, large hatpins, razor blades, chains were in larger envelopes. Mommy, my mother, had somehow taken these weapons from students, and then cataloged them. There were lots of envelopes. She came back in with her class; it was graduation day. Her female students had been required to make their dress as a final exercise.

"Glenda, you can't wear that."

"Why not?"

"Because it is not proper for a young lady to wear a dress like that."

"Whas wrong with it? Ah made it." The exposed cleft of Glenda's full bosom was a dark divide on smooth, brown flesh, contrasted by the white of her dress.

"Come, we will fix this." The younger, guided by the elder, made the alteration. A harmoniously added section to the outfit thwarted both the high school décolletage and an increased release of adolescent male hormones. Glenda marched in the dress, but her bosom was lovely to the eye. She had been correct about the glory of her expressed exposure.

With a precise, calming facility, my mother moved among the students. They were rough, unlike the more mannerly ones from Holy Ghost. I felt the difference lay more in public versus parochial rather than north and south. The un-tethered behavior I saw in public school students held no appeal for me. Order and discipline gave me comfort. I had never attended a public school in New Orleans, and I never wanted to, even if the teachers had my mother's prowess. No pressure was needed on me to continue my high school education at a colored, Catholic school. The only issue would be: the coed one (with my sister) taught by nuns or the all-male school taught by males? Far, further, and furthest from the nuns were the shores I set out for. I took the entrance exam and won a four-year scholarship to Saint Augustine's High School manned by the Josephite Fathers.

My choice and my sister's choice of schools were the antithesis of the common. The reputations of the "raw" colored schools were the fortresses that Aunt Alice's fulminations sought. She and my mother, twins, in lockstep in ambition and fervor and career, had Jim Crow bisect the oneness of their two twin eyes. They both taught different students, who, by looks, were indistinguishable. My aunt taught colored/Nigra students in The South. My mother taught Negro/nigger students in The North. For different students, different methods, and for me, different women, with the sameness of one face, trying to hew me into a fitting form.

The slurs of the students, being primal, shaped the emotions. Nigra was a southern construction; its destruction would have to be the undoing of Dixie. As I understood it: my aunt, and all other southern "proper" colored folk, and those others, who sought to help, had a curriculum whose binding glue was hope-from-rectitude. One day "Fly Away Blackbird" Jim Crow would occur because the law, requiring separate racial worlds, would vanish: if and when would lead to then.

If:
If all the colored students mastered every one of their subjects,
If the colored students always were properly behaving,
If proper behavior always led to proper adult behavior,
If all colored students became law-abiding citizens,
If all colored students appreciated the universal arts,
If all colored students dressed properly,
If all colored students would not overeat and get lazy,
If every colored student would not act like the whites' colored-stereotype,
If every colored student understood that they would have to work twice as hard as white students,
If the colored would not act common, and,
When: "The Daily Dose" understood, it no longer had colored awful to sustain Jim Crow's brew, millennial calm would come upon the times.

Then: Given the notice of the coloreds' now-classic facade, the white society, with fully opened Christian eyes, would embrace their not-white brothers, and change state law.

However: Sovereign state law went from KKK space in west Louisiana to the border of race-besotted Mississippi in the east. In the middle lay white land, where status, so set in the generations, was retained by passion renewed: scion of, then father to pedigrees of pride: graduates from Tulane University, Loyola University, and LSU. These, the doctors, lawyers, judges, and principals led society's waltz. But they, and the fireman, or the policeman, or the bus conductor, or the bank cashier, and the all-those-that-need-not-be-menial, within white land, would need pull back, and then contest for place by means of fresh-mixed exams.

Therefore: Aunt Alice (a drum major and a drill sergeant for a suitable propriety for coloreds) taught forward, toward this New Jerusalem. But all knew that no one, neither white nor colored, could fathom the shape of this unseen land, and even less certain: in a region begot of spoils, who would get the new spoils and who be despoiled?

Being a nigger, instead of a Nigra, freed northern behavior. There was no need to fight for fastidious posturing, for no laws need be repealed. My mother's white students also had slurred titles, but because of the disassembly of the composite word "white," there were more of them: Irish/mick; Italian/wop & dago; Jew/kike; Puerto Rican/spic; Spanish/dago; German/kraut; Polish/polack; Asian/chink, and the exotics. Each, in their own way, seemed well matched. All the groups acted with a bravado of coarseness that leveled the discipline required to settle them. And with de facto equality, there should not have been the need for ethnic-specific guidelines in teaching.

But the Negro students had an additional sticky referent of two numerical quantities, one was about 100 in value, the other about 80: respectively, excellence in grades and IQ. The numbers (GPA & g), as a defining duo, came from the mouths and pens of those who purported to know and then describe "Negroes", but the slur word "niggers" was what everyone heard. Negroes (by science called): niggers (by what they are) can never get anywhere near a 100 on a test. Why? Because Negroes (by science called): niggers (by what they are) have an average IQ of about 80.

"William, that's low!"

"Yes, it is. For whites, the average measure of g is about 105."

"My God! Wickliffe, Jason, they're both dumb and black?"

"No! They are dumb because they are black."

"Richard, Charles, what can teachers do?"

"You will educate them to the extent of their abilities."

"Arthur, how far do these extend?"

"Not very far. Any further, and your efforts will be in vain."

"Linda, how will I know what is too much to give them?"

"You will come to understand. Remember though, most are unsuited for sophisticated instructions." The North also had its purveyors of a "Daily Dose."

My mother, the twin, countered north Jim's twins. She filed away g as she had done with the weapons. For the GPA, with the summit-rigor of 100 in mind, she labored. Her students' achievements stood on the windward slopes of right-shifted bell curves. From there, they could have been seen to exhibit *les flammes de la Négritude*, if the leukomas of the g-men&women had been less thick.

She paid a high price for her northern rise: she lived alone most of her life, and she met men who advantaged her for her competence in the domestic arts.

Words For My Mother's Possibly Perturbed Shade

The Crime: Capital.

Verdict: Guilty.

Sentence: Death.

Method: La guillotine.

When: "At the end of the wee hours."

The Blade falls.

The head, with its eyes blinking in abject horror,

Is quickly picked up by a cotton-stained, dark hand.

The mouth gyrates in the silence of Adam's split apple,

While the tongue flaps and laps obscenely

In its last tastes of air.

The crowd roars.

Some piss themselves.

Others soil their breeches.

And several find partners and copulate in a frenzy.

The Cakewalk, The Black Bottom, and The Stroll break out.

Jook-Joint songs vie with Church-hymns,

For finally, at long last,

The wily old murderer:

The word

igger

N

Has been decapitated.

35

"You are now students of St. Augustine's High School. You will act accordingly," said Father O'Rourke, the principal. The freshman assembly kept their eyes focused on this unsmiling man with a stern face colored sun-made red. His hands were in the pockets of his soutane as he stood on the dais in the schoolyard. It was difficult to know how tall he was, but he was fit and strong looking. I was overjoyed at having a male as the head of my school after the nine years with women as principals. Though the nuns had shaped and trained and encouraged me, I closed their door behind me. I never thought about them again.

My homeroom teacher, Father Hall, wore glasses that kept slipping down his nose, and reflexively his index finger pushed them back up. The sections were A, B, C, and D. I placed no significance on the alphabets, because the obvious could not be: that these were rankings of some sort. No one would be so unkind to students. I was proud, but my scholarship proved nothing. In my class at Holy Ghost, some did better than others, but no one was better than another. Segregation because of book skills remained unfathomable in my world. From kindergarten through eighth grade, the nuns had made me feel so.

About a third of the class came from Corpus Christi and Epiphany (two, downtown, colored, elementary Catholic Schools). To me, most of them looked white. Their names added to my confusion: Bernal, Beverotte, Bocage, Boissiere, Chauvin, Dapremont, Decou, Glapion, Parent. It took several weeks for my eyes to adjust, and then I saw them as colored.

Peeled away from my environs, because of age and choice, I awoke to the consistencies of the various textures of the city. I had heard the names from infancy; downtown, uptown, back-ah-town, and out-front-ah-town were broad and general in sound. But The Irish Channel, Gerttown, Broadmore, Carrolton, The Callopie, The Desire, Gentily, hinted at habitation rather than just location.

A short walk, then two public bus rides put me (after forty-five minutes) at St. Bernard and Broad Street, a corner of wide merit. There were wonderful stores in its space: a supermarket, a large poor boy shop (specializing in seafood), and on the catacomb corner, Dixiana Bakery. I never had any extra money but just the presence of these comforted me. My L shaped school route had a small hanging foot at the beginning of the bottom limb (the walk from my house to Washington Street). The two limbs of the L, going from uptown to downtown, cut through layers and were tangential to white-lands, colored-lands, section boundaries, and lands in transition. I had passed each of these places before, but never as a commuter. Now, each day, along the route, I would learn to travel as a disinterested tourist.

Saint Augustine's dress code only demanded a tie. Holy Ghost's brown khaki pants and shirt and black tie had been grafted onto me for nine years. Without them, I felt odd; now I had choice. I opted for the practical: grey khaki pants (my grandfather wore this type), new shirts and several new ties. But always the question remained, excluding jeans (which were not allowed), what was better and more comfortable than khaki pants? Dress pants, but only because sometimes one had to dress up. Without my knowledge or approval, the nuns had deftly excised my sartorial genes. Fashion, by habits, became excrescences when changed.

Saint Augustine's amazed me; everyone seemed huge. Teachers came to the classes except when there were labs. Sounds, traveling and bouncing about, told the not-visible state of the floors. What was quickly learned, by its frequency, was that paddles were a noticeable part of learning; there were no more pam-pams in the hands with rulers. Personalized, hand crafted paddles (and one razor strap) were now the lords (not mistresses) of sting and bruise. Each paddle spoke in a staccato tongue, with its accent driven by the personality of the wielding hand. Within the classrooms, teachers held sway, but on common ground, Father O'Rourke (called "Chief" outside of his earshot) was, first and foremost, magisterial in dispensing impartial justice. In the process, his countenance could be terrible to behold, more reddened, implacable, and fierce.

The whistle blew.

Instantly, a near complete silence came upon five hundred young men in the schoolyard.

Chief, platformed, looked out over the assembly.

"When I blew the whistle, some of you continued talking," he said gravely.

"I am going to blow the whistle again, and there will be silence," he said ex-dais.

The whistle blew again.

Most had been silent from the first; the second raised the volume of prudent heartbeats. Within the loud silence, Chief hurled himself down and forward into the ranks. He ploughed. I saw only the part of the furrow in front of me. Then came the sound of blows. Heavy blows. Blows made to bring submission. Chief returned to high space, ire-roasted red, snorting heat to out his fire. Who? I never knew. Why was doubled queried. Why the violation from the first whistle? Why the insanity of scoffing in High Father's face after the second whistle?

The laws of the grounds had been stated; transgression was unacceptable. Neither masochist nor sadist walked the halls of St. Augustine's, but a belief infused the school. This world was a physical place; physics had rules. "For every contrary action there would be an equal reaction, like it or leave the place." And men were unruly (by nature), and then by inference: At a man's school, corporal punishment was the font in the writ that was its charter. It was impossible to justify this belief to others; they saw the world differently.

Within my newly stretched world, occasionally on the bus, I encountered white Catholic students (their book covers revealed them). I watched their behavior as curiously as one might spy on a nearby resting fly. But they were not insects, so I began to wonder at the difference between St. Augustine's and these other Catholic schools. I encountered in "The Daily Dose" two names: Jesuit (High School) and Ben Franklin (High School). On asking about the latter, Aunt Alice praise-gush spigot turned on full. Jesuit's name produced just a smidgen less flow. "Oh, you have to be smart to get in them. You have to have at least a 120 IQ to get in Ben Franklin."

These two schools were the gold standard: the repository of the "top notch" students within the public and parochial systems. The two sticky numbers used in The North (for Negro downgrading) found place as tags on the skulls of the southern gentry's children. This grouping, among the colored, I gathered, was not done or was not necessary. Disappointment, in this lack of Negro democracy, came when I learned that "A class" meant just as the designation implied. I didn't like it, for six of my Holy Ghost classmates were in other sections. Separation, in this kind of way, from my lifelong friends had an unpleasant smell, the kind that made me turn up my mouth from the offense given to my nose.

Father Grant: "All of you (A section) could be in Jesuit or Ben Franklin." (The entrance examination to St. Aug seemingly had an I.Q. section.) How others in the class took this, I didn't know. For me, some pride, but mainly disdain. Though dearly loved by my aunt, I was always suspect, Father Grant notwithstanding. She correctly understood my far from golden intellect and my secret love of much that was common. To me, even with the potential passkey to unlock the white doors, I could think of no worse fate than to walk through them.

Father Grant's paddle was an aesthetic and scientific construction. Short, thick, shaped by regular geometric curves that ended in a molding, it was painted white. Its aerodynamic logic had bored holes in it, to reduce air resistance while in motion. The paddle's ascent was physics demonstrating order in the cold firmament of discipline. With but one stroke, my lifelong friend and classmate Arnold said that a hot, bright yellow star had instantly blazed before his eyes. But he would not cry; he held his tears as he walked back into his cooling seat.

Father Mac was serious, short, balding, and a bodybuilder; his t-shirts were filled up and swollen with muscles. He red-colored quickly and boomed when angry. It was most, most unpleasant to witness; his paddle's accent was red-raw anger. Years before he had leapt from the passenger seat in a car to tackle and rain down blows on a malefactor (still surrounded by his buddies). The bad boy yielded, more precisely, he crumbled and both he and his cronies capitulated. The hooligans' animus, given to high jinks after a football game, changed; they began to rampage through a quiet area adjacent to St. Augustine's. Father Mac both ended the disturbance and entered legend at the same time.

His civic classes could often be turned from his lesson plan and toward a discussion of the inequity of racial separation. There were times, when some used this as a ploy, covering their lack of homework. But scratching the itching foot of a fire demon could be risky. Kindled and smoldering inside him, he truly loathed racial segregation. The South's willful malice, evinced by the impetigo-studded visage of its society, was an affront to his priesthood. "St. Aug" was the man version of Katherine Drexel's training injunctions, sixty years after her start. When the time came for them, the Josephite Fathers used the edge of Saint Augustine to repeatedly lance the large, segregated, Catholic School System of New Orleans. Lacerated by their cuts, it bled, until gouts of fetid blood had drained out from its sores.

In my second year, Father McKenna taught religion and Father Pavalac geometry; two priests who brought proofs, from the elders, into the class. Carrying their respective worlds in their heads, Saint Thomas Aquinas and Euclid sat facing one another on the two ends of the lever. Five weights in Aquinas's faith proved God's gravity; the world of religion upheld the world of line and angle. Hardly undone, the Greek pushed down with his five axioms and moved God's world, QED. The inconstant pivot point rested inside soft brains. Hal's brains were hard with thought, and because of this, his hard head was locker chastised.

Father McKenna, large, powerful, and ancient, felt that Hal's desire for geometric rigor was out of place when dealing with Aquinas's "soft" proofs of God's existence.

"Little boy, see me after class." Obedient but imprudent, Hal waited outside the door after class.

"Father, you wanted to see me?"

Father McKenna looked down.

"Huh?"

Then Hal, the dark, fledgling heresiarch, came into focus.

"Oh! Yes!" growled Father McKenna.

No excommunication, but a simple warning of the life to come, came from one hard-handed cuff that sent Hal's head into the lockers. It was violent; Hal's static, kinky hair went askew. Then the two of them, protector and upstart, marched down to the office to see Chief. Lesson learned. Render unto old fathers the words of belief, and unto the strictures in logic provisionally plausible geometries for the structure of the universe.

36

In late winter, Father Grant, now principal, walked into the room and called out a list of names. "All of you will report to Loyola University's auditorium this Saturday at 10 AM. You will take the Westinghouse Science Exam. The top thirty scorers will participate in the Joe Berg Science Seminars. These will be held every Saturday at Loyola and Tulane. The Archdiocese is sponsoring this."

Of course, this edict would be obeyed without question or thought. Aunt Alice was sternly proud, and Grandma Adele was the time warden. A short 10-minute bus ride would carry me to the school, but I was directed to be ready by 8AM. The bus trip carried me, in reverse, to a new country not more than two miles from my house. I took the Feret at the corner where I normally got off. I had never ridden the bus past my stop. This new stop, at the end of the line, rested within the deep innards of the Garden District—white land. Young white people dotted the huge campus. I asked someone where the auditorium was located, and with a not-unpleasant look at me, the student pointed out the way. When I arrived at the location, I saw a huge space filled with whites. After this visual dawning, questions and understandings began to drop on me.

I'm in this room with a large number of white people.
I'm taking a test to see if I can be in a thing that is all white.
Is that legal?
Look at them; some of them are looking at me.
Pay attention, someone is about to speak.
I am not comfortable here.

A priest stood in front of the room and began giving directions; the tests were passed out, and the pencils given. "Begin," said the priest holding the mike.

It was hardest test I had ever taken. When done, I located my fellow "Purple Knights" and we all agreed as to its difficulty. With certainty, I knew that my score would not be high enough to beat my classmates or the whites. One day during the following week, Father Grant came into homeroom and announced that four students had been admitted. Mo, Hips, Bo, and I had all made the cut. There was no doubt in my mind who was the last one admitted. Jesuit High School had six, the highest number. The next highest number was St. Aug. Xavier Prep had two. The initial class would be Saturday. Colored feet would soon step upon the white landscape; Loyola and Tulane did not admit colored into their schools.

The bus moved with retrograde spirit down Feret Street, away from my world. At the school, again, directions asked; directions given, but with the same quizzical look; upon arrival there was an immersion into a large white pool, filled with white students and a few white adults. I found my fellows and the two students from Prep: Hal's youngest sister and her classmate, Ethedra, who made me gasp, sigh and then realize that I was smitten.

I am Walter the page, and the songs I sing beneath thy window are my only heritage.

The play I had played in, in eighth grade, awoke from dumb repose, and sought to make me, with true-courtly love, bow my head and re-bend my knee. A bronze-brown queen, solid upon her two feet, stood before me. Would that her glasses could see through to my pounding heart.

"I am brother Wendal Adams. I want to thank you all for participating in what, we hope, will be a wonderful experience for high school students."

The speaker's mouth attempted to show his spirit. It gave the impression of a gentle soul whose expression was summarized in a smile that came from a sphincter-type closing of the mouth. With a polite interruption, a white adult called out:

"I see there are colored students here."

A small noise arose; his eyes had not failed him; indeed, we were present. The man was of a proper pedigree. He was well dressed and well-tailored (*maybe his clothes were from "Lord and Taylor"*). His thick-sole wingtip shoes looked expensive and they were highly polished. The pedantic aura he exuded, cadenced with his southern drawl, spoke to lawyerly pomp.

"I don't think that they should be here."

More hum.

"I don't want my daughter to be accused of fostering integration."

A slim young girl standing next to the man materialized to my sight. Her spine bone congealed from the firm distress in her father's contention. Brother Wendal was lost. The Old South continued.

"I think that they should be made to leave."

Brother Wendal's quick thinking turned this direct hit about.

"Then we should let the students decide. Would the students who want the colored students to stay, please raise their hands?"

The warmth of this limp democracy became frost in my heart. We six all had fixed faces. The vote was overwhelming; the colored students could stay. But the Old South did not accept defeat.

"I recommend that all those, who don't want to be accused of fostering integration, leave."

He turned and left with his daughter along with several others and some parents. Brother Wendal, ascendant through relief, sphincter-smiled beamed and outlined the marvelous program. Now on Saturdays, Loyola, Tulane, hospitals, factories, etc. became places of wonder. Doctor Debleau described the geometry of the orbitals of electrons. We saw the functioning innards of dogs. We saw chocolate made and how railroad tanker cars moved staggeringly large amounts of it. We saw and saw, week after week, which tallied into years. And I also could see the strong mind of Ethedra, housed in its vessel of splendor.

Father Berrigan taught religion in the third and fourth years. He was tall, but his height made him appear thin; he wasn't. A wound he had received during the war, made his gait a little odd. Because local naming made things real, my private name for Father Phil was "shell-shocked Phil." I had heard the term on a TV show that had soldiers in it. Father Phil made the class worth being interested in and he rarely got angry. Besides, students never pressed him; it neither seemed appropriate nor wise.

Book-taught religion had begun to wilt. Fine line graduations, intricate patterns of thought and above all, the insolvability of seeing into death (Grandpa George had died my freshman May) dulled the academic side of faith. The most potent image in my final four years of formal faith learning came from "shell-shocked Phil."

"I think that many of the people in insane asylums are really possessed by devils."

This most catholic seed, planted in the twitter-fright gardens of my brain, found rich soil. Father Messina, the English teacher, without malice, called forth the germ-life from the kernel.

"Devils can enter a person at will."

"Is it because the person is bad?"

"No, it is the whim of the demon."

"Prayers? What can stop them?"

"Nothing."

"God?"

"He does not interfere."

"Then there is nothing we can do to prevent this?"

"That is true."

Watered by this logic, strong vines of terror grew and passed through accommodating locations inside my mind. The abominations of the insane could become part of one's reputation. Self-willed propriety and demonically produced social opprobrium butted heads. The champions, if numbers indicated victories, were an enormous set of vile demons. Without Christ driving out the invaders and forcing them into herd upon herd of swine, proper social behavior became impossible to secure. Freedom from God-guilt because of demiurge domination was sorry comfort. A general paralysis of expanding panic had now fully encompassed my mind. At any instant, at the whim of a fallen, but extant evil, I could be made to do the most despicable actions in the human canon.

"Even the man who is pure in heart will become a wolf when wolf bane blooms and the full moon beams," became a kinder fate. By the human actions of blocking sight and smell, the transformation could be stopped. Against those entities in the God realm, no human action could thwart their potency in the world of physics. My faith had given me no weapon to defend myself. Rather, it offered up my social flesh as a casualty of the rules of engagement. I would become an object of loathing.

The pressure of this logic was unsupportable. Without a countermeasure, true insanity was likely or inevitable. I forged my own weapon in self-defense: the will to fight, unto death, against the entity. Consummate hatred toward anything that would force me into public contumely was the unflagging source of my weapon's tenacity. I healed myself, but my faith's rational seat was supplanted; faith in my own mind saw into both worlds, Aquinas's and Euclid's, at times with flippancy.

"Father Coffee."

"Yes?"

"What happens when you bless us? Like, do rays come out of your fingers or something like that?"

"Sit down, before I kill you."

"Yes, father."

That summer, on a Sunday during my Philadelphia vacation, a dispirited "I'm going to church, Mommy," left my mouth as I closed the back door. I walked down Greenway Avenue and turned at the corner of 71st Street.

Massive and stony St. Michael's eyed me the entire two blocks up to Woodland Ave. The grey granite structure, on the other side of the street, offered only stone, not the living body of Christ. My feet did not cross Woodland Ave, but this was not open rebellion, the obligation to worship fixedly remained. It was the location that had become intolerable, that church, full with those pale, icy eyes that always colored-gawked. I turned right and walked toward Cobbs Creek Parkway. Sitting upon the first park bench I came to, I worshiped. For four weeks, this almost-bower became my place to reason and give God his due. After the fifth week, god no longer came to the Parkway, and I no longer went.

Schism.

My reasoning mind, and Catholic beliefs could no longer live together inside me. The inevitable war had begun. The neural wiring of Catholicism inside my brain cared little for my reasoning. The straightforwardness and elegance of nothing beyond grave death was slippery, and it had many enemies to overcome. The synaptic fortresses guarding the roads, in the labyrinthine city of my faith, did not have Jericho's walls; no clarion blasts would crumble them.

37

But I let them down too. Having been given every advantage that a student could ask, I had ill-used most of them. I wore the dunce cap, turned upside down. By this inversion of the popular hat, I myself had choked the sluice gate of excellence to a point. But even the fool's cap bit could not bore through my hard head.

What to be? How to be? With whom to be? "To be or not to be..." Kendell, flawlessly, had delivered the great soliloquy in English class. When he was done the class applauded. The options had been offered: a term paper (with the full number of steps) or Hamlet's full meditation on the dagger of choice. Everyone else chose the pen. Note cards, drafts, the final paper, all seemed less foreboding. Father Hughes, the senior year English teacher, was the only priest whose persona labeled him as a don. He was tall and wide, and he wore flowing white soutanes. The Marlboro cigarettes he smoked and his constant slight cough (which he never covered with his hand) bespoke the aristocrat and not the cowboy. Egalitarian sentiments were not strong in him. His intelligence and great learning had little tolerance for anyone who refused to work. He was a snob.

"Your term paper theme is a critique of Milton's *Aeropagitica*."

"*Huh?*"

Paradise Lost, vaguely familiar by name and hugely known by Catholic dour, made Milton less foreign. But, "critique" and *Aeropagitica* lived in the out-world. The first must have resided in a fancy house, where manners were excessive; the second lived in the clouds. I did try to climb and look blind Milton in the eye, several times. What became evident were Milton's sight and my own blindness: I could not understand the text with enough clarity to make judgments on it. Yet I had read at college level in grammar school, and I had passed the Joe Berg science test, and I had… and I had… and I had… The pilot-light heat from my small heap of had's had become a fading ego of place: I was still in the A class. The erosion of my standing in the class was a minor; the major was that term paper coming due. I could not finish in time. Failing English was not a thought; what was to be done, was. God may indeed love fools and children, but the devil is more practical: he gives ideas on co-opting the right (way) by using the sinner's strengths, thus reinforcing how to be strongly wrong. Narrative was the saving temptation; I told a story. I took Milton's sentiments on publishing freedom, and made from it a world, wherein some of those ideas (the ones I could understand) became the laws of the land. I got an A- and the comment that there were many ideas in the text that could have been discussed. But I had cheated. The prided A- was plated with iron pyrite (a sheen, but not from true gold). I had not gone through the steps, most of the note cards were blank and the rough drafts had little or nothing in them. Pop-pop had gotten a C, but he had done it the right way. At first, I felt as the trickster always does, triumphant, but "Breh Rabbit," and his kind were not Catholic characters. Deception had but one source: Satan. And by the transitivity of taint, I had sinned. My breached Catholicism took this to heart as a matter of ethics: It was not right, but there would be no confessional entered upon the point. The blossom of four years of Josephite efforts and my family's labors had wilted inside the bud. I was a dreadful student; only on occasion was this verdict surmounted. Fortunately, good luck did not despise me.

With a kindness (I would have wished from my blood father) Father Grant steered me to Lake Forest College. Gestation could take place within any womb, even one drafted by Chicago's icy winds. The encased seventeen years of wisdom I would carry along with my luggage was small:

"What to be? How to be? With whom to be?"

"Be."

"How?"

"Je ne sais pas."

"Who does?"

"The same answer: 'Mon pas connais.'"

Part Three

THE PIELBALD HORSE

38

Lake Forest train station impressed by what was not there: no noise, no frantic human traffic, and no hungry stares from the two taxi drivers. The station was a speck of attractive desert amid a vast oasis where elegance and wealth pushed themselves into your face, almost with effrontery. The drive to the college brought a mixture of two contradictory perspectives. Novelty and deja vous sat side by side in my eyes. The stunning dwellings overwhelmed but being from New Orleans I merged them within the magnificent garden district. The trees in Lake Forest were tall enough to support the sky, but in Audubon Park, the live oaks had been there before the time of Proteus. My Southern self had finally gained my desired distance from the warm bosom of New Orleans. Now I would be lodged in the forest of the frost giants. Titans, who had stepped into the American mind, rested their bones and their wealth amongst these trees. Every day, Armour, Swift, Rockefeller, and others of this race had brought, from Chicago to Lake Forest, Santa's full sack for Christmas. Their diluted scion and the new admissions now contended with the husbandry of so well-heeled a world. Lake Forest, no longer "a suitcase college," now domiciled most of its students on weekends, but wealth and crass had hardly given up the union they often formed.

My lifelong friend, Arnold, had chosen the same school. He and I, and two others, D. P. Dross and Blount Apel, both white, were roommates in a quad on the top floor of Harlan Hall. Dross was a "jock" whose fellowship in the fraternity of the superior athletes was both his "cool" and his joy. He hailed from the Midwest. Apel (self-described as a "ski bum" or a "shit bum") was from New York. With an askew fringe of hair covering one eye, and a cigarette dangling from his lips, he would weary on the guitar. Blount belonged to the fraternity of the "black dressers," who, when possible, sealed their personas by only wearing black clothes. Dross was form and Apel was scatter. Within four days of moving in, reciprocal contempt toward one another became their only bond. D-P asked for and received a room-transfer. The quad became a triple. In his desperation to be seen as "cool" Blount, easily, had made enemies. They short-sheeted his bed; shaving cream and sand were added inside the insult.

Formal freshman orientation joined inspirational speeches with roughhouse frolic. In the middle of a field, behind the gym, a long, stout, greased pole had been placed. Atop it sat a freshman beanie; the sophomore men guarded it with their bodies and noisy intimidation. The task of the incoming men was to get the beanie. Mêlée, of course, was the object and that is what ensued. Freshmen who managed to get to the pole and climb would be hauled down, often losing their trousers in the struggle. Strategy, for the freshmen, was to peel away the upperclassmen. I joined in, but all those contending, on both sides, were much larger than me. If I got trapped inside the crowd, being trampled and suffocated were very possible. But at the edge I could pull away the guardians.

"Boy, don't do that!"

I looked at this scowling, thickset white upperclassman. Then a grin, of uncertain origin, was shown. The noise of the contest retreated.

"I say, boy, get away from here!" was done in a rasping seriousness that fully isolated the game both from this person and me. I looked again at the grinning intimidator.

Is this for real? Why is he calling me "boy"?

There was some fright, but overwhelmingly,

This is going too far, and this person may be insane, white people frequently are.

"Move, boy!"

I walked away and went back to my dorm and cleaned up. Arnold arrived later and said that the freshmen had triumphed. He and Don (a colossus from Florida) had a wonderful time. They pitched around some defenders and allowed a rapid-climbing class member to get the beanie. But it was impossible, for me, to forget this incident with the strange person. At supper that night, Paul Walker (a Negro sophomore from New Jersey) came over and sat at my table. Paul began laughing:

"Roach frightened you today at the beanie pole, huh?"

"Roach?"

"Dave Toledo. He's a really nice guy. He just likes jokes."

"Hmmm."

"He was in the Marines."

Respect for soldiers put a thin cap on my bare disquiet at Roach's behavior, but I didn't know the man. And I had never joked with a white person on so personal an issue. Russian class brought an opportunity to make a final judgment on this two-toned humor. Arriving early on the first day, I chose a seat mid-way in the room, which was about three quarter filled with students. A sound alerted me that someone had taken the seat next to me; it was Roach. "Hey boy", he said with a grin. Persistent, unpleasant foolishness marked the man. Saying nothing, my attention turned on distraction. The open space of the doorway had been abruptly filled by a figure.

"здравствуйте."

The beautifully flowing, but startlingly foreign word came from the teacher as she entered. She was tall, as the greeting word was long. Middle age, and attractive, she wore a simple, but well-tailored white dress. And, her heavy bosom bounced. The movement was ordinary, natural, and wonderful. With her blonde hair in a pompadour, and with the heels she wore, statuesque was an adjective required in any sound description of her. Every male's mouth dropped open. Agape: to speak Russian.

Eros: to faux nurse from the milk of her benediction.

"как вы поживаете?"

"*Cock we paush she va,*" a student raised a hand.

"Yes."

"Would you please pronounce the first thing you said when you entered?"

"здравствуйте, it means hello. I'll write it on the board." She picked up a stick of chalk and wrote the word. Syllable by syllable, she took the complex sound apart. As I began to learn, her breasts heaved less and less. Until finally, my cock-eye closed; she became Teacher.

Latvia, not Russia, was her home. Regardless, both places were lairs for beasts that drew red cartoons of dying prey on white snow. A wolf, bearing sanguine canines, was the face I gave to the Russian winter. Vodka, its counter, lay clear and heavy in its vein bottles. This nourishment gave both heat and flammable misery to the Russians' immensely cold life. Movies and stories had written this gloomy text on the Kremlin's domes. Also written, in this dreary land of Ursa Major, was mastery of the inscrutable world of pure mathematics. In cold logic and in caviar, Russian itself was the czar. Many of these treatises had not been translated and remained bound in the beautiful Cyrillic symbols of the Russian alphabet; my major was mathematics. There existed a natural coupling between the two subjects, and my language requirement would be fulfilled.

39

"Language! How exquisite the shapes it took as it walked, upright, out of the human mind."

Russian and Latin, which I studied in high school, shared the same love of inflection. So polite a word, it called for the changing of every ending of every adjective and every noun and every pronoun with each grammatical case. For those who liked to use long, vivid, pertinent, colorful, robust descriptions, the Russian bear sat waiting. English, curtly dismissive to the cases, voiced itself strongly to its thickly robed, distant kin:

Good God!	Хороший Богх!
I saw the **good god**.	Я увидел хорошего бога.
How?	Как?
I prayed to the **good god**.	Я помолил к хорошему богу.
When?	Когда?
I sat upon the **good god**.	Я сидел на хорошем боге.
What?	Что?
I sat with the **good god**.	Я сидел хорошим богом.
Where?	Где?
Go to hell!	Пойдите к аду!
Может Быть? Кто знает?	Maybe? Who knows?

Of course, man was the not same as woman, or a thing. Masculine words, feminine words, and neuter endings were all different. And since one is not equal to two, single and plural were given their unique endings. The first sentence in an additional small text stated, "Russian verbs of motion often prove difficult for beginners." The entire book covered two verbs: to move under self-propulsion and to move with external power; such a cleavage partitioned all objects that move. Speaking Russian correctly would be a hell made on the cold flat of the steppes.

Along with its grammar came the pronunciation. The opulence of the pasha had been trapped within its sounds; gibbosity, with the round of the long, fat pearl; the bubbling within the samovar; the bulge of the ermine coat as it soft-warms the full belly from the pelting sleet. Attempts at clever intonations and unwarranted assumptions of facility could let loose faulty plops.

"No! You just said that he is sucking himself."

Really? What did I just say? I wonder how you ask for some?

"Try again."

The reel-to-reel tapes in the language lab were lullabies in the pitch of a speeding high C. The voice of the native speaking female paid back English ears, for the years of tonal hegemony given to the "Songs of the Volga Boatmen." Not a low note, nor an evident breath pause, nor a lessening of express pace came forth. She sped on, unchecked in ear by understanding. Without texts to follow, and with the room being cool and not brightly lit, it soon became, "Wake me when it's done." Or "Ouch!" as my head dropped forward to hit the panel that held the tape mechanism.

Calculus, the other morning class, mixed students with Doc Sam's folksy brilliance, and his Pall Mall cigarette smoke. With hard chalk in his right hand he wrote on the blackboard. And with his smoking brand in the other, he wrote, on the air, his frustration with dull students. He was one of those hairy white men, who never seemed clean-shaven. His skin color and his dark hair follicles were always in high contrast. He was never rumpled in appearance, but the dandy was at the opposite end of his dressing. His New York accent capped his earthy image.

No one shone in the class, which I felt was odd, for at least one student had used the same text in high school. This impressive preamble slipped through my pedestrian memory (it meandered about pleasure), which was both my sensual gift and intellectual failing. I had forgotten the book my class used for our senior year's math course, "Allandoffer and Oakley": a "new math" text of density, complexity, and foolish hope. It was a bellowing, grey covered pachyderm let loose in the wilderness of mathematical instructions after Sputnik (the "Co-Traveler") went on high. The earth's first new moon (tiny, squeaking, calling home, and made in the USSR) stiffened our nation's will to prey also from the higher sky. Irving Adler's paperback, *The New Mathematics* captured the vogue but as an adjunct, not a primary source. New words, new symbols, and new grammar were splashed upon the humdrum world of addition, subtraction, multiplication, and division. However, these four old legs still bore, firmly, the ancient cow Mathematics, whose sweet milk had nourished the Russian high leap. The old math of calculus (exotic unto itself) was more tedious than difficult, regardless of aptitude. But without the tedium, of working countless problems to gain facility, only the talented would do well. Not being so made, my study habits rapidly put me into the lower depths of the class. But I read. With my few dollars, I bought Dover books on math from the bookstore and pondered over the arcane forms and ideas that composed higher math. Occasionally this coincided, tangentially, with class topics.

"Doc, how can a definitive choice of function be made?" remembering an argument from an almost incomprehensible book.

"The Axiom of Choice allows it."

"Okay."

Doc's kindly answer, to a faltering student's after-class question, was beyond kind; it spoke to the warmth of the man. Years later, I learned that this non-kin had written to my mother entreating her to rouse me, some-how, to study. But this was impossible.

"What to be? How to be? With whom to be?"

The now modified response was *"BE!"*

Gestation, within the cold womb of Lake Forest College, until a responsible me left after four years was not a feasible response to the imperative. Instead there was a chronic, chaotic delirium of new being.

40

It had turned chilly when we arrived that freshman September; nostalgic autumn was only beginning to unfold. For the first time, I would see this colored spectacle as it fell upon the days, with the smoke-gray grimace of hard winter lying in wait.

Sharing the town's contrived, but masterful sylvan grace, the campus (though technically small) boasted of sumptuous woodland themes. There were large grassy areas whose counterpoint of steeply wooded ravines let birds roost undisturbed. North Chapel, so wedded to its position, seemed as if it were a graceful stone up-thrust amidst flanking pillars of trees. North Gym was old; its weathered red-stone coat and conical spires bespoke of protected royalty. The Japanese garden, the first I had seen, was a precise, small wonder. It made me want to bow my head in respect to its beauty and cleverness.

Of the twelve hundred students at the school, twenty-four were colored.

With this ratio of almost fifty-to-one, colored students became the accent marks in any gathering. There were no colored workers: no cooks, no maids, no maintenance staff, no gardeners, and no teachers either. In the kitchen, this dearth disheartened the most. Despite choices, each dish was as tasteless as the next. Whether colored hands could have transformed "mystery meat" into edible food is questionable, but the thought of a colored miracle made me feel less alone. Mealtime was social time; this became its purpose. Waiting in line, sitting at a table, and talking.

Two lines, through two sets of doors, entered "Commons." The accommodations resembled a stout crescent with the tapering ends near the doors. The seating was not open; various groups had laid claim to sections, and all maintained this order. The world of the Greeks exposed itself both in my afternoon class of Western Civilization and in the taking of daily meals. The men of Delta Sigma Chi, Phi Pi Epsilon, Alpha Stigma Nigh, Digamma Alpha Epsilon, and Tau Kappa Epsilon broke only fraternal bread. The women of Chi Omega Chi, Gamma Phi Theta, and Tau Delta Theta only broke into smiles for the proper fraternal type. The few Gamma Delta Iotas (God Damn Independents, proclaimed by loud self-assertion) broke wind at both. A new type of fractionating of "white people" presented itself. These brotherhoods, sisterhoods, and dissidents reverse-refracted through complex prisms. Means, backgrounds, and veneers recombined into the specific white lights desired by each group. Their place, on the gigantic stage of white world, would be illuminated by their own self-defined uniqueness. The groups preened within these self-made beams. The presentations entered my mind as Technicolor-white documentaries, done in montage. Meaning, teased out of fragments of conversations, slivers of sight (staring was impolite), courtship postures, nocturnes of drunken howling, and a stubborn insistence on the high height of their worth formed "The Greeks'" social attributes.

At first, I found it difficult to categorize the physicality of whites. A homogenous opacity, broken by occasional Negro-bumps, met my eyes as I cleared the food line and faced the cafeteria. However, with a necessary, but uneasy focus, the individual features of the Caucasians began to emerge in relief. One fact became apparent, if "white" was one thing, then that one thing was a mulligan stew. Primordial Adam White and Mitochondrial-mother White must have spent a good deal of time apart, dallying, with unknown others, in the raw.

College dissolved both day and night and reformed it into one-time. The singularity of any student, at any time, could open. Such intimate views of strangers were bewildering. My simplistic feelings of either "like" or "dislike" toward others had been shaped in black and white. But Lake Forest was green, like my eyes. Here, the old fermentations distilled the sour mash of race and class in mid-western vats. Novel sights and misunderstandings were the free drinks always at hand.

"Hey, come on, let's go to see the soccer game," said Sybil, a white freshman who sparkled with friendliness.

"That's where they kick the ball, right?"

"Yeah, Roy is playing." Roy and Sybil liked each other.

Sybil and I walked to the South Campus field where the game was being played and attended by a small noisy crowd, but the tiny bleacher section still had enough space for us to find seats together. Roy wasn't in the game, but two Africans were. In a half-hearted manner I began to watch the game. Goss, one of the Africans, was light-skinned and slim in build. The volleyball-size ball came to him. A thickset white boy from the other side rushed at him. Tackling, as in football, was not done, but somehow the boy was legally going to take the ball away, so I figured. Goss did something (just exactly what, was unclear) but the charging lad fell on his ass and Goss, still with the ball at his feet, went toward the opponent's goal. I focused strongly on Goss. Another charged. This one fell in such an awkward manner that laughter was the first impulse, but it was checked. What mattered more was, what was going on? Goss kicked the ball to a team member. I excused myself, left the bleachers and joined several people standing at the line marking off the side of the field. The other African, Derek (short, thick, and dark), intercepted a pass made by the opposition. Men surrounded him and came at him. They fell like bowling pins; he then kicked the ball out of bounds. Before the end of the game, Goss did his unknown magic trick again: men came at him (as he went forward with speed) and they fell, as if by command. Two African Mandrakes had appeared, each their own scantily dressed Lothar. But they gestured hypnotically with the feet, not the hands. When the match was done, I walked up to Goss and with serious passion said, "Teach me this game." Goss father-smiled and laughed, without offense being intended, "Uh, well, we'll talk about it later." The All-American player was kind. Derek's temperament was different, more akin to the rhino. Both were effective in a match: one bruised the body, the other the ego. About a week later, Goss gave me an old soccer ball and told me to practice. I did so, nearly every day. When my Western Civilization class ended at two-thirty, I would leave the Persians and the Greeks slaughtering each other, and themselves, and take to my gymnasium: the grass in the middle of the quad. I practiced by myself or with others until dinner. Overwhelmingly these others were male, white students who were labeled as "preps," (a seemingly conflicted word like bourgeois) many of whom would doff their studiously mangled loafers and kick in bare feet.

Before soccer, for me, there was the six-man, intramural touch football team of the freshmen. At 120 pounds I was always the smallest person on the field, I could neither catch well nor throw a football with any accuracy, but I was reasonably agile and somewhat tough. They made me a blocking shield along with Bob Mavic. In the first game, vs. the Phipes, lining up to rush against me was a blond man named Kraft, five eleven or so and about two hundred and fifty pounds. He did not appear particularly agile, but parts of my body were going to sustain large deformational stresses. Over the course of the game Kraft tired which made my job easier. At the end of the game (the freshmen won) there were handshakes and good feelings. We played Alpha Stigma in the next game. There were large men on the squad, but these were much more agile than Kraft. The freshmen won but the spirit was ugly.

The third game was the watershed, and the last I played for the team. I won most of the battles but was bruised to the point of severe pain all week. The foolishness of my position, given my size and the obvious tactics of opponents, made no sense. Every ex-football player or large man with a combative disposition, who wanted action, chose to rush. Their aggression would focus solely on the blocking back, for all they had to do was touch the quarterback. A failed test, a fight with their girlfriend, a dispute with another or whatever, all found a way to enter. **Rush**, the naked infinitive, became the swollen, grunting bitch that gave release. Without protection and without adequate practice, and with no medical assistance, such unequal jousting was absurd. And most of all, I had seen the magic show of soccer.

41

The snow ended my first soccer season.

Life in the dormitory encouraged studying to be done elsewhere, or, if one used a hearing aid, then to turn it completely off. There were periods of quiet, but more often than not, freshmen passions were boisterous. The weekends became the official time to celebrate, with more ceremony, the (almost quasi-religious) love of beer. In the quad at the other end of the hall, quart bottles were emptied at an astonishing rate. I heard the clinks, the laughter, and the boasting of how many quarts each drinker had consumed. How could humans put that much into their stomachs became a biological question I put to them? Almost to a man, they said they pissed it out in short order. I did not urinate copiously, even if I drank large amounts of fluid; I became bloated. But sweat would pour out of me with any small amount of physical exertion. This was biology; white people had different types of kidneys. As the term wore on, quarts became a half-keg. This upped their ease of getting "shit-faced."

Jay Stein lived on the floor. He was short, left-handed, and he had a good sense of humor. He also enlightened me as to certain laws of physics that operated in obscure sections of white land. A profoundly disturbing trend has been occurring that was inexplicable. Under certain circumstances, I became de facto invisible. The notice of this transformation didn't occur suddenly; after weeks of puzzling observations it revealed itself. In the hallways of buildings, or in other public places, students, who were in my classes or in my dorm, missed me. Recognizing them, from afar, walking directly toward me, I assumed they saw me. But just as the distance closed to within greeting range something averted their attention and they passed by me. The diversions were subtle: perhaps a thought forced an inward meditation, and they passed by (this was the most common); a book needed tucking up in a bag, they passed by; their shoes suddenly absorbed their mental focus, they passed by. Since the schedules were set, this became a frequent occurrence. At first, given my upbringing, I would be reflexively poised to say "Good Morning" or some other greeting. However, realizing that there was no notice of my presence, I would stifle the reflex, causing my mouth to seize, and produce a sound akin to a dry heave. Not a frown, not a scowl was shown on the faces, just diversion. Finally, I asked Jay about it. Jay laughed.

"Don't you understand? They don't want to speak to you because you are colored."

"Oh."

This was additional white-light beamed into my colored eyes. Naively, feeling somewhat hurt, with a growing feeling of loss, I longed to hear the greeting "Hey baby, whas going on?" from a colored voice. Instead, I had been isolated, within alabaster halls, by my nigger-pox. Memories of home, friends, and politeness entered, producing sentiments, which were simply out of place. It would take time, but I would learn that when an enemy has been exposed, it was risky to try and feel too much. Contempt (not anger), as a good, sustainable armor, had low emotional costs. The twenty-four Negro students (almost equally divided between freshmen and sopho-mores) moved in their own ways among the twelve hundred whites. The sophomores, the year before, had been ten out of twelve hundred. This year they were seasoned, wiser, hardened, and comfortable with the situation, as their individual temperaments would allow.

The forms of diversion, common to most college campuses, were both novel and social to me. Curiosity fed the first, and a recoil from isolation fed the second. Arnold was more mature, and stable. He had adapted to the requirements of college life and in doing so, he and Don (who was of a friendly, but sober temperament) both realized the similarity of perspec-tives. Also, each one was a good athlete. I found community in my nomadic dispersal. Watching bid-whist, which was normally played exclusively by Negro students, semi-taught me the game and allowed me to admire the attractive, Negro sophomore women. Sassy independence (most were from the New York area) and card skills made for pleasurable viewing. Of course, there were also attractive white females, but they dematerialized when I thought of them as physical women. Occasionally, given the large number of them, spectral images of parts, e.g. breasts or thighs or lips could, by quantity weight, reassemble, at an unexpected moment, and cause a solid reaction in my groin. My warm erection, snuggled against my cold thigh, were sustained opposites that made dreams vivid, when finally, I turned off into sleep.

The most potent discovery was the weekend films. With no admission charge, no segregated seating requirements, and in isolation, I saw new forms of storytelling that compelled, and were remembered like etches from acids spilled on marble. Dali, Eisenstein, Cocteau, and Bergman became the new magicians. They induced worlds where hands bred ants, stone lions rose, and death was the poet's thrall, or the dance master of all. Old fibs cast anew.

The life and vitality of the campus moved indoors as late fall began to cede its place to the incoming bite of winter. Dress became less carefree and community more deliberate; bundling and unbundling took its toll. My wanderings shrank when the pavement's cold assault moved routinely inside my "winter" shoes, causing my feet to ache. Commons, sealed off from the cold by closed windows, filled itself with the unappealing impotency of meat without aroma, but which did emit a faint scent, when brought under the nose by the act of eating. This bewildering smell matched the meat's unknown ever-present, grisly pieces that could neither be chewed nor cut. The potato, the pleasure of the northern palette, dominated all. The dreary sturdiness it lent to meal after flavorless meal even displaced the social pleasure of going to Commons. It now required effort to go. But I had a begrudging admiration toward people who could eat such unendingly dull food and remain in good spirits. Mortised to blandness, they were rugged and sturdy like the log cabin of the Lincoln legend. Lake Forest (though of a higher standard) seemed what The Midwest had to be. Wealth could rest calmly upon its own weight without the disruption of a spice palate. Of course, I didn't starve; my stomach would not allow that. Whatever leftover money I had from working in the Common's dishwasher section, I used to buy food outside of Commons. However, moving through the hours of college life in Lake Forest was a dreary exercise that had no remission. What could I expect? I was a large part of the problem; I lacked social skills. I was again invisible, but now, not through another's malice. The days became mushy, and time smeared them into a joyless streak.

Only memory, exaggerated and polished, offered comfort.

Final exams for the first trimester were coming, then Christmas. Arnold and I made plans to go to New Orleans together. By the time we left Lake Forest for the holidays, winter had come to the Chicago area. There was no exaggeration in the stories we had heard about it. Both of us were dressed, not only warmly, but also thickly. However, Chicago was not Lake Forest; it was the goring bull, not the hornless calf. In walking the short distance between the commuter train station and the regular one, we saw whirlpools made of snow and dirt perform dart dances in alleys. Reaching the station, we both looked at each other and said in unison the same thing in different words, "I feel like I ain got no clothes on!" "I feel naked!" An elderly white woman was struggling to get the door open. It was impossible. The wind, blowing face on to the entrance, sealed it. Whistling noises and her focused attention rendered Arnold and me as invisible parts of a background she was trying to flee. This stalemate was changing from discomfort into pain as the wind-buffeted suitcases beat into our legs. Arnold cried out: "Lady, you better open the door or I'm gonna push you aside and open it myself." This broke through. She ceded her position and Arnold opened the door. She went in first, then I fought to keep it open for Arnold. By the time we had entered, the woman had moved off into the warmth of the station.

Both of us squeezed our dollars when buying food. We arrived in New Orleans the next day. The elastic tug drawing us home was now without tension. My large suitcase, guilt-weighted with Russian and calculus textbooks, was opened only once. I took out my clothes and the gifts I had brought.

42

Grandmother Adele was well into her baking preparations. At least a week was needed to go from raw materials to the finished products. The candied fruits were soaking in whiskey. Large quantities of pecans had already been shelled, for the cakes, and, in addition, for the pralines and the brownies. The big mixing bowl was out. Caramel colored, with a broad strip of pale green blue near its middle, I had known it since childhood. Objects in my world did not go away easily. The wooden mixing spoon, the speckled enamel pan (candied sweet potatoes were made in it or at another time baked fish), the white-enamel coffee pot, and the devotional pieces on the mantel in Mamma Adele's room were all transports carrying the past, spilling their contents from a glance or a sound or a smell. The handed downs: my crib, my highchair, and my rocking chair (which could have brained an ox) were at Aunt Vonnie's house. Her children, my younger cousins, now possessed well-lineaged items of family.

Aunt Vonnie was making gumbo; it was impossible to convince her that it was not worthy of being imitated by a fancy restaurant. It was good, better than many. But, as always, "best" in New Orleans was an impossible judgment. This added to the delight of Christmas or any other time when above average kitchen performances were expected. The normal greeting given when visiting someone's house: "Yah want something to eat?" now had seasonal weight. Judgments on holiday fare would be made with a Christmas tongue.

It snowed that Christmas, a wet, heavy, four-inch snow. Though this was the most the city had seen in sixty-seven years, within days the ground had forgotten the melted history. Christmas was not solid anymore. The fireplace was no longer in use, for Daddy George had been dead three years. My mother and sister (she was in college now) stayed in Philadelphia at Aunt Grace's. A visit to St. Augustine's was fun, but I wasn't in high school anymore. My ex-classmates, who had stayed, and gone to colleges in New Orleans, had their lives centered in the city. I took to my bike. The physical pleasure of pedaling freely about the spacious city (in areas that were not dangerous) was comforting. I rode and looked, as New Orleans passed through me as an incorporeal wind. My grades arrived; they were poor. Then, the time was done. I traveled back to LFC alone. Finally opening my textbooks, I found pleasure in studying on the train.

The quad-mate, Blount Apel, left school after the first term. John Preston was assigned to our quad. He was tall and white and of two standards in his appearance: soft and viral. When he went to shower, he always left the room smoking a cigarette and naked, with his towel flung over his right shoulder. He had no upper body muscularity to the point of a concave chest, but his legs were powerful. And his literal slack ass was fronted by a huge penis which slapped against his thigh like a meaty clapper making a "plap, plap" sound. He was uncircumcised, which made his dick look bizarre. Arnold and I gave him the name "prick-face." Without inflammation from harsh word or broad gesture, John's and my mutual dislike of each other slowly grew. It fed on air-thin spites. The assumed new fraternity of the three dissolved over the term. John treated Arnold differently. He began to ignore me. Again, I had vanished, but this time, the prestidigitator was my roommate. The mutual antagonism was too unpleasant; home should never be like that. I ceded the room to John and avoided it as much as possible.

The sun would simply go out of sight for weeks on end, leaving a grayness that became noticeable by a desire to be constantly indoors. This was an artificial emotion, fed by the brightness inside buildings. Western Civilization had reached Chaucer proto-English. With the goading of "don't read the ribald stories such as the *Miller's Tale*, for you will be scandalized," the dangers of English kissing and behavior were humorously exposed. Russian pronunciation and reading were tamed, and calculus had mellowed out into addition, how to integrate (functions). The bookstore became more of a place of wonder. Dover paperbacks on mathematics offered more glimpses into a world of giants: Riemann, Minkowsky, Gauss, and especially Poincaré. These foreign men became my new heroes, demi-gods, moving through the narrows of equal signs as "Plastic Man" did through keyholes, but speaking in the equa-tongue: logic. I fled from English, and would, if possible, never take a course in it during my college career. Understanding of this desire for distance would come later. The term ended with reasonable grades and elation when I saw the green sprouts of my first spring. This famed, and celebrated rebirth was not as warm as I thought was implied, by the grand praise it received in verse and story. In New Orleans, the end of March had no outright flirtations with either jacket or sweater. Spring term lived up to its promise of new growth. Alcohol, (*that profound spirit that flowed out of spent fruit and grain*) held the magic of delightful deliriums. Stupor drunk and propped up by an outside wall.

A Spring Nocturne:

Bacchantes: the huge, new constellation of savage angels, earthbound, going to lie in the bed of the west, my virginal bed: Betsy, Jeanie, Josie, Christine, Cheryl, Caroline, Carol, Barbara, Susan, Fran, … the stilted winnowing of my sight. I had seen them in their fall down, then in their winter fleece, now I longed for them spring-shorn, to waylay me, and play out the night with me kept in their keeps.

Passing out, my reverie broke apart on the fracture of an open sigh.

Soccer reappeared with muddy feet from the spring rain. Academics took its subservient, sitting posture to the coursing blood. I wore down the impudent grass in the quadrangle.

I had used my springtime-credits unwisely. The school responded by giving me low grades in calculus and Russian. I had sinned; punishment was due. Two consequences followed. I had to make up the courses and I was not allowed back for the fall term. Taking a calculus course during the summer at St. Joseph's balanced the first negative. Some of Doc Sam's instructions had sifted through my thick skull; I got an A. The second phase of punishment was served in New Orleans. With a Grundig portable tape recorder pouring out Russian speech, and studying page after page of Russian grammar, the fatigue of repetition broke my will to daydream. My unpardonable sin of profligacy had shamed the family. I was fed and clothed, and I could walk about, but I had no money to go anywhere. I lived out my three months of house arrest within the confines of my home. My aunt wanted no one to see me. And I myself took the same shame to heart. I saw no one. Religion, as a solace, was gone, and as a flail for my failure, I had surpassed it: I had myself. Food, though I ate little, was still a friend; it passed no judgment; it was always agreeable. Christmas brought the joy of knowing that release would be soon. I took to the train, going to cold Chicago, with near tears in my eyes. The sweetness of home had been demolished, but a pragmatism of place nestled inside: I would fail no more courses. Also, my whirligig had been shattered. Legal Jim Crow was moribund. Only the duality of Negro&nigger was still in effect. Settling into my single dorm room, in the winter of '65, I closed my southern door behind me.

43

The new winter continued to reform the face of discontent. Increased loss, my boyhood friend had moved on. Our bond was indissoluble, but it had attenuated and took its new shape in the convolutions of our uneven maturities. Beidler, my new dorm, had been an attractive fraternal residence in an isolated section of the campus. It had withered under the years. Now in its dotage, it gave license to a motley group of young men to perform their acts of youth. But unlike freshman year, most in the dorm behaved reasonably. There was a stable mixture of study, booze, and (for the lucky ones) women. The rare explosions, normally caused by outsiders, and usually on the weekends, could have enormous hilarity, if the damping of charitable decency were omitted.

When the term ended, I met my mother in Chicago. We stayed at the Y. Its just-above shabby atmosphere was home to many and perhaps a possible warning, of descent, to some. There were two Y's in New Orleans: one for colored and one for white. The colored Y was a small, attractive, two story, blonde brick building on Draydes, just up the street from the local colored library, itself a fine-looking old building of red brick, with imposing staircases on each side of the façade. Both structures were clean, orderly, and hollow. The other Y, for whites, was grand with rooms, facilities and, of course, it was forbidden. My mother butted her head, and my sister's and mine against what would not be given to her children. She wanted us to continue swimming (Shakespeare's park pool had been closed). Northern Y's had pools, the colored Y, in New Orleans, did not. Off to the white Y, one Christmas, she carried us. The person at the desk spoke of the facilities at the other Y and how happy she and her children would be there. The lack, of the use of a pool, was something that he could not remedy. Not once was race mentioned, only textured words winding around it. Time had passed and the situation was different in Chicago. Its Y had always been egalitarian; its complex funk was cosmopolitan in origin.

I would have one week in Chicago with my mother, "Mommy." A week alone with a presence known by letters, pictures, bits of communal time, and loving surrogates, who shared much of her sameness. Chastisement was the edgy phantom that might grow real and push its thorn into the seven days. But she gave no speeches; no exhortations slipped out. Only once, a stern face reminded me of my obligation to be silent and not draw embarrassment on top of my kin's misfortune. Cousin Uriel lived in Chicago; we visited her. The bus ride was ordinary, but as the stop drew near, the area had taken a single face: it had seen better days, and still lower was where it had to go. I had never visited a relative who lived in such a section. A pleasantness, still seated in Cousin Uriel's weary face, met us at the door. The house had no smell, which was a labor of work, but still this was nothing it could call its own.

"Yall, want something to eat?" A speechless perplexity froze my mouth.

"No thank you, we've just eaten."

"Then you want something to drink?"

"I'll take a glass of water, if you don't mind?" politely came from my mother. Cousin Uriel turned her back and went to the kitchen. The ugly green paneling covering the lower half of the walls was torn and rotted away in small sections near the floor. As she returned and approached my mother with the glass, a rat, sporting a large backside, came out of a torn section, and moved to the next opening five feet away. Cousin Uriel could not see it; her back was to it. But my mother and I saw the thing. To me, the most deviant aspect of the sight was the vermin's lack of terror. Giving one furtive look at Uriel's back, it moved across the floor with the restive pace of a tenant who tries to avoid the landlord, due to the rent in arrears. I looked at my mother whose face spoke, for less than an instant, in red-hot eye talk: "Don't you open your mouth!" No words could have come out of my open mouth, for the cord to my tongue had been severed. When the visit was over, we thanked Cousin Uriel for her hospitality and left, my mother's glass of water still untouched. We didn't speak of it, or much of anything else. While waiting for the bus, two men passed by, one said: "I bet she take all his money." Bursting hate, even to a chattering of my teeth, ignited me. In my mind, my beloved mother was of a gender, but she was never to be dwelt upon as a sex. Though the men could have no knowledge of our blood relationship, the imputation still struck as incestuous and bestial. In the spike of mindless-anger, I would have used a weapon against the two.

Chicago was wide and fat; it had the spirit of New Orleans, but it was not squat. Its substantial vertical rested on huge, meaty thighs. Both the Merchandise Mart and the Marshall Field Building were high mass. In contrast, Marina Towers, which faced the Y, were uncomfortable to observe, they seemed to disfigure the vertical. From most angles, the thin projecting curves of the coverings over every porch presented themselves as articulated cutting surfaces. These, ribbed around and stacked symmetrically forty stories high, made the towers seem like industrial scraping tools.

The twenty-story helical parking ramps below were the bellows, pushing, in reciprocating action, these devices. With such thoughts, viewing the buildings brought visceral discomfort.

Carson, Pirie and Scott Department Store provided a nature trip. I asked my mother if we could go to the seventh floor, which had the sporting goods section. She said yes. We had been the last to enter the elevator on the sixth floor. She had entered first; I would exit first. When the doors of the car opened, due sight on, towering over several rows of counters (which concealed its lower half) was the torso of a huge bear (easily nine feet tall). Its enormous head, with the fierce eyes and teeth bared, was frozen in the intensity of its malice, *while its heated breath moved in imperceptible flows.* Its arms were not chained; the claws were at the ready. Instant terror of the uncertain, the improbable, and the impossible reigned, not long, but long enough to make a calculus palpable. A bear was alive and loose and looking in my direction. The how and why were not important, though possible ideas whizzed by. In three charging strides, crashing down and over counters, I would meet Ursa Major. A crowd was waiting to enter the car. But there was no panic, however they could not see the bear; it was behind them. Still no growl, no anticipated charge, no out rushing human chaos.

False fright.

Holding boundless awe in my open eyes, I went and met the clothed statue of the brown god, who, when alive, could blot out the sun in Seward's Folly. Credit was due both to the taxidermist for his skill, and to the floor designer for the efficacy of the display. Because a hunter, (true or mock), could not be without feelings upon emerging from the elevator, and immediately sighting an upright, enraged Kodiak. A hunter's heart would be made glad and calm.

Eye, finger, gun, poised, and as one.

I have earned this kill. I will blood myself with it. I will call the tribe and tell them the tale of it. I will wear its skin. I will set its head high on a red cypress pole: a baton rouge.

"Winter clearance sale on Hunting Gear. Up To 30% Off."

I will burn its fat.

"Coleman Equipment: Stoves, Lanterns and Coolers. Big Discount."

In the smoky light from the "Yayapahthawah," I will see its spirit enter me.

"Pretty big fella, huh? How'ja like to meet him?"

"I would soil myself."

"Not if you had a Leupold scope on a Remington 700 with some 458

Magnum rounds in it." Sales-pitch gold to be turned into the lead of a hunter's nerve: reverse alchemy.

When we entered the elevator to do down, it was empty. From two stops, it picked up four colored passengers; on the third floor, two poorly dressed white boys faced the entrance. One entered and said in a loud voice: "It smells like shit in here." The other entered and said: "Yeah, it smells like shit in here." Before the doors could fully close, one pushed the open-door button repeatedly, until both doors pulled back. The two left, with similar words said at an even higher volume: "It smelled like shit in dere." Stressing the word shit with vigorous nods of their heads. The doors closed. Unwilling to let the incident pass without a mental comeback, I remembered a concept Jack Reins had taught in psychology. The "white trash" had engaged in "projection." Words were good friends; without fail, they let one pin some-kind-of ass-marker on the donkeys.

A tacit understanding ended the trip. Without censure, in any way, "Mommy" conveyed the essence of my situation: Keep your wits about you, finish school, and you will be all right. Academics, supplemental work, alcohol, lack of sex, new friends, and soccer could bubble in the pot, as before, but now, perspective had been thrown in. Relegating the first two items of the list to the status of chores, without grumble or inordinate slack, they must be given their due.

44

I joined an intramural basketball team that was truly a ragtag bunch. Our main opposition would be the fraternities. The games were hard fought, but without rancor; the contests meant so little. We played in the huge barn-like gym, where a gusting wind, hitting the thin metal sides, shook clattering sounds from the normally empty (at least for these games), corrugated box. Fluttering clapping as randomly given praise was the effect. In one mid-week game, Alpha Stigma, for some reason, came swollen with bile to do enraged battle. Dross, the ex-roommate, and the Alpha Stigma floor leader was the sole mouth in the taunting directed exclusively at me. Perhaps fearing the eruption potential in the constant baiting, my team took the taunts to heart in an inverse way, and dropped out, leaving the scoring burden on me, who could not bear the weight. The roughness of the game pushed the heat higher between Dross and me. We collided; Dross threw one more taunt. "Fuck you!" exploded out of me. The goading had been effective; restraint had crumbled; my torrent of anger flowed openly now. "Fuck you!" again hurled at Dross.

"Shut up, you god damned nigger!"

Sticks and stone can break my bones, but words can never hurt me.

Imprecise reflexive-sensibility, spawn of Hamm.

White people always sound funny when they say "nigger."

It sounds like a foreigner trying to speak English: sometimes wrong intonation or maybe it's the phrasing. I should react, I guess. He is standing in a wide stance. Maybe I can kick him in the nuts with a front snap kick? If I miss, he will have advantage. If I do get in the kick, and it is a good one, the school will want to expel me. They will not condone the damage I have done. His face is not showing rage; yet he raged the situation with his word. His brat brothers will help him. Some are smiling at his affront now, especially the tall pock-faced one. He must have to pay for pussy; he thinks his height buys away his lunar face. Want some sandpaper, asshole? Dross is looking confused: he knows that if I report this, he might have problems. My teammates won't back me, except maybe Sidney.

Nigger! Nigger. Nigger?

"le mot nègre "
"the word nigger"

"sorti tout arme du hurlement"
"Emerged fully armed from the howling"

"d'une fleur veneneuse"
"Of a poisonous flower"

"le mot nègre"
"the word nigger"

"tout pouacre de parasites"
"all filthy with parasites"

"le mot nègre"
"The word nigger"

"tout plein de brigands qui rodent"
"Loaded with roaming bandits"

"des meres qui crient"
"With screaming mothers"

"d'enfants qui pleurent"
"Crying children"

"le mot nègre"

Global fire: T Rex-destroying comet; Glacial tear: rodent kingmaker.

"le mot nègre"

Limit point for all sequences, bounded and unbounded, in the colored manifold. The rotten sum of residues around the branch points at infinity: the global measure. QED by using complex-real analysis.

"le mot nègre"

A prism of razors, splitting black life into a shifted spectrum of thin, blood red slices.

The Golden Rule of The Law of Regal Harmony

Be able to speak unto others
As
They have spoken unto you.

I would have a word to contain you, Mr. Dross, un autre mot, un mot de renom, un mot généreuses, que tous les englobant et crasseux vers vous que le vôtre vers moi: (another word, a renowned word, a bountiful word, as all-encompassing and filthy toward you as yours toward me)

"Man, you know I don't think that way about you."
Reaction:
Dross, your childish plastering of affectations is trying to mold a "cool."

That word, your word for you, was strongly "nigger" born, fool.
   Observation:

Probably Dross meant it when he thought about segments of me, but as a full man-enemy, he said what he meant. So, he lied through his words of assuagement. Mother Math precisely defined the limits of Mother Tongue. "I'm not some nigger!" cried "Brideshead's" Rex, to protest Catholicism's pointedly negative description of his Protestant status. In self-defense, Rex's world's universal denial-of-negative had been the reflexive counter.

"le mot nègre"
"the word nigger"

"un gresillement de chairs qui brulent"
"a sizzling of flesh and horn matter"

"acre et de corne"
"Burning, acrid"

"le mot nègre"
"The word nigger"

"comme le soleil qui saigne de la griffe"
"Like the sun bleeding from its claw"

"sur le trottoir de nuages"
"Onto the sidewalk of clouds"

I walked away. Before the final whistle, one of Dross's brothers pushed me (in a clever spite) in the small of the back directly toward a stanchion. Barely avoiding the damaging collision, I turned, and found Khoffman running away and laughing. "Punk, mophfahdie, sissy, you got a cock-up booty and its shakes like a woman's": ad hominem vegetal blobs, thought-hurdled. To have no word ally sagged the spirit in battle, slipping on triteness into triteness. *How sweet it is going to be, to curl into the unlit womb of sleep, and be covered by black time, a respite from Mother Math's unflinching light.*
   Soon after came Raven. We met in flight. Raven, wild bent to explore; she took my cherry. I hers, maybe, I never asked, she never said. I was taken

into her fancy by the jade in my eyes. She sat firmly lodged in my brain by the scent of her sex. Then she turned her eyes and winged to a new pitch. I replayed the taste of her mouth till the record wore smooth; then I scratched its blankness till I was black and blue.

"Why she leave me? It hurt me so bad, my food don taste good no mo. Wha she leave me for? She ain't gon find nobody sweet like me. I could make her sing like a bird sitting in ah tree. Lord, I hate to see that empty bed. Ima go out and get me a pint of gin and a bag of weed. And Sweet Jesus, Oh Sweet Jesus, nobody better mess with me."

Summer's arrival again brought Philadelphia's hugeness and, in addition, this time, my mother's new dwelling. I met Raven there in a simple way that satisfied me. When my mother was not in the apartment, I locked the bathroom door, and from inventions of passion grander than our brief couplings, I came on the tile floor. Then she was gone. I unlocked the door, free, now, of bruised memories, unburdened of semen, grateful.

45

My mother's first and only step, in leaving her almost twenty-year, one-room domicile, led her to center city. Provincial Greenway Avenue was gone; its replacement was Ben Franklin Parkway: a short road studded with the crown jewels of the city's culture and scaled for Brobdingnag.

Entering her building, I walked past the spacious, well-furnished lobby to the elevators and rode to the seventeenth floor (out of a possible nineteen). My mother's three sets of windows faced The Parkway and 22nd Street. Directly below her apartment, across a wide, splendidly shaded, grassy strip, The Thinker sat, brood-guarding the iron gates of a museum to his creator.

Mommy was one of two "coloreds," out of six hundred residents, in the Park Towne East building, so I, the son, needed several visits to my mother's building before the doormen would acknowledge my legitimacy. This initiation period moved on coarsely civil moments. The doormen would balk after opening the door for me until they called my mother. Even after I had been given a key, some still regarded me with suspicion, asking where I was going. My mother argued for understanding from me about them; I agreed. However, I confronted one of them, the most asinine by virtue of the doorman's scowl each time he faced me.

"How come you can't remember my face?"

"I'm here to protect the entrance."

"I understand that, so take a good look at my face, so you won't have to ask me what I'm doing here next time."

"I'm just doing my job."

"I know, but I want to help you do it better." We both looked at each other, with blank faces, and thought, *"Fuck you!"* But this settled the matter, for the present.

The doorman returned his comeuppance four months later, at Christmas, when he claimed to have forgotten my face, and again asked: "Where are you going?"

"I just visited my mother during the summer."

"I can't be expected to remember everybody who visits."

We both thought: *"Touché, fucker!"*

Only Nikolai, the large and amiable Russian doorman, spoke freely. "здравствуйте. как вы поживаете?" "Хорошо, и вы." I took out a pack of Pall Malls. "Вы хотите сигарету? " "Да. " Looking at the brand. " Хорошие сигареты. Спасибо. " "Пожалуйста." If no one was near, we would light up. Together, we would have drunk vodka, toasting to each other's health, for an hour or two. Then I would have collapsed. Nikolai was a mountain, the Urals made man.

After the newness faded, the plaque of the ordinary began to accrete. From now on, summers meant work, for pay. I found a job at Stein's Linen and Towel Service, a huge professional laundry, one of whose tasks was to provide clean linen to several large Atlantic City hotels. Every day, forty-foot long trailers, crammed full of sheets, towels, and pillowcases, would pull up to the unloading dock. When unloaded, piles of linen could rise ten feet high. The do-rag wearing young black men, who unloaded them, sometimes frolicked by bounding on the white heaps. These, many times on individual items, showed visible stains of varying hues. But when the workers hid inside the linen mountains or ate their lunch, laying on them, I wanted to gag. The soil and smell of strangers still remained repugnant.

Forty-five minutes of travel brought me from center city to the laundry in Frankfort. For the first time I saw "the elevated." The stations and the trains and the ride, all cheese-mold green from paint or age, carried me into old Philadelphia, where the deep hollow of thick culture could retain its own. "No, I've never been outside Frankfort," said one young worker in the laundry. No center city, no highway, no "Jersey", rather, square blocks girdled from the swaddling bands to the winding cloths.

Cool, warm, hot, extra hot, and inside the oven were the temperature settings in the laundry. Normal, loud, and din were the sound-volume levels. Dry, sweating, and drenched/soaked were the possible workers' states. It all depended on one's job. Daily, clean work clothes, in size-labeled bins, were waiting for the new day's efforts to soak in. The office staff lived air-conditioned lives, so they did not change clothes. Sweat and white smocks on the women's bodies let bra lines and panty curves become visible. But inside the hive, the logic of dangerous work kept the attention focused. Moving with pace, while gulping ice water from large mason jars, women labored alongside sweating men

One day going to work, I noticed a bicycle in the window of a shop on Lancaster Ave. It quickly went out of sight, but its shape, done in royal blue and chrome, had been exquisite. The next day I got off the bus; the store was closed. Staring through the window, a name, Fiorelli, was painted, in lacquered gold, on the down tube. It was a "racer", but more elegant than my three-speed in New Orleans or any I had ever seen. On Saturday, I went into the small shop. Mr. Fabiano (sixty or so) greeted me. Gushing at the beauty of the machine:

"Is it a racing bike?"

"It's not a true racer; it doesn't have the proper rims."

Mr. Fabiano loved bikes, and in his youth, in Italy, he had raced them, and he told me of seeing the magnificent Coppi race. When his eyes looked back into the past, his silver moustache widened with his smile. His store had been located on Lancaster for many years, and his sons would take over when he retired. Old Philadelphia, again, and it had no pretense, comfortable with itself, and its harbored treasures.

"How Much?"

"One twenty-five."

(Hmmm. The clarinet, in high school, had been bought on time at Werline's.)

"Can I buy it on time?"

"Sure."

The Saturday I made the last payment I thanked Mr. Fabiano and shook his hand with gratitude.

It still took forty-five minutes to get to work. But now, during the rush hours, I was on the busy Philly streets myself, moving with my attention focused on not getting crunched by accidental mishaps, or willful drivers; it was exhilarating and novel. Trolley tracks and narrow tires were opposite magnetic poles; beware. Sewer grates (which I had never seen in New Orleans) were occasionally slotted. If these were turned parallel to the traffic's flow, and if I were pinned to the line of the slots by a car, problems; approach them with caution. A laughing white boy, in the front passenger seat of a car, plucked at me through the open window. I just escaped being knocked down; be ready for quick evasion. In ecstasy, I overtook and passed a sclerotic, clunking T-bird going down a hill. A very-labored surging-gurgle sounded, and the red T-bird pulled up alongside. Quickly turning my head, I looked at a heavy, brown, unhappy face, "Don't you ever pass me again!" Accepting the rebuke, I shook my head, saying: "No Sir, I won't." Lucky escape: point noted, curb excessive freedom of expression.

I was never late, but my bike allowed flirtations with it. If I had missed a bus, I couldn't recover, but with the bike, I could power through the seven miles and arrive on time in a sweat, equating it with a type of work. For by now, the job had become boring. The summer ended, and Frankfort, tolerant for the season, permanently replaced me with a Frankfordian.

46

I began my sophomore/junior year isolated, and sane. The latter state did not flow from my willed cohesion; I had been disciplined to maintain the rigors necessary for routine sanity. Seeing Raven still hurt. That pit was not so easily avoided; it pulled; I fought. Lying in the bed of a new lover was the palliative for a broken heart, so said Casanova, and the advice seemed reasonable. Finding that new lover, possibly in an unknown bed, within a mysterious room became a detective puzzle. Solutions presented themselves in incomplete, fantasy forms that were drawn from the solid press of the earth.

Making the soccer team allowed me to travel into parts of The Midwest—a foreign place. If the trip required an overnight stay, I was always given a room to myself, a double, in fact. I tried to notice (with my smile ready to woo) if there were single women in the rooms to the right and left of mine. The doors leading to these adjoining rooms were erotic portals in my mind. By unlocking my side and the person on the other side unlocking theirs, a solution for heartache might be encountered. In the two years I was on the team and traveled with them, I met no one. Never having a roommate was not troubling, but it was odd when I thought about it. There were two main groupings on the team, frat brothers and Africans, but these were small in number. A diverse core made up the majority of the team, with me being the only colored. And as far as I gathered (by the chat at meals) most players had roommates; the coach, I think, decided who stayed with whom.

Real Analysis was the math for the year. The text was unusually attractive: a bi-color book, the bottom in blue, and the top in black with the bisection giving more area to the black. It was one of those curious math texts that gave more space to words than formulae. A naive glance held that the topic was both moderate in difficulty and in implication, but this would be incorrect. Words like function, compact, cut, and integral were dense. From the precise notions of a mathematical function came Gregor Cantor's discovery of numbers, each describing a larger infinity than the one below it: , , and so on.

"What foolishness! Infinity is infinity, that is what it means: without end. There are no sizes of infinity. Let alone, an infinity of infinities of infinites beyond end."

"Cantor demonstrated that meaning can be put to these concepts: Alephs without any possibility for an Omega. Like Darwin, he was reviled as a devil and a corruptor of youth by theologians, even by some mathematicians."

The Vanity-of-Ignorance (a broad-beamed scow) floats without a keel. Yet even when hard rocked, causing it to tip and sink, it still gives up but little of its pride. "You're a fool if you believe such nonsense. He was an ass." *No, fool and ass are your crown and throne.*

Another introductory Russian language text (much more demanding than the first year's), and Soviet Literature were my minor's requirements. For the first time I read poems where the rhythm-drum, in a verse, was struck with short sound-sticks.

Greep.	Гриб.
Graap.	Грабь.
Grop.	Гроб.
Group.	Груб.

The facile movement of a horse's hoofs clacking in the stanza.
Or, the stamping of soldiers' feet:

Left!	Левой!
Left!	Левой!
Left!"	Левой!

There were other types of poems that spoke to my emotions by an immediacy of empathy with its sound (the way a cello would in the future).

"Ты помнишь, Алёша, дороги Смоленщины,"
(Do you remember, Dear Alyosha, Smolensk,)

The palatalized pronoun and the fleshy pout of the verb were a mix of glorious sounds both to say and to hear. The line surrounded the dead with memory and sorrow and love. When finally learning of the hell at Smolensk, sighing breaths were the only proper offering I could give, with the promise never to forget my past: the dark cover that gave me understanding. I knew that I would master neither the Russian language, nor the scope of mathematics, but they were not college vistas, soon to be forgotten. They would be enduring rents in the opacity of my ignorance. Despite my vast limitations, my journey was my own, the stumbles and the leaps and the loves, all carrying me forward toward the finality of the unconscious darkness. Regrets, at the end, possibly, regardless, time's blade, dull or sharp, will loose me. The impassive eyes of the old ones will see the banquet begin. I hoped that the worms grow "fat and happy" feeding upon my flesh.

During the spring term, through word of mouth, I got a one-time job raking leaves at a house in Lake Forest. The yard was lovely. With piles of leaves to my front and the house to my back, I revisited New Orleans through the chore.

"Hey, you!

Hey, you!"

The voice that had come through to me was a child's. Snapped back up north, I turned my head. It was a four-year-old or so white child who had come from the house and was addressing me as he walked toward me.

"Hey, you!"

In amazement, I looked down at this child who would address anyone, let alone an adult, in such a manner. Without thought (perhaps part of my mind was still in New Orleans) I reached down with one hand, and slowly, and carefully lifted the child by the front of his shirt. I stopped when our faces looked at each other, eye to eye. The boy no longer demanded acknowledgment. His unchecked incivility had been replaced by the precocious intelligence of fear.

"What is my name?"

"I don't know."

"I will tell you my name." I told the child my last name prefaced by Mr. The boy's now-widened young eyes, and his elevated breath rate showed the imprinting process at work.

"Now, what is my name?" Without an error, he repeated it.

"Again, what is my name?" As before, he said it correctly. With the gentleness of a slowing moving hydraulic arm, I lowered the experienced child. We went about our respective tasks. I raked leaves, and the boy played, nearby, until the colored maid came outside and called him.

About a year afterwards, I was in the overwrought supermarket of Lake Forest. One of its decorative features was a panel of frenzied cerulean, extending from the ceiling to one-third down the back wall. Mounted on it were highly colored models of edible marine life and an old, brass diving helmet. This mural-in-relief was visually aggressive, but it was devoid of any aesthetic grace: pretense without the sea. The garish display always forced my vision toward it when I entered the store.

"I know your name." Looking down, I saw a smiling white child. "Huh?" Then that memory awoke in me. I nodded and returned the smile. With the rising motion of the nod, I glimpsed the mother's face. It was not upset, but it was looking at the child with the look of someone who wondered where her son had met this person not of her world. "It's Mr." Immediately, the woman face turned to me with a look of annoyed surprise. As soon as the child said my name, I nodded and smiled again at the polite young man, then turned and walked, with a steady pace, down another aisle. More amity (as was implied desirable by the boy's face) might provoke questions. The complete answers, to which, could only have been understood in the now-dissolved past. Also, there had been one-sidedness in the first encounter: I had not asked the young man his name.

However sufficient trespass upon the privilege of arrogance, in this land of the old gods, taught its own lessons. One tranquil Saturday afternoon in April, Drey, Sneaky, Arnold, Slim and I decided to walk about in Lake Forest. We were marked as a group: Drey and Sneaky were wearing their LFC letter jackets. Spring had loaded winter's skeletal trees with leaves, blunting the fractured grayness of the sky. Jokes were being told; laughter took its place as the sixth member of the group. The wide sidewalks and the large yards—in which the houses were deeply set back—combined. We were in the forest where we saw no one but ourselves. But five Negro men massed together (four of whom were quite large) was a gravity source. Trouble would seek us.

Absorbed, no one noticed, an elderly white woman appeared as though by a conjurer's trick. She was given ample space and she walked past us. Drey, with too much Negro license and not enough colored caution, said in a comic voice (the kind attributed to startled "darkies" in the movies), "An old white lady walking down the street." It was doubtful that she could even hear, let alone, understand him, but Arnold was miffed. "Don't say anything around those people." I said nothing, but I knew he was correct: the less said around white people the better. The walkabout rounded; we decided to return to the campus. About fifteen minutes passed when two police cars also materialized from ever-pregnant space. The red lights were flashing. All of us looked at the two policemen who were emerging from the vehicles. Arnold and I immediately knew the situation. The old white woman had been disturbed, and she called the police to report her disturbance. The police said that a complaint had been made. All five must come to the station while the issue was sorted out. Arnold, Slim and I got into the same car, driven by a young white policeman. He tried to make light of the awkward situation. "Come on, guys, that woman was so old and wrinkled. You should have picked on someone young who looked better than her." This was a laudable effort by him that probably would not have been made in many other jurisdictions, or it might have been an attempt at a ploy. Despite whatever, the grossness of being taken away in a police car kept us silent. At the station, we all were brought together in the central room. Everyone was identified as a student of LFC. The second policeman, short and bulldog like in his posture and manner, was snarling. "It's five against one, but in cases like *this*, we tend to believe the one."

The nature of the complaint was never stated, nor were we ever asked anything. The police had to understand the lack of substance in the unspecified accusation, for they took no precautions against the accused, and our previously astonished faces had grown sullen. The young officer, trying to ease the growing tension, gratuitously, told us where the rest room was located and where drinking water could be found. After an hour or so, something was resolved, and we were released; no explanation was given. The police offered us a ride back to campus, but no one accepted it. We all walked back in silence; each keeping their thoughts to themselves. By the time we reached Commons, the light of the day was fading, with the evening chill already having set in.

"April is the cruelest month, breeding"
[Nettles] "out of the dead land, mixing
Memory and" [spooks], "stirring"
[Foul] "roots with spring rain."

138

47

The summer of 1966 was England's glory; they won the World Cup for the first time. I, a provisional Brit by this common interest, talked of football, all summer, with the English workers in the ground's crew. We were working on the renovation of a women's dorm. I had never been in a woman's room before, save for those who were close relatives, and one punishment day at the convent. In the shotgun houses of my friends, I had averted my eyes until reaching the kitchen. At LFC, the concealing walls were being torn out and the spaces altered for new configurations. The old rooms had been sturdy suites that had sheltered coeds I had dreamt of. The mirrors had watched them move about naked, and the beds had known the press of their bodies. I searched out and found the room of a wished-for love angel. *Sanctus, Sanctus, Sanctus:* Holy, Holy, Holy was written on the carpet, in my mind's approach, to this cloister for the wet pearl. Entering it, my eyes and breath, all askew with excitement, were taken away. Dust, some of it round rolled to marble size, was under the bed, inside closets, and above cabinets. It was much like a man's room, slightly cleaner than some, but not so much as others. This astonished me. An enduring regard for buckets, mops, brooms, and disinfectant (one of women's supposed genetic imperatives) had not been there. Smell had left nothing of itself for me to latch to. It was a dusty, dormitory room, where the mons had had hairs plucked away as soiled underwear was loosed upon the floor. Then a body, full with exhaustion, fell to its rest on an unmade bed. I got no less of an erection thinking about my now ground-walking angel. The thought of drunken rutting on the damp earthen floor of a forest, alive with the cries of Bacchantes, de-sexed the cleaning-genes. "Pine Oil" lost its gender.

Male student workers (the ones who did the smashing and hauling) stayed in dorms on campus, along with male students attending summer classes. Without supervision, and the restraint engendered by having the full complement of both students and administrators' eyes watching, asi-nine behavior inflated itself to building-engulfing size. One worker used the same pair of sneakers everyday (without socks) as his work shoes. The smell became so rank that his roommate made him keep them in the hall. This caused the area, near the door, then the hall, and soon, the entire floor, to gag upon itself. I avoided the place.

Telephones were operational only in rooms that had requested them through a signed contract between the occupants and the phone company. A mistake had been made; the phone in my room could not receive calls but calling out was enabled. My roommate, well intentioned, but foolishly, mentioned the error to others. At first, polite requests were made for its use. Then the assumption of privilege entered: demands were made based on "It's free. Why should you mind?" I was admittedly puzzled. The room was a double, and the phone was "free," supposedly. I spoke to the room-mate about it. Eric, having opened the door, did not know how to close it. His disposition was not cowardly, but size and a loud mouth could sway it. The knocks on the door were incessant; they came from a mix of white people, some of whom, I had never seen before. And emergencies were always occurring. A muscle-bound lad bought a malamute puppy and kenneled it in his room. The dog became ill, and its owner, in paroxysms of worry, became belligerent in the phone's use. Not for calls to the vet, but to those with whom he could lament the situation. One day (by my magic hand, which had never used the phone) it ceased to work, and dismissive coarseness did. The latter was a simple solution, that when hardened into place, took no notice of scowling white faces.

The telephone company rejected the idea of a "free" phone. When the summer session ended, a bill, in the thousands, was sent to me. Coarse attitudes still worked, though with a quasi-legal prelude. "Did I pay you a deposit to have the phone turned on in my name?" "No, you did not." "Was it required that a contract be made for the responsibility to be mine?" "Yes." "I signed no contract; then how can I be responsible for the bill?" "You have a moral obligation to pay for the services used." "No! I don't!" Continual badgering finally produced, "Lady, kiss my ass." Thus, it ended, for me.

With these summer lessons, I better understood the sentiments that shaped the Globe Theater's Pit, and enjoyed bear baiting, and wassail. I saw celibate Newton joyous at having a counterfeiter hanged. The direct-ed intelligence, the lack of manners (despite wide ruffs), and the noth-ing-amiss-with-aggression attitude were never sheathed. For in an instant, all with them could be rough and tumble. In the future, students, here and from other schools, would control the country with their passions having available the mechanisms of power. Arguments for personal manifest des-tiny would be based on licenses carried inside their genes. A rant of cocky, southern black men was showing its applicability to life in general: "All I'm giving out is hard dick and bubble gum, and I'm fresh outta bubble gum."

BLESSED ARE THE MEEK, FOR THEY SHALL INHERIT THE EARTH.

"Really!?"

48

In the fall term I met TJ. He had one of those faces you occasionally see on Negroes: it has "chinee-like" eyes. That would have been enough to make him unusual. But a Russian phrase, used to describe Asians, in a poem by Алекса⬛ндр Блок had stuck in my mind: "С раскосыми и жадными очами!" (with slanted and greedy eyes). This made him literarily odd too. Physically he was a thickset, average height, colored man. He was "country" from Texas, getting his masters/doctorate, from Northwestern University, in Renaissance drama of England and Italy. This latter almost made him bizarre. He had been "discovered" at his Texas undergraduate school, and proclaimed, by the admission coordinator, "a diamond in the rough," because of his graduate school's application's IQ score: 180. He never spoke of this to anyone at LFC. It slipped off an alcohol-lubed tongue, a year after I came to know him. By that time, he was the wished-for older brother, albeit, no possible imaginings, on my part, could have predicted such a fraternity.

LFC hired TJ as a counselor for a South Campus dorm where Arnold, Don, Sneaky and Drey lived. They told me (I lived on North Campus) of the brother who everyday drove an old black Mercedes coupe to Northwestern. Occasionally, at night, he let them use it to go and get food or pizza. The food-crave struck one night; en masse we descended upon TJ's suite. He came to the door and admitted all five of us. The apartment had a good smell. Opera was playing on a stereo system. The music was pleasant; normally it was not, despite the efforts my aunt had made by taking me to several operas, playing it on the radio, and disparaging "trashy" (R&B) music.

TJ was pleasant and gracious. An attractive white woman was sitting down on a couch in the large parlor; she nodded to everyone. The request, for the use of the car, was phrased as the desired to render a service. "Could we use the car to buy some food, and get you anything you might like?" The sight of empty dinner plates nullified the service angle, but.

"Sorry, guys, I'm taking Joan back to Evanston right now." With agreeable disappointment, all bade both good night.

I saw Arnold and Don only infrequently, usually in Commons, sometimes at the gym; our different worlds rarely overlapped. In the flow of one such meeting, TJ was mentioned. He and Joan were having trouble. How this was brought up remains unclear. In a rare concurrence, we three met at the gym and walked to Common together. Passing the window in TJ's apt we saw Joan inside. Quickly forming the idea, we stood outside the window: "The feeling we used to get, whenever out lips met, like smoke for a cigarette, is fading away...." The song brought Joan and TJ to the window. Each smiled a warm smile and waved.

Christmas inched forward and finally arrived. In Philadelphia, my mother, my sister and I would be together, for the first time, since my sister left for her Catholic college, which was replete with nuns. I had never been there nor to her graduation. Attending would have been "nice," but since it was over, there was nothing to feel bad about; I could not change anything. And the sight of gathered nuns was a sight I could do without. They had the power to alter a space by inducing the tension from a dark twittering of white-beaked birds, eager to dig at flesh.

I never thought how my sister and mother related to one another. Between my mother and me, there was a bond of my freedom to do, and of my guilt for not doing my chores. She had knitted the large socks of great promise, for her boy child. It was different with the two women. For the girl child, she made the nettled skin-wrap of a non-Creole colored woman. I saw their faces—when neutral and kind—rapidly shift to battle ready, and then to war visage. Perplexing dismay filled me when these family battles raged. Christmas was bringing a light to my world, a blood red flame. To avoid them both was my wish, but this was impossible. For the first time, I was viewing another cosmos and it was a horror.

It had to do with men, specifically my sister's ex-fiancé, viewed differently by the two. I had the license of ignorance in their quarrels, but I saw a reservoir of anger: hidden, full, and fueling their rage. A theoretical self-hate had been infused into each of them, by the southern mind. Both had all save the one quality: Creole looks. Each hurled, in complex arcs, this lack toward one other. Mother and daughter were back-facing twins, who when near one another found no dearth of causes to ignite combustion.

Immersed in this skirmish, I saw the stakes in their war become unbearable. This battle has escalated to capitulate or leave my apartment. The hour was late. My sister could not go wandering out into the street; her safety would be at risk. Yet such was her angry defiance, she took on the mantle of not caring. The familial terror drama was enfolding, as mother and sister picked up each other's gauntlet, but a soft, comforting babble, with a tremulous bobbing of the head, came upon me. In my mind, I was moving toward: I saw it as a space opening, unfolding itself: a beckoning which compelled with immense power. Inside was the insulated oblivion of unconcerned insanity. My induction into this protection was being kibitzed on by my receding, terrified, and ineffectual rational mind. "I am going insane; there will be no easy exit from this place." I had no idea what my face looked like, but my mother and sister were staring at me. Their eyes were wide, and their rage had turned to fright. My shaking babble was counter-moved by both screaming out my name and vigorously shaking me. The entrance to my new habitation vanished; I stared at both of them. They hugged me tightly. The severed anger between mother and daughter would have to re-knit in their dreams and take its shape in the morning air. Morning arrived and the two relented. Each took the posture of avoidance. When the Christmas break ended, I left bewildered at the level of my ignorance of "women things." Mine was the world of the penis. Theirs was the world of the sanitary napkin. Semen and menstrual blood were like oil and water, though probably mixed at times, they did not need to share philosophies. I flew for the first time. Half drunk, I hoped that the cigarette smoke (I smelled from my second-class seat) would be an additional buoyant in keeping the flying sardine can aloft.

49

Winter arrived, and it brought no surprises; it was a known beast. I unpacked my "long johns", and settled in, ready to do my chores. One job was cleaning the library at night. After everyone left, the large building became unsettling. Both the racks of books and students' cubicles parsed off sight. The ventilation blowing on empty and nearly empty shelves vibrated them into making clattering sounds. Books that were re-stacked or lent outweighed or un-weighed on these metallic tongues. This nightly chatter came and went in abrupt spasms as the air from the ducts was released or choked off by the thermostat's command. Fluorescent illumination, carried within a cadaverous-green hue, guided my path through the tomes. Though the building was deemed empty, three floors of nothing would become three floors of a large something, if I encountered a presence. At every turn I steeled myself with a tight stomach. To do battle, maybe, but more to prevent the rush from a fright "turning my adrenaline brown," a conceivable response to a "Tale From This New Crypt."

I spent my small earnings on Laren, a freshman. She was pretty and finding her had been most unexpected. She was a friend of Ben's girl, Joselen. Ben, who was known as the Philly Flash, knew, as soon as he met Joselen, that he would marry her. Such certainties for me were not in my nature. Being married to Laren was a sweet fiction that might have unfolded in imaginative bliss, but I had no ground to walk upon. My solid vision for my future would not have burdened a wisp. Laren saw me better than I saw myself; she was horrified when I tried to remove her bra in my dorm's basement. Fittingly called "the pit," it eschewed light and let out only sound. "What would my mother think?" Her question spread into the darkness as my hands retreated. I had fallen in love with her small breasts. A memory, sensual and sweet, would be stored forever, but the engagement was done. She left me, and I duly went through the ritual of heartbreak.

Ringing the entire campus were stories, (possibly flowing out of the legend-make-works machine) telling of prodigious appetites stoked and satisfied—by students and staff alike. The Pill: science gone to rut, let many, formerly, taught legs open with slack. "The Kama Sutra", "The Prophet", and "Mary Jane" spun the fancy-free. Ubiquitous, ad hoc pallets, of grass or whatever, were being constantly moistened with the do. But I was one of the anomalies who could not find a simple path to the libertine "tenor of the times." But some others were more patterned. There were those who had rank odor, or those who were crushingly unattractive. Some seemed still to be inside the womb, where no one else wanted to go. Some swung at everything and set records for swings and misses. These generators of new hope lived with the fresh possibility that given sufficient night quests, at some party, they should stumble upon opposite kindred. Both stoned, they would find seclusion (or not) and pluck at each other. This would be in no way different from the madras-ringed spectacles that were made, I had heard, by "les beaux gens," in the frat houses.

Math, for the trimester, was Linear Algebra, taught from a thin, un-attractive text. Its notions, when turned into formal principles, cut the "straightness" of line (or path) into concepts. Then it built models by adding and multiplying together (in stunningly brilliant ways) stretched or com-pressed or rotated (or left alone) "kindred" bits of "straight." One example, illustrating the potency of the constructions, rested in their ability to tell the tale of the world, according to modern physics, general relativity excepted. Linearity is to necessary explication in particle physics, as inscrutability is to a god. However, the argument does exist, that the latter notion is more easily accepted and accessible than the former. In describing the "observables" of reality, the German Heisenberg's quantum description of particle physics makes use of infinitely large arrays of horizontal lines and columns, where each junction has a specific type of mathematical "thing", rotating in spaces were 3D had been upped to infinite, imaginary D. Despite this arcana, the normal world believes in linear algebra: solid-state components, especially in TV's & computers & smart-phones, are expected to work.

Introduction to Western Philosophy, with Doctor Guessing, was more fanciful than math. The trimester journey from Socrates to Sartre was dizzying and humorous. Vertigo came from being spun round from "Know Thyself" to "No Authentic Self" without effort. And humor flowed from these polar-opposite points of view, because of the originators. One was a young-boy-liking old Greek, and the other was a French intellectual who don Juan-ed the second sex, using the sexiness of his brains, so intimated Doctor Guessing. Both of them, and all in between concocted verbal-logical systems, based on "man." Because this was taught in a liberal arts college, I, fancifully, called all the studied systems "classical," all classes were eligible. The Übermensch could be applied both to a German and Spinoza, technically.

When I paused to catch my breath, after this catapult ride from The Academy to The Left Bank, I felt duped. I had been enlightened by "Rufus and Razmus" humor, which had been given to me by a naïve and well-meaning member of a fraternity. This peek, into a place for the well-heeled, became another instructive landmark in the terra incognita of bias toward my kind. (Rufus hears Razmus, who is in the barn, saying, in a voice, (as imitated by the storyteller) filled with the drawling speech of coloreds in minstrel movies, "Whoa Donkey, Back Up Hawse. Whoa Donkey, Back Up Hawse." Rufus peeks in to see what this is about. He sees Razmus, pants about his ankles, with an erection, lying back on the donkey, as a support, while having sex with the horse. But Razmus is fucking lazy. He directs the animals to perform the copulation, calling each to move forward or backwards by giving out instructions in a passion of lassitude. Upon hearing this joke, and feeling no malice, for the teller had none, I did wonder if the capacity to successfully copulate with a mare was part of the joke also.

The remarkable systems of logical cogency that I enjoyed learning were not relevant to Nigras or niggers (coded as coloreds or Negroes). Both in The South and in The North, my people were not species-e-fied as Homo sapiens, but as arrested Homo erecti living in the midst of "knowing men." And that division was immutable. "Cogito ergo sum" (*pas un nègre stupide*). The dumbest white ass was "superior" to the smartest black man. This ordering was unacceptable. Nietzsche's term "will to power," as a living phrase, especially when inherent capacity was considered, seemed closer to how the world might work. It was technically unsatisfying though because it was rendered null by this overarching assumption. A black man of genius, with the will to power, could not move toward the notion of the Übermensch in any Western eye, because the assumption of such a creature was considered absurd, for mensch (human being or man) did not apply to the black. Only as the unter (below/under) could mensch conjoin. Philosophy did hold truth (despite Nietzsche's objection): it pointed toward an exclusionary vision. The Negro/colored was without relevancy in the issues labored over in Western Philosophy. The proper discipline to examine his mental turbulations would be deemed, by the others, to be some type of anthropological investigation: the anthropoid ape of the former. My misdirected anger sparked and confirmed a bias. I vowed that would never take a course in anthropology.

The faux spring that year was kinder than ever before. It was warm and liquid-filled with whimsy. Spring term brought soccer in the quad; the liberation of running and dancing with the ball on the green sweetly returned to me. While the mud caked in the cleats of my boots rejoined me to Madre: terra cognita. The class I had arrived with would graduate at the end of the term. This finality, given the additional year I needed, tore them totally from me. And in volume through the gash, a purity of flow, which would both define and summarize the sixties, came unabated.

50

"A pipe full of keef in the morning makes a man as strong as a camel in the courtyard during the day." My liking for Pall Malls and Camels joined the newly discovered "herb" to these staunch, old fellows who still pleasured me in the draw. I got drunk, at times, dreadfully so, but marijuana took my heart. Alcohol became a poor second. One of the "smokers" on campus showed me a small book that spoke to the differences in the personalities of individuals who favored one over the other inebriant. The pamphlet told story after story, where in subtle battles of wit and commerce and place in daily life, the keef smoker bested the alcohol drinker. On campus, far from the Middle East, there were not such nuanced differences. Alcohol was loud, red, and belligerent; marijuana was pompous, purple and mushy. Both centrifuged, into dreadful purity, mounds of asinine behavior.

Dave, a quiet dorm mate, whose cowboy boots literally turned up at the toes, making them look like the front of the runners on a rocking chair, pushed his privacy away one Friday afternoon by turning up his music. He lived at the end of a hall, which spread out like a T. The music came through his door and down the funneled outlet of the narrow channel.

???... *Abana killem die-ooooh... Oh Sophia, ooh my darling....???* Then came drums, but not in the manner of the nimble pocking and scratching of Gene Krupa "letting loose." It was not a "Drum Boogie." These new skin mouths that were speaking told of battles with the lion; they had heard the aggression of father elephant asserting his will to stamp-shake the earth. And they were the gruff voices of engines growling. *?? Ah-ga-dun, ah-ga-dun, awe dund de, awe dund de...??"* The human spirals in these paeans were from lands red with blood and stout with flesh. In them I heard no promise for a future vapor-life blowing on harps or singing done by flying castrati. Drawn by the sound, I nevertheless remained frozen at the foot of the T. For I had been molded by manners, respect must be shown. Understanding what must be acknowledged, Я кланяются вам, Господину (I bow to you, Sir) came automatically out of my mouth. Thus freed, I walked down the hall and knocked on the door. It opened. "Dave, what is that playing?" A pale, pleasant face, bearing the vitality and overt friendliness of a circus clown, laughed. "It's good, uh?" "Yes, yes, but what is it?" "*Drums of Passion.*" "Who's playing?" "Batbatunde Olatunji." It was intense Ray Charles "man sound" but from a different, though kindred world. It unshackled my want and need to listen longer, and more closely to the new types of foreign music. The album jacket said: produced in 1960. Again, I had been slow on the uptake.

When it came from England, the only white sound that matched my tastes was The Rolling Stones'. Their theme song "Satisfaction" had working class grit, but the lyrics in "The Salt of the Earth" were monumental.

> "Let's drink to the hard working people,
> let's drink to the lowly of birth,
> raise your glass to the good and the evil,

let's drink to the salt of the earth
let's drink to the two thousand million
let's drink to the lowly of birth."

The Stones talked of a land hard with the sensibilities of the "paroles," but not with the dystopian brutality of *Nineteen Eighty-Four*.

As far as I understood the Stones were not different in origins than the Beatles. Both groups were from the working class, and both groups were dope takers and were laying, as much as capacity would allow, every groupie between Moscow and LA, traveling westward. But I despised the Beatles' song: "I Wanna Hold Your Hand." Its "goodness" was appalling. Only as, I Wanna Hold Your Gland, could I phrase it as a title in my mind. It then became milk mixed with blood (as the Maasai drank). I would have wished to think of the milk as not from the udder, but from the breast. The public controversies, over the saccharine lyrics, merged into a tracing back of origins of sickeningly pious elements that turned my stomach, which for me meant a strong dislike. Fulton J Sheen, TV's first Catholic preacher of renown (he was popular in my house), remained, in memory, as the face of sugared piety. The broadcasts of Sheen's versions of right and wrong were made through the science the archbishop held in mind. The world was flat, like a pie, with a section, my own colored world, unseen. The area was blackened over, deliberately painted out of time. The catechism had told me one (Catholic) plus one (Catholic) equals two (Catholics) in the sight and love of Jesus. I believed this. Sheen, the learned, entertaining exemplar of the church, ruptured this balance publicly on TV. One Catholic plus one Catholic (colored) equaled something vastly more complicated. It was not two, but one Catholic plus the nullity of the Catholic (colored) thing, whose existence had been crushed out of consciousness. The chaos of childhood and an intrinsic dislike of the man's posturing protected me from strong harm. Together, they diffused the edged observations that would have outlined the questions: Speak, prelate of my church, where is my world? Where are my people, who are faithful members of the flock? Where am I? Do you not see this omission as a great evil? Is yours not the sin of complicity? Sheen, with his melodramatics, was too much of Shakespeare's counseled-against thespian. Neither Hamlet nor Othello could ever rise from his prancing words. In college, I read the harsh pronouncement of Rimbaud: "O justes, nous chieron dan vos ventres de gres!" ("Oh, just men, we will shit in your bellies of stoneware!")

Sometimes, I found weekend parties that were interesting, and had unattached women that were fine and seemed to like me. At one, I met Nina. We danced, talked, danced, and toward its end, we began kissing. Her breath was smothered in the smell of bourbon, and I licked its fleeing taste from her lips. Her gifted body was country and western bounty without exaggerations of perm and lacquered pomp. She and I, both dripping, walked to her apartment. We undressed. My heart rate went to high counts; she groaned and writhed, and then she balked: "I can't! I can't!" *Huh?* I just can't make love to a colored man. I want to, but I can't." *Don't! You don't have to, just fuck.* Naked, she turned her back to me and I curved to spoon. We went to sleep or passed out. When I awoke in the early morning, we were still spooned with my finger moored in her sopping crotch. I left her still asleep and went back to my dorm with the old, unfickle pleasure eating breakfast high in my mind, some type of something, any type of anything. At lunch I walked in and saw her at one of my regular tables. Embarrassed, I wanted to go to another, but I couldn't. She had done me no ill; it had been her call. I sat down. She said, "Did we have sex last night?" "No, we did not." "Hummm, well I had orgasms all night long," Her words carried no hint of embarrassment. They were not softly spoken (not loudly either), but delivered in a normal tone, though coated with a raiment of smugness. No one at the table seemed to find her words unusual. I heard no response or giggle. But I didn't look anyone in the eyes, to make a judgment from their faces. I ate my lunch-mush in wordless perplexity.

After classes it was still bright outside, but the light had softened, allowing me to look at the sky without strain. I walked to the ravine behind my dorm and climbed down far enough to let LFC vanish. My side of the glacier's cut was the side of men; across the gulf it was wild. The moist air carried and let linger in my nose the smells of the place. Sitting among the leaves and twigs and tiny life, I myself vanished, a Gulliver, irrelevant, ignored. **BAP-BAP-BAP** The sound cupped by the valley and flung against the trees made its location difficult to fix. **BAP-BAP-BAP-BAP-BAP** The longer interval let me focus on a stand of trees. Something red was moving high upon one. An immediate instinct of denial: It can't be. **BAP-BAP-BAP-BAP** From the head I traced the body. **BAP-BAP-BAP-BAP** It was. The name leapt from books and stories and rooted itself in my eyes and ears. My memory owned it. **BAP-BAP-BAP** But the woodpecker owned the day, all of it, as Rex did Mardi Gras.

I (Lemuel), while lying back on a Brobdingnag's dug, looked up into an ashen sky, needing to travel, to be renewed. A grey-white bird entered from the left of the bleak canvas and cut the line of the rift with its flight. From a point on its underbelly the bird let loose something that streamed out into a perfect triangle, then fell apart, almost immediately, into a chaotic dispersal of small clumped elements. The traveler passed out of my vision to the right. It was what it seemed. *That's how it looks!* From odeur, molded by forces, perfection had appeared, then its destruction. I watched it fall until it reached the ground less than half a foot from my face. The splat woke me to my almost open-mouth fate. A biting smell quickly rose from the small platter of leaves; these few had been chosen by caprice. I nodded in appreciation to the uncountable contingent elements that had shaped my good luck. Smiling (I could afford to, I was not running back to my dorm gagging), my fingers touched the down that would not mature into a mustache. I smelled soap and pencil and leaf and earth, and under it all, Nina. Her scent fit into a domesticity of my mind's own ordering that was mine, not hers. But I welcomed a new ardor into my home. I wanted to see her in Commons, at dinner. Not to talk to her, the moment had passed; I would never get that close again. But I felt my pride surge. Bereft of understanding, I had set a standard that in the future beaucoup de bois blanc would fail to match. While waiting in the food line, I casually put my fingers, cleansed of all but Nina's resolute cling, under my nose, and I left them there. For the first time inside the school's cafeteria, I was pleasured with the faint waft of a heavenly smell.

What a day!

Math and Russian, as always, defined the term. The third subject looked into the eyes of a stranger. Chemistry held interest. (Linus Pauling's "The Nature of the Chemical Bond" had clogged my craw with its difficulty when I tried to read it in high school.) I had matured, to this extent, it was not the difficulty of the course that dissuaded; it was the smell. The chemistry lab held bizarre, unpleasant odors. Symbolic logic won the day, and Ms. Gibbings, the teacher, was cool. She smoked Camels, she looked like a mature hippie, and the tips of her thin shoes were dimpled and turned up.

My battles with my faith had primed my nose; I smelled religion or its impulses or its sentiments lurking all about in the Russian novels, which was fine, but this had no more heft than anything else. Also, there were morals implied because wretched behavior was cut into relief by the brilliant descriptions. For example, Poppa Karamazov pondering the nature of lust, by watching the village idiot, stinking Lizaveta, sleeping, partially naked, in a ditch. What was off kilter, in this fiction, resided in the notion of redemption through constant suffering. Freezing out rebellious personality traits, moral or political, in the ice-land of Siberia might work. But as a righteous scourge, unrelenting torment was чушь собачья (bullshit).

Stalin, the great tyrant, had not died under the dispatching knife his policies had created. "But Stalin (or any other such ruler) will suffer in hell" had been the lifelong, comeuppance principle that I had heard espoused by the supernatural-believing moralists. Maybe? Stalin, who had screwed millions of people, sloughed off his pockmarked mortality in agony, with more to come after his mortal rupture? Maybe not? If great wrongs lay in the past, and eternal punishment lay in the future, the assurance of the nature of the continuity between these two, possibly infinite, epochs became troublesome. The only known link was a mysterious, moving (almost unfathomable) instant: the present. Saint Augustine said that the continuum (past, present, and future) existed in the eternal "now" of God. Einstein and Gödel, both felt that there was no such thing as time. The separation of past, present, and future was an illusion (witness the photon: it does not move within this tri-part division). "нет ответов, только может быть (there are no answers, only perhaps)."

Professor Smith taught number theory: the study of whole counting numbers. Kindergarten learned, by rote, using large pencils on coarse paper. You could add, subtract, multiply and divide them; simple arithmetic, and many mysteries were based on them. **1** (the number of gods worshiped in Christianity, Islam, and Judaism), **2** (the smallest even counting number), **3** (the number of divine beings in the "Hindu Triad" and the Catholic Trinity), **4, 5, 6** (the number of faces on a die), **7** (the number of "days" in a week on the planet earth), **8, 9, 10, 11,**…, **100** (the number of gods in the Akashino creed), **101, 102,**…, **609** (the price, in dollars, of "company" at Maison Rouge),…, **666** (The number of the "Beast"), **667, 668** (the number of false gods in the Paaupaa Mantagaa religion),…, **690** ("the number of beings of one substance in a five-dimensional godhead"—Leonid Oupenski),…, **999** (a famous Bourbon Street lesbian's house number),…, **90,039** (the dollar cost of an inexpensive house), **90,040,**…, **199,000** (the distance, in light years, to the Small Magellanic Cloud),…, **4,734,871, 4,734,872, 4,734,873** (the guilder amount for an expensive car),…, **13,700,000** (time, in millennia, since the Big Bang),…, **250,000,000**(a power ball winning jackpot in pesos), **250,000,001,**…, **13,000,000,000,000** (a small national debt in rands),…, **322,560,000,000,000,000** (the span for a "short" human

life in nano-seconds),..., and on and on, **71,658,775,912,346,987,676,58**
7,000,000,000,000,000,000,000 (a female number indicating the time, in
years, according to some GUT's: Grand Unification Theories, after which
all protons will have evaporated),..., and on and on and getting larger,...,
5,728,910,567,345,275,962,845,643,521,839,990,111,567,289,105,673,45
2,759,628,457,643,521,839,990* (maximum length of time, in centuries, a
sinner would spend in purgatory if they bought sufficient indulgences),...,
and on and on and getting bigger,..., and on and on and getting larger,...,
8,111,527,596,284,576,435,273,452,759,628,457,643,527,345,275,962,8
45,764,352,734,527,596,284,576,435,273,452,759,628,457,643,527,345,2
75,962,845,764,352,734,527,596,284,576,435,098 (minimum number of
lines in a "large" Feynman diagram for the entire universe "soon after" the
Big Bang had cooled enough to allow the integral separation of energy and
matter),..., and the numbers continue on and on and getting larger, **66,999**
,666,999,666,999,666,999,666,999,666,999,666,712,357,111,31
7,192,329,313,741,434,701,010,101,201,201,201,230,123,012,340,123,40
1,234,501,234,501,234,560,123,456,023,034,527,528,457,643,527,345,27
5,628,457,643,527,345,275,362,845,764,352,734,527,562,845,764,352,7
34,527,562,845,764,352,734,527,562,845,764,352,734,527,562,845,764,
352,734,527,596,284,576,435,273,452,759,628,457,643,527,345,275,962,
845,764,352,734,527,596,284,576,435,273,452,759,628,457,643,527,345,
275,962,845,743,520,000,000,000,001,111,111,111,122,222,222,222,333,
333,333,444,444,455,555,777,778,888,891,234,123,412,345,678,567,898
,765,432,123,456,789,098,765,432,166,666,000,666,660,006,666,600,06
6,666,666,675,962,845,764,352,734,527,562,845,764,352,734,527,562,84
5,764,352,696,666,666,616,669,666,696,969,696,666,969,696,666,969,66
6,696,966,699,966,699,966,626,000,000,000,002,626,007** (this famous
666 digit number—given the popular name "wooh buu dung: 我不知道" -
was a winning lottery draw from the pool of prime numbers with less than
one million digits. In addition, certain un-gendered seers, near Guangdow,
strongly argued that the number portended the coming of the green monk,
Pei Huay Shii),..., **and the counting numbers continue on and on and**
on, getting larger and larger and larger and larger,..., Graham's number
minus 2, Graham's number minus 1, Graham's number (the number of
angels who want to dance on a pin's head) (while discussing a property
of prime numbers) is so large that there is not enough space in the entire
universe to write it down*, ... and the counting numbers continue on**
and on, getting larger and larger and so on. Since the deity's favor rested

on things that sat to the right ("Sits at the right hand of The Father"), these numbers shared that bounty. Somewhere in that direction, a long way off to be sure, rested their end. The use of the word infinity finished them off. Normally it was best not to delve into or trouble that word for its innards, just as the word "God" should not be anatomically examined. But before reaching the Omega, there were relationships of harmony and order that were for mortal eyes. These proofs spread out into the modern world, settled, and hardened, like a concrete slab, and supported the hierarchy of our lofty sciences. 1,2,3, ... I learned to view these kindergarten scribbles respectfully.

* Vatican numerologists called this 73-digit number **"Heaven's Door."**
* **"The Number of Creation"** in Southern Taoist texts. Also, allegations swirled concerning the "randomness" of so famous a number. (Commentaries of Pei Poo Pai: pp.324-331)
** **The size of each written digit (a Planck length) is a proton divided by 100, trillion, trillion.**

The blandness of the time outside classes smacked me in the groin, a region never at peace for long. The placidness of "Roll Jordan Roll" was dismissed by the ache of Spill Seed Spill. I had the two weekend evenings to roam and mingle. Innocence suffered, though it had been doing this for a while. There were some "folk" who despite being capable of acting otherwise, darkly died themselves a puckered brown. Brian, from Kansas City, showed his backside every time he got loaded. When stoned, he flouted the law of asshole fatigue: he never tired of being one. Lesson learned. "Febbel, foubul, fobull", the tongue has been led to fail by booze or weed. Retreat. Stagger home or find a commodious place to crash. But "don't be no fool." It may be forgiven, but never forgotten. With this principle fixed in mind, parties became what they might be. At one, I met Arda, a sophomore, who had an odd reputation; she was known to be tough and to walk with a knife. She was also very cute. We talked. I expected nothing, and my chat freed itself by that expectation. After telling her where my dorm was, she asked a simple question. "Oh, so your window is the one with the light over it?" "Yes, it's a pain sometimes, but the curtains are thick." I left before drunkenness and enjoyed the walk to my dorm. Sitting on my bed, and feeling like a pleased seducer, I smiled at her ghost presence, while listening to her over and over, in my mind. The sound, a rapping at the window, stunned by its inexplicable nature. For an instant, and I knew it, there was fear. Drawing the curtain aside, I saw a figure, indistinct because of the light in my own room bouncing back at me from off the panes. I opened the window, and there stood Arda. Stupid boy, I still remained puzzled. Inside the cascade of the light she smiled, that kind of smile. Fumbling as with a bra hook, I loosed the screen, and with agility she mounted the windowsill and entered. Her smile had not changed; I entered it. I took her in a manner akin to how I ate my grandmother's fruitcake, whose whiskey undercurrent kept it moist, and made it wanton, in an adult fashion. "Bad habits" had paid off. With a still intact right hand, I had relieved myself earlier that day. So that now, without the mad impetus from my thousands of seed-progenies waiting in the vestibule, I felt to perform, stacking my manhood up groan by groan as they came from her. She wanted; I gave; she gave; I took: a completed coupling. Knowledge flowed upward from my cock to my brain. Closing my eyes and in athletic zeal, I wound my hips in figure eights. Awkwardly at first, in time, control came. I opened my eyes to see the effect. Her gaze had no outward focus; her eyes were drowning in their own swoon. Jolts of ego delight ran through me, annealing my hot "iron" in the I of Man, the dick giver, the stylish ploughman: gentleman farmer without peers. The look on her face was addictive, if not again from her, then from another. I pulled in a breath and curled my lips in ficken pride. A grimaced sigh rose from her, next, a spasm, made with a body-long quake, then came a jet of obscenities, "Oh shit, you mother fucker, look what you done done, you gonna fucking make me cum!" Hoping my face could still maintain the look of a mature man-of-the-cock, I marveled at the places where orgasm could traverse. Dense, gated regions would flash open in the moments of its passage, sounding out their salutation. Men were pridefully foolish who thought their phallus Pharaohnic. Arda-free sought, and she found. I (mercifully) understood; she would not remain in any one bed. She was a night minx moving to her own moon cycles. She came and went, and left nothing, not even her scent.

The day after my last exam I reported to my summer job in Lake Forest. The town rested upon feet that, while not gilded, were marvels of fine stone padded by stacked green wads. Blanchard's was a primary local source of building materials. The company, both neat and complete, had Mr. Blanchard chewing and smoking his stogies while selling his sand, cement, lime, gravel, topsoil, flagstone, grit, and sundries for affluent customers' projects. A railroad spur (that crossed a well-traveled highway) ran into the yard. Rail cars were shunted to the proper locations and then unloaded. Customers could have materials delivered to them by a fleet of robustly aged yellow trucks. Somehow the ethos of the town, the correct deportment consistent with genteel propriety pervaded the yard; sound volume was never at proportionate levels. Despite their origins from clacking bin loaders or front loaders abrading concrete or six wheelers needing tune-ups, the decibels comported themselves in an attenuated manner. The massed fortunes in the town commanded a certain degree of magic.

Summer, the traditionally busy season, normally had Blanchard's take on a student worker. Unexpectedly for me, my education continued, both in and outside the yard, because unorthodox texts would be pushed before my eyes. Necessity required a mandatory reading of them. The job description, written in large print, was that of performing dumb labor. I knew the first half of this. The unknown second part would be, who would direct me to do the dumb labor? Mr. Blanchard gave me over to Dwayne Dropson, the yard foreman, a good-old country white-boy from Mississippi. After the introduction, Dwayne put his cigar-stump back into his mouth, and said, "Com awn," while walking through the door leading into the yard.

52

Dwayne was a large man in his late thirties or early forties. His brown kaki shirt had ample sweat stains and his baseball cap sat as though it were part of his head, a grey, beaked scalp: a pecker-head. Comically, his neck was sun-boiled red. He moved with an indefatigable slow lope like a man accustomed to continual hard work. Following behind Dwayne allowed my eyes and mind to gape in wonder without notice from anyone. *How did a Mississippi red neck get to Lake Forest? He can't live in the town. They wouldn't allow him to walk around the street looking like that; it would sully their image. Dwayne at the Onwensia Country Club? Lord have mercy!*

"Higgy, this here is…

whas yoh name again?"

Actually, I wished that I could be called "Whas yoh name again." They didn't need to know anything about me. Higgy, a driver in his fifties or sixties, walked ramrod stiff and grimaced any time a flexible action was required. His face wasn't tanned, but parboiled red, which set off his blue eyes. I met the remaining three drivers as they came in during the day.

Herb, a Swede, and at least seventy, stood near the storehouse for cement bags. Dwayne read my thoughts. "Don let that old man fool you. He gon outwork you, just like he does everybody heer." *Yeah, right.* Dwayne put me to task immediately: he directed me to get a shovel and then to go to the sand bin; someone had called in an order; bags were to be filled. Wet sand and large scoops, each shovelful weights at least thirty pounds; an ambitious one could top forty. The three-and-half-foot-high bags, with their damp-puckered narrow mouths, caused me to spill sand. "I don't need no sand all over me, now." Less sand in the scoop solved that problem, but it lengthened the time. "We ain got all day, yah know." I finished; my wrists ached all that day, evening, and night. I couldn't fault the old red neck, but I could out fox him. Next time, I so quickened my pace, with less sand in each accurately placed scoopful, that I finished quickly. Dwayne just looked at me but said nothing.

With no traffic, it took five minutes, by bike, to get from the dorm to work. When it finished, I went immediately to the practice field, to soothe myself. Between soccer and the boredom of my dorm lay TJ's apartment. We nodded when we saw each other, and after a short time, conversations started. Quickly this turned into brightly intelligent chat. Names: James Joyce, "Uncle Erish" (Erich Heller), Richard Elleman, Proust, Ira Aldrige entered the discussions, paused them, as necessary questions presented themselves, and explanatory responses brought me up to speed, as much as could be. The interchange never weakened; T, as smart a human as I had ever known, had both a vast and precise memory. With the strong logic in T's arguments and his "colored-country" sense of humor, I was agog at these chats. I had never met another person with such capacities in literature and music. What made the conversations truly enjoyable rested in T's trying to seat his understanding of science and math as corollaries flowing from the arts. I would have none of it. A spongy equivalence, like "astrology is astronomy made practical", was made to wring itself of science and become what it was: an embroidered corset, holding a body bereft of bones. We battled, in wonderful humor, as equals, though I came to recognize T's vastly superior intellect. It bordered on the spectacular.

A huge contrast existed between this and being at work and having to deal with Dwayne. Quizzical glances, emanating from Dwayne's intelligent eyes, were always directed toward me. All four of the drivers (two Oakies—an uncle and a nephew, and Roy and Higgy) made allowances for my mistakes, without any anger, and even joined me in a "praise of Herb" moment. The incident came from my second unloading of an open hopper car full of sand. The first unloading had been touched with magic, though

I decried having to intimate this necessary explanation. The unloading procedure was simple. The bifurcated railroad car was pushed over the pit. Two hopper doors, one to a side, were opened. Sledgehammers were swung against hoppers' sides, one man to one hopper. Each pounded their hopper, until the sand (normally wet) began flowing. Fully covered in bib overalls, a long sleeve shirt and a baseball cap, Herb walked with his sledge in his slow skipping stride to the rail car. Swinging his bludgeon, he hit the side of the hopper; I mirrored him by beating my own. Herb's flow started first, then mine began. Both were trickles. Each carrying a shovel, we climbed into the thirteen-foot high car. Poking and goading, the sand began flowing freely. Herb's side started flowing faster. While a good portion of sand still remained in his part of the car, Herb walked on the sand to the front edge and climbed out. By the time I got mine flowing, the sand had fallen from the edge. It was impossible to climb the sloped side. Only when the sand finished did I carefully slide out the hopper door. The entire matter was a fluke, and due to the sand being mostly dry on Herb's side and wet on mine. How this was possible remained somewhat mysterious; I kept my mouth shut over this biased allocation of wet. The awakening occurred the second time, but even then, "forces" might have been at work. Somehow, I kept to Herb's pace from the onset to the point where we were standing on our respective heaps of sand. With roughly the same funnel opening, we began. Herb took no notice of me. With huge scoops and many of them, I matched the diameter of Herb's drain opening, for several minutes. Then Herb's side fell apart; it sluiced down into the hopper mouth possessed or directed or enticed (I had a choice of the motive force involved). Herb rode the descending pile and straddled the hopper door. With his side empty, he gracefully exited through the opening. I did the same, without grace, about five minutes later. I avoided Herb and went into the shed. All the drivers were there. "Herb! That old man! He, how could he? You know what he did?" Laughter (good, wide mouthed laughter), smiles, chuckles, and smirks took over the shed. Ray, whose voice sounded like deep frogy croak, said: "Don't feel bad, he did that to all of us." "What the hell is with him?" "He's worked here for so long, and he wants to die on the job. So, they are gonna let him. And besides, nobody can out work him."

Herb's emanations reminded me of my grandfather. *This is what father should be*, unlike my blood one. I told this to T. He responded by changing the bloody Marys' we were drinking into a clotted tale of a bloody Pater. Within a huge sour note T spoke, this one and only time, of his father. The short tale and its epilogue were extremely disconcerting. Hard work and hard luck had been the twin nubs that rubbed T's father into a gleam of spiked glints that stabbed his own heart. He gave love as the lawfully thrown rock does when it meets flesh: the terrible bludgeoning admonishment from the father who allowed no weakness under his rule. Crossing a barbed wire fence, Lil J, one of T's older brothers, slipped and severely tore his scrotum. Father, when presented with the wounded son, pronounced: "I ain't got no money to send you to no god-damn hospital. Don't be so clumsy next time." A brutal lesson was given, drawn from hard lessons learned. T also spoke, only once, of his mother; she sheltered him, her favorite. His big head laid closest to his mother's heart; "You're the smartest of my children, see how the skin on your forehead moves, that a sure sign of brains." For this favoritism, his brothers, he obscurely hinted, exacted dues one day in the barn.

53

"Come over here," Dwayne hollered, but in a suspiciously chummy manner. He and Higgy were standing in front of the topsoil bin. He said it again, "Come on over here." Without my knowing, the sub-brain took over. All my instincts and apprehensions were removed from my voluntary control. Caution let me move toward Dwayne but kept me well away. When a "proper" distance had been achieved, I froze and just looked at the two of them. Dwayne saw that I would not come closer. "Heh, heh. You lucky." Then his hand touched a switch on the loader, and it started. The scoop buckets began to move, going up and over, following their track, spilling their contents of black, mud-slick water; it had rained the night before. I would have been fully drenched with the smelly fluid. The summer student's rite of passage? A nasty joke given to the colored kid? Dwayne's sense of humor? But Dwayne said other things that gave me some insight into his alien country world. "We didn't get no lectricity til 1955." *Damn!*

Three weeks were left in the summer. The old dorm where I stayed would be torn down the following week; I had to find a new location. What little money I had saved would be savaged if I had to pay for lodging. It came to me. "T, can I say at your place for three weeks?" I could sleep on the couch. T said "Yes." The friendship became fellowship and then a brotherhood. I, the younger, bounded about, and talked of all my notions to my elder male sibling. I shed the title of "the old weird one" and brought to the table (that both my brother and I cooked for and cleaned) all manner of ideas. However, the idea of not offering a lodging fee, for its equivalence in cleaning (since this had not been agreed to), was as spongy as T's science. But T said nothing.

By the time the fall term started, the small apartment had become catholic well beyond my old religion's capitalization of the adjective. TJ's was a place of universal spice and savor where the penitent mind was not only unnecessary, but also strictly forbidden. We cooked, drank unusual liquor, listened to opera and jazz and in-vogue music, and talked. T's black cat, Brother, ran himself into a frenzy begging for bits of meal meat: chicken livers, calf's livers, and kidneys.

One week before I quit my job at Blanchard's, Dwayne let fly. "Yah know, I read what that fella Rap Brown said." The words stunned me. First off because the verb "read" was used rather than the verb "heard." The topic was not neutral, and the slightly combative tone put me on edge. "You gon burn down somebody property. Don need no trial. I'd be judge, jury, and executioner." Having no wish to discuss this with Dwayne, but being forced to say something, and being still dazed, the sub-brain worked. "Dwayne, you from Mississippi, right?" "Yeah." "You saying that colored people get a fair deal there most of the time?" "Well no, but you can't goh round burning people's property. I ain't saying that some things ain't wrong, but that don make *that* kanna thing right." The talk ended there. Dwayne's Mississippi and my Louisiana would never agree. But we both knew that the impulse to slaughter each other, out of hand, could be held in thoughtful check. I learned that Dwayne moved back to Mississippi that same year. According to Mr. Blanchard, "He just didn't like it up here." (A conceit formed in my mind: Maybe Dwayne felt it better to deal with the poverty of his original white/colored world rather than with the many rich shits that inhabited Lake Forest.)

Finally, I had to leave home: I left T's apartment. Summer with T nurtured in me the most un-Catholic trait possible: freedom from the notion of innate guilt for having been born human. I had an original life, not an original sin.

I was working 40 hours a week and my only courses were math and physics. And in the math course, I found a type of love. Complex numbers were as profoundly beautiful to me as any creation my mind could envision.

$$1=e^2\pi i$$

One (1), completeness, the fullness thereof (able to multiply or divide with all, without disruption), emerged from a quartet. The transcendental number e, the base of natural logarithms, made smooth the way of change. The union of the number 2 with the iconic number pi (was emblematic of the constancy of the circle. "Will the circle be unbroken?"— the square root of -1: the imaginary unit, leapt from the infinitely flowing, "dense" river of real numbers onto the dry land, where one could travel not only from the small to the large, but also up and down and all around. Surprisingly, these elements helped described, thus far, a world, our world.

Why these symbolic notations need be useful, in the telling of the provisional, physical understanding of the world, was unanswerable. But these probable fictions, which conjured up "the flesh of our universe," were more soothing to me than "to know, love, and serve" one of the many incompatible I-am/What-is entities (natural or supernatural). These were normally chosen and fixed by the lottery of birthplace. To be in awe of physical reality, especially with its description backed by a strong evidentially based system, seemed moral, and could possibly lead to like behavior. To have the certainty of knowledge, from a belief in an I-am/What-is, that so easily justified subjugation, violence, and murder, though possibly imbedded with "tender mercy," seemed less moral. Especially when, each I-am/What-is normally made their incontrovertible pronouncements using human tongues, graven or lingual, that could be straight, forked, curved, brilliant, stupid, ignorant, learned, idiotic, ordinary, tricky, vague, inspired or plainly insane.

Every day after soccer practice I stopped by T's place. On the weekends we ate a meal together. The novelty of home being on campus, but not in my dorm, remained fresh. In late October, unable to play due to injury, I broke training and drank a good many Daiquiris at T's. We were both sloshing about with stories and wants. I admitted that I had had the hots for Joan, T's ex. It wasn't right but, at that time, I would have liked to have had sex with her. But now, I didn't because T was my brother. Secrets had no place. The booze flowed. I told T how my simple heart related to the world. The unconscious might exist with its stewing machinations, but face forward, food and sex and thought were the drives, while trust became the human bond I responded to. It didn't emerge with difficulty; it was natural and just due. "I love you, brother. Wow! I never thought that I would have one." From two different wombs had come the oneness of the fraternal knot.

Both he and I were teetering on the edge that went from very high to drunk. T's face was drooping; his eyes were sinking under the booze.

"You don't know what I'm like."

"What do yah mean?"

"You trust too much."

"Not really."

Now T's eyes were drunk and carnally lowered. Then he softened his mouth oddly.

"You don't see me."

Lost within these words, and T's odd visage, I just stared.

"What if I told you that I am a punk?

A sissy?

I'd suck your dick?"

The sentences hung apart, then coagulated and dropped as a scalding lump onto my brain. "Huh?"

"Imma punk. I want to suck your dick."

Good God, A Punk!

The whole summer with a punk!

Just let me get out of here.

I furtively looked about to see if the walls were closing in, or if the door had vanished, to hem or trap me inside the space with the self-proclaimed punk.

"Yeah man, it's kahna late, ah better go."

"Go."

T went into the kitchen; I moved toward the door. With my hand on the knob, I heard glass breaking. It was a single shattering in the sink. The basin gave the tinny clank of a hand hitting the metal of the sink. Then another shattering, *I don't want to know what is going on.* Two seconds of quiet, then a faint wheezing sob began. Glass was now being crunched. *Ah shit!* Things were being assessed in my mind at neural transmission limits. I felt it, without the specifics surfacing. **PUNK, HORROR, PUNK, "I WANNA SUCK YOUR DICK!"** All the hidden shame and nastiness of T's real world (as I understood it) were losing their mass. A fleeing of their gravity was occurring. T might be hurting himself; T the older brother; T, who first said that my mind was both sound and sane; T, my friend! I walked back toward the kitchen and found T staring into the sink of broken glass, clenching his teeth and crying.

"Hey man, why don't you get some sleep?

Go lie down, come on. Come on T, get some sleep, man."

Words spoken only through a charity rote.

T went into his room and I locked the front door as I left. I had done my righteous duty; I need never go back into the apartment. My lungs drew breath as though they had been hard scorched.

Awaking, still dizzy, and with no idea of how to handle my feelings, I wished for a blank day, without thought, like the Zombie man, "Carrefour", who did his chores with no understanding. This couldn't last long. IT would loom over every attempt at distraction, just waiting, to drop again. Of course, IT, an inarticulate nasty thing, has its full horror lay lightly aground. The homosexual could not walk among men as a man, **and** this loss of respect was contagious. Besides, punks were never neutral; they always wanted dick, some dick, any dick, truths gleaned from my world's common wisdoms.

After lunch, a resident of T's dorm knocked on my door and delivered a note from T. I thanked the message carrier, closed the door, and opened the envelope. Written in a dreadful scrawl:

"Please come over so we can talk. T"

Willingly, I would cut off the relationship. Putting the note down, I watched it. Maybe it had been written in vanishing ink leaving me the choice of ignoring its presence. Seeking neither explanation nor confrontation, I just wanted to erase five months of memories. An impossibility, I had to face him. I would make it just another nasty chore, like picking up crab and shrimp remains that had been thrown in front of the house in New Orleans. Walking to South Campus, and bracing myself, I knocked on T's door.

"Come in."

I walked in. T's tiny chinee eyes, swollen (almost shut), and his fleshy face, contoured by contriteness, were offensive. It was a bizarre un-manning of his looks, be he punk or not. "Look man," came from both of us, but the directions they implied were different. *Puccini was playing on the stereo.* Losing words, I let T speak, but I didn't like its abject quality (despite it being necessary). T made words, good words, probably, but the apartment because of its new resident, a declared punk—an abomination in admission—was not the same. I tried for a blank expression. The couch, the kitchen, the bath, the books, and the table were all there, and so was the alien: knowledge. *The album wasn't a full score; the next track began to play. I recognized its opening, "Un bell di" from Madam Butterfly.* T talked more words with his mobile contrite face; he "would not bother me." T made gestures and reasoned from the posture of the sinner. Leontine Price *was not singing. This voice was as beautiful but less robust than* Price's, *and more ethereal. Waiting with a stout heart for Pinkerton, her seducer, the stars were*

twinning about her longing for the lover. The ideal brightness of that day bore
her up and yet pierced her throughout. The day was not now, but it would
be. This was sung in a tone of plaintiveness, done with such art, it made the
saccharine seem revolting, when compared with this, its master. It was both
a magnificent voice and a brilliant rendition.

"T. Who's that singing?"

T put out a chuckle (which I did recognize) and said "Mah brother. It's
Felecia Weathers."

"Jesus, that woman can sing!"

In the overflow of the induced emotion and the caution inspired by the
song, for Butterfly did kill herself, I spontaneously wagged my finger in
a serious reprimand. "Donh be trying to hurt yoself no moh, yah hear?"

From then on, a frankness of speech emerged, which was revelatory to
me. T's incisive intelligence showed a new edged motion; a flaying of surface
layers opened his bi-closeted sight to my still-green eyes. The pulse of sex
so strongly orders the mind's eye toward sight or blindness.

54

October 1967, the war was half-a-generation old by then; "Charlie",
napalm, and body count were its collective nouns. I never got the why of
it. "Necessity," it was said. The full "why" was lost in the thicket of Bundy's
and Rostow's reasoning, and LBJ's drawl. McNamara, a new type of Mars: a
facilitator for the bloody fields, guided the thing. By body count, America's
destruction of the enemy seemed effective; the living VC, being turned into
the tally, must run out. How many could they have? But dressed in black
pajamas, planting punji sticks, scurrying through tunnels, and subsisting
on "a little rat meat," "Charlie" had endured. I had my student deferment,
and a blank mind regarding the thing. The slaughter seemed righteous to
some. I'd heard a fellow say that he wanted to join up to get some "action."
Weapons were potent things, oozing with power. Handling them and dispensing the bearer's might had appeal. What always presented itself when
these thoughts occurred was the equal sign. Charlie and his comrades
might do unto one what one would do unto them. Then, disfigured at best,
one would walk or be wheeled or lie broken among the still normal; why
became WHY?

Muhammad Ali's position brought celebrity notice to WHY? "Ain't no
Viet Cong ever called me nigger" was tight reasoning. The counter of "Were

you ever around them?" was a reasonable response. Ethnic groups picked up foul foreign words quickly, and without difficulty. But the thrust of the objection to serve was plain, there was still plenty of right-here ugly, freely moving about, from sea to shining sea. Bob Dylan put musical poetry to some of it and sat this starkly before the face: the poor always got screwed. They got the short end of the broken stick, and they were often manipulated to wield, as a splintered lance, the end of their own short stick. That's the way it was. Pray to rise to the middle class, and then still pray more for a loftier ascension. *"The canards against the poor rose from the bottoms of the Cristal-filled flutes."*

By math and reason there were not enough riches on the earth for a million Carnegies, let alone a full nation of them. The country could not be all Lake Forest or Kenilworth or Winnetka. The towns of grit and grunt must exist, in abundance. I didn't know which type to prefer as a permanent home. At the end of the year though, a choice would have to be made. A longing to see my kin and New Orleans spawned the decision to go there for the holidays. Chance gave me an easy road home. Pete, an Alpha Stigma, but raised as an army brat, was driving there for the season. Somehow, we met and shared our destination. Pete needed help to drive straight down to "the city that care forgot."

When I first drove, in the initial part of the journey, I put Pete at ease. Also, I kept my assessment of the car's quality to myself. It was fast, but the steering wasn't tight, at least to my liking; it had a loose, soupy quality to it. Be that as it may, when Pete snoozed, I, not fully but almost, floored it. That sucker sped down the road: The Galaxy (Ford's private one) was moving toward Andromeda. Moderating this, less the flying wake Pete, became an art. However, Pete noticed that his light sleeping was not long enough to account for the many miles we had traveled during the nap. I kept saying that the roads were not crowded, and I was making good, legal time. The first part was true. The second needed the "legal" cut out, but the folks on those roads did it too. Pete had to know the movie *Thunder Road*, and his car looked, just a bit, like Robert Mitchum's bootlegging car. It was all Lake Forest good feelings until we left Tennessee.

Mississippi State Line

When I was young, my friends called Mississippi "Mississlippi" - it seemed like a better name. The state, though poor even among the poorer ones, had ascended to a coarse and brutal royalty, where it wore a crown of adders, and wielded a scepter of vileness. Emmett Till's broken face, and the laughing faces of white murderers, being acquitted of mixed deaths, were indelible national images. What I saw beneath the state sign was its coat of arms. Backgrounded by the Confederate Flag, emblazoned was the mark of the beast: **KKK**. The highway became the divide between high walls of poplar and cottonwoods (un-fruited "southern trees") behind which were places of disquiet and dread. When we drove, I peeled back my reason, and eyed the road for tormented phantoms rising from shallow-earth graves. Late that night, for the first time in both our lives, we came upon ground fog. It lay, bumper high, crawling and bobbing, seeping from one tree stand to the next. Neither Pete nor I slept. I drove; then Pete wanted to drive, but the effect was the same. The mist flew upward and enveloped the car in an impossibility of sight. High beams shot back their reflections, broken by the fog's water droplets, as a glare of doom. Only with a funereal pace, illuminated with low beams, could safe passage be made. The solitary road was beautiful: our search and peck movement for the road's way was seen by none but ourselves.

At some hour, during the pre-light of the morning, the fog's back was broken. Mississippi's ground became visible and solid again. Our food was gone well before dawn. By eleven, two grumbling stomachs demanded renewed offerings. Along a well-laid road, we saw a Dairy Queen; its parking lot was full. And every car's signature said: "I am owned by a young white person who, more than likely, lives in this small Mississippi town." A density of bias compressed itself both with tales from Faulkner's word-full mill, and the still of warm-brewed death lawfully sitting on its roads: "Mississippi Goddamn!"

"Pete, you get the food and I'll stay here and watch the car. I just want a hamburger and fries." Pete didn't buy the attempt at a subterfuge; there was no need to be wary around his white kind.

"Hey, you come on inside. Things are not that way now."

"I understand that, but somebody needs to watch the car."

"No-no, you, come on."

"Aw right."

The restaurant sat in a broad space chopped out of a large wooded area that extended for miles on either side. The highway was the primary road in, but a gap, in the trees in back, hinted at a wooded entrance. Neon tubing girdled-round the huge ice-cream-cone display; at night it would be the hangout's flare, a tan cone topped with an ice-cream-white flame. It was a bright Saturday morning in autumn, and the high-risen sun in a cloudless sky lit everything beneath it. The walk to the door was long enough for everyone looking at their "cool" cars to have seconds of free view of the two of us. I walked with Pete but slightly behind him, so that only those inside with an angled view could see me. Pete opened the door; country music was playing, which was a little odd, in that I had never heard that kind of music on a jukebox before. Pete walked toward the counter through the gathering looks. I stared directly at the small of Pete's back. Heads snapped, necks twisted, eyes widened. I saw a white boy with a crew cut turn his face from astonishment to tight-lip strangeness. Then the new physics began. The few seconds of silence became bees buzzing. So many heads were turning I swore I felt a breeze. The country music joined in. The phrasing, long anyway, took to freezing. Whole notes would not end; wailing was the effect. I didn't see the clerk's face; I let Pete order, while I looked at the pretty countertop. *It was white plastic, with a cash register on it, a dispenser for straws too, napkins were kept in a neat chrome dispenser. Also, the sugar container had a chrome top that was very clean. Its bottom section was made of ribbed glass, possibly to facilitate holding it firmly.* The hive was on notice; the bees were now fidgety. I was the lead on the way out. I saw their faces. Trying not to prejudge less my face portrait fright lines, I came to the weak conclusion that I had never seen such looks on either neutral or friendly faces. Then again, my ignorance of whites could be in play. This thought let me get out of the place with a reasonable expression. Outside, Pete took offense at the behavior of his kind. He voiced this sentiment all the way to the car. "You would think people wouldn't act that way anymore." He kept at it as we got into the vehicle. Pete's hand put the key into the ignition. "Pete, shush, just drive." We were not followed, and we spoke sparingly to each other for the remainder of the trip. The experience had to be handled by us in our own separate way. In my mind, I saw too many ghosts lying in the southern swamps. I could never live in The South comfortably, at least not then. Pete and I parted in New Orleans, as friends.

The holidays were wonderful, and I ate up to my standard: prodigious amounts were consumed. These were farewell meals. I flew back to freezing Chicago, though this time like a seasoned air traveler.

55

Vera strode into Commons with a complex stride that let her cover ground in an exceptionally graceful manner. She sat alone. I walked to her table and asked to be excused for the interruption. "How did you get your stride?" "I learned it. My mother taught me." Talk bloomed. Weeks later she and I were lovers… "I missed my period" "Okay, what do we do now?" I had caused a pregnancy. I now had the status of an almost father; there was no strain in this learning, only joy. Vera made a doctor's appointment for Saturday. We lay with each other on Friday night sparking from what would be confirmed the next day. We rose early, and Vera went to take her shower while I kept watch at the bathroom door. It was sweet to protect her and her privacy. Me and my "old lady": a duet of groans. And maybe another duo was coming: one of sucklings. I loved her breasts too much to stop wanting them in my mouth. (I would stop, of course, for the baby, that lucky little…). I peeked at her when the shower curtain opened, moved by a jet of spray or her body's motions. The contrast of her skin with her pubic hair remained a magical sight: the dark marquee, which heralded the greatest thing on earth—new, living earth. She stepped out of the shower and stood on the towel I'd placed outside it. She was all-aglow in her flesh; my heart just took to thumping. I began to dry her. Nothing could have been more sacred. I stopped at her mons, but she knew me. "Hey, not now, we have business, remember?" We did, and it terrified me.

After the examination, she came out into the waiting room laughing. "When the doctor finished, I asked am I pregnant? And he chuckled 'Yes, very!'"

As usual, we ate dinner together. The thought of being separated for the night, after such news, was too jarring. I told T of my impending fatherhood and asked if Vera and I could spend the night on the couch. T said yes. In the late evening we went back to the apartment and made up the couch. Vera lay on me. Then she rose and sat by my feet. In the tiny lights from a clock's face, and a radio's dial, and the kitchen's nightlight, she moved toward me. When she got to my waist, she looked down. She lowered her head; I could see nothing but the darkness of her hair. An unknown warmth began that rose to a nervous weakness in me. I was immobile through the fear of her moistened lips abandonment. Her head moved slowly. Nothing in my life, thus far, had produced such a sensation; its continuance was the sum of the world's existence or its irrelevance. Short, quick gutturals cluttered my throat.

The knock came first then "Counselor." We quickly jumped up and went toward T's room. He came out and looked at Vera, in her bra and underwear, and said, "She surely **does** get comfortable."

That's some lame shit to say. What did you expect her to sleep in?

A dorm resident had come to the door. Hidden in T's bedroom, we heard the interchange. We dressed and chose to spend the rest of the night at my dorm. But in our approach we would have to be vigilant, for I knew one of the night watchmen: an ogre of pink, hugely-muscled flesh, who had bragged to me, in confidence, of his pleasure and prowess in "catching" couples.

For two weeks, every day, Vera and I talked with a newly discovered rational maturity about the future. When possible, we spent the nights in my dorm twined about each other, sometimes in hope, at other times in confusion. We decided not to see each other anymore. We could never separate again, and, together, we knew, we would ruin each other. Our paths could not merge. We made the trip to Chicago with Vera's best friend, Kay. She didn't drive well, but she knew the way, the open-secret path to the doctor. Vera and I kept Kay calm when her nerves were being riled by bad driving from passing motorists. We arrived. The abortion was done. On the ride back to campus, Vera rested against me; she was still so fiercely placed in my heart.

The following week, for the last time, we traveled with each other. The train was not bound to my time, it refused to be slow. Its duty was to make measured haste, to see the end. The ride to Chicago had no duration; the stops lumped themselves together. There were only two, where we entered and where we would leave. We arrived at her mother's vacant apartment and we sat and looked at each other. I knelt and buried my face in her lap and encircled her waist with my arms. She placed a hand on my head. "It would have been such a beautiful child." I came apart. Tears and the effort to stifle them were one and the same. I wanted to wail, but I wouldn't; the deed was done. My stretched heart covering we three, it would not be. She and I, it would not be. The tiny hand clutching my finger, it would not be. It would not be. It would not be. …

56

The last term was at hand. Its arrival brought no emotion; Lake Forest had become a comfortable location, though knowingly not permanent. Maturity titrated itself through what had to be done. To graduate, comprehensives must be passed. The small blue exam books would hold my future; I would not fail. Again, I induced the mentality of doing chores. For seven weeks, every day, I reviewed the world of math that I had been taught. Occasionally, with mild curses, I railed at my foolish lack of concentrated study during the last five years, with the more biting imprecations reserved when studying in my weak areas.

I passed my comps, writing on one question ("Develop complex numbers") almost too much, given the time of the exam. It was my homage to Riemann; I received a commendation on the section. My grandmother, my mother, her twin, my sister and her husband came to the ceremony. All, in gratitude for my awakening, had said silent prayers (these I saw by reading the large thought bubbles above their heads).

Jig, a senior with a sizeable mixture of weight, athletic ability, and means, lived on Cape Cod, and had a house in Boston's South End that needed renovation. "Hey, come to Boston and work on the house with the guys." The "guys" were six seniors: five men and Freda (whose sensuality deserved an award). All were from the area. Cambridge & Boston were places well beyond my imaginative powers. The weekends spent on the Cape at Buzzards Bay or at Sturbridge extended this limitation, surrounding me in a world panoramically alien. Neither New Orleans nor Philly nor Lake Forest nor New York, nor my glimpses of Chicago, combined with my experiences in each place, prepared me. Chipping away, at marvel by marvel, I aligned the sharp pieces into a mosaic of understanding; but it still left me breathless. I imagined the "big sky" country out west to be as awe inspiring as the massively vibrant spectacles of life before me.

I lived in Cambridge with two of the "guys" and, a friend of theirs in a three-room apartment on Western Ave, two blocks from the Charles River. Technically, I wasn't a resident; I didn't have a room; I slept on the couch. Daily, we four gutted the old house on Rutland St, and returned home covered with the steadfast resistance to its memory's destruction: its dust and its grime. Hugh, a lifelong resident (he said "Hah-vard yah-ard" without affectation) liked his own body odor without it being gussied up by deodorants. With his door open, his room bore testimony to this preference. Nightly he searched, as a moderato woodpecker, on his manual typewriter for words to grow the lines in his enormous manuscript. It rose as leavening dough, laden with excess yeast. Under his bed, he kept a rifle, a bolt-action thing; it seemed old. Hugh had no passion for a weapon; he had only a vague fear stoked by the times of revolt and a desire to protect himself. The angry looking and spouting black men, selling the radical newspapers, convinced him of an impending race war, or at least widespread public disturbances. He, a raconteur, with a capacious memory, was not a fighter, but definitely not a coward. He would not succumb without a fight. The thoughtfulness and efficacy and coolness of his decisions were suspect though. His weapon and a rumor-induced situation might accidentally lead him to slip down on a path, tiled with both panic and blood.

All three roommates shared a birthright fealty to the Boston Red Sox. Toward the end of summer, a nervous sentiment emerged; it showed itself as a visible agitation in both Hugh and Charlie. They began pondering on "the chances." Charlie lingered over the newspaper's sports section with a furrowed brow and a grimaced face; Hugh settled his nerves with Bronx cheers against the coming heartache; Neil said, "Que sera, sera." The routinely occurring beauty of residences that existed in both New Orleans and Lake Forest was not present in Cambridge. To my eye the houses were, if not unattractive, profoundly plain. Drab, shingled-skinned dwellings (bleak as the winters they bore) sat on ill lit and tree-darkened streets. The innards of Cambridge were quiet and reserved. To love such a place, roots must be set down, and then let grow. Stimulation was the nutrient-water for growth. This, in the summer of '68, was given skin and face for show. Vision could never rest; something gaudier, pretty, outlandish or brilliant could be in the next block.

Working with Freda everyday gave an exquisite itch to the skin-tension of the day. We had dallied, ever so slightly, in college, but it never clouded my vision; she was an intoxication that did not wane. I could not win her; I had tried. I learned to live with the sensation and accept it as knowledge. I wrote her name and mine on dymo tape and stuck it on an inside panel of the mailbox; thus, conjoined by this hidden plastic-bond, she and I would weather the years.

The weekdays passed as "easy" weekends did in college: simple working-frolic bounded only by time. But the new weekends were of a different savory. Outside Boston/Cambridge, paths of leisure had been carved, over generations, on which the mundane ticks of the weekend clock burst into soft-decibeled fireworks. And for contrast, there were two poles (visited on alternate weekends), one for the ordinary - Sturbridge, the other for those with means - Buzzards Bay. These slivers of the country, my country, America, were so easily enjoyable in this oddly scoured landscape.

Brief moments burst out of the mundane like end-of-fireworks' climaxes. In Sturbridge, a five-foot long water snake moved past Charlie and me and slithered into the water as we walked by the banks of the lake. On a dark night on the Cape, those who smoked tried some Vietnamese Black while sitting on the shore watching a surf churn up (cud-like) green phosphorescence. I looked up toward the house on the left and glimpsed a naked boy and two naked girls frolicking. They ran past a window and into another room. Their summer laughter, and the girls' bouncing breasts and sweet-shaped rears were mine, forever. Oh, how divine memory! Worth an "Aye!" In Sturbridge while walking in the woods, I heard a shout. In an indelible horror, a horse pitched a young girl off its back. Her short legs flew over her head as she went to ground. I heard (and remembered) the sounds. First, a longish thump/crunch, then came the moan. On the Cape, meteors fell, and by their dark endings they healed their own livid burns made on the face of night.

The work of destruction ceased on the house. Now rebuilding skills were required. Also, my fellow lodgers were tiring of my paid usurpation of the couch; I needed a proper living space. Charlie broached the subject, which hurt my feelings, surmising it to be rejection. I began looking for an apartment; the search lingered. Charlie, probably desperate, found a place for me. A former classmate from Lake Forest was moving. I knew her and asked to see the apartment. I arrived early. The building was horrid. Four stories of brutally weathered wood were shedding its ugly green paint like tiny undead leaves wanting to peel off and drop before autumn's command. On the ground floor, a dented, orange and black REXALL DRUGS sign hung above a large, storefront window. "Laundromat" had been painted, in an unsteady cursive, on the glass. Fronting on ill-lit Brookline St, the yawning entrance to the apartments, a cutout without a light, would turn to pitch at night. The staircase rose immediately from the first step into the entrance, so one could not hide in it. The passageway went upward and past each apartment without flourish. The smells of the hallway and stairs were not offensive.

Waiting on the small fourth-floor landing, near the door, were two people, a tall, slim black-man, and a tall, slim, attractive black-woman. The man's face, noticeably pockmarked, exuded unruffled male smugness. Not knowing what to say I introduced myself and stated my purpose. They said nothing of theirs, only that they were waiting for the tenant. Janet appeared. She spoke first to me, then to the man: "How are you Tan?" She ignored the woman. Janet opened the door; I walked past the two and followed her. The narrow hall opened onto three rooms on the left-hand side; a wall was on the right. Inside, Janet turned at the third room to face the hall door. The woman rushed past me and hollered "Bitch!" Nails raking, she hurled her body into Janet's. Janet held. They tussled; Janet's large breasts seemed to be a target. Her blouse had been torn and her bra exposed. The man did nothing but watch with a marvelously detached face. Dumbfounded, I instinctively pushed the two apart. "Bitch!" It had been her first and only word, and now it became her last. The couple left. I looked at Janet; she said nothing. A long, red score went along the pale skin on top of her right breast. She went into a room and put on a new blouse; then she showed me the apartment. Spacious, most unattractive, and it had a reasonable rent. "I would be more than willing to take it." (Maybe Janet has been seeking to flee from the couple, or at least from the woman. Janet's bad fortune may have been my good luck).

Now I lived a new life of isolated freedom in Cambridge, the east coast mecca, if not medina, for the new age. My LFC friends had not left me without moorings; in fact, they resolutely, time after time, held me aloft in their land. I had been introduced to several people who became good friends, thus my tether lines branched and then branched again.

57

My new jobs were doubly odd in that they were both sundry, and they brought into question the legitimate scope of the quasi-moral work relationship: $(paid out) FOR Work Done. As in all pairings, assumptions about the terms gave this juxtaposition its validity. My proper colored culture and my pious religious teachings sought to stiffen the FOR into an (=) equal sign. "Why did God make you?" "To know, love, and serve Him," and to do my duty. "Why are you being paid?" "To do that which has been stated as my duty." AND "As a colored person, what is also required of you when working?" "To work twice as hard as a white person would work." So, I was told; so I was trained; so I did. (Why this principle wasn't applied to my kin's "pay" for my schoolwork apparently skipped my mind). I worked at Zaire's warehouse loading goods onto pallets meant for distribution to their various stores. The rule of the job (though never possible to enforce): THE LINE MUST NEVER STOP! But the conveyor belt was always full, so it was always stopping. The workers couldn't have cared less, just as "No Smoking" was ignored. There were four hours, until lunch or quitting time, of walking along the line of the belt, putting objects on wooden sheets that rolled up to the backs of the waiting trucks. Always there were hustle-up exhortations from some worker or the occasional bitching supervisor who came out from the forbidden innards of the warehouse. The terminal illness of such work displayed itself from the first hour on the job, boredom unto mischief, possibly to malicious mischief, regardless of the above-minimum pay. The potential for injury became evident. My background would make me weak in moments when careless disregard for the employer's interests evinced itself as the safest course of action.

After two weeks, I left. "Manpower" came next. One could not envision a simpler form of non-committed work. Each day, from the pool of men who assembled in the office, some were chosen for work at sundry jobs sites. Three enormous boons were laved on the chosen workers: no permanent obligation, immediate credit given through "the draw," and lack of censure for drinking—not being drunk though. Up to fifty percent of a yet-to-be-earned day's pay could be drawn. This cash advance allowed for a world of possibilities, the main one being the capacity to buy booze. The downside of the draw, at the week's end, was a paycheck reduced almost to pocket change.

A large factory that made industrial plastic items was being relocated using its regular workers and Manpower's help. On my first day, in a friendly encounter, I met "Garble-face," a huge white man whose features were not arranged to make proper sense. Workers were taking six-foot-long pieces of heavy angle iron from the trucks to the empty insides of the cavernous building. I put mine down; Garble-face let his fall or perhaps it slipped. The deafening sound rang through the hollow volume as from a gigantic clapper striking a titan's bell. I turned back and saw Garble-face poised over the fallen iron, not moving, staring downward. When the man did turn his face, it showed a joy that moved toward ecstasy. On the next load, he threw down the iron with force. The sound matched his effort. I then put myself out of sequence. When I came to the area again, a foreman for the company stood screaming at the man, threatening to send him home if he dropped the shelving once more. When Garble-face finally caught my eye, I shrugged in sympathy; then I maneuvered my work to avoid any contact with the man.

A forklift moved the heavy items. Somehow, I became the driver, carefully driving the forklift for the entire day. The next day, several of the white workers wanted to operate it. "Goh head on." Some were foolish, others incompetent, but most were careless with the one-ton toy. The levity of the new drivers, both constant and loud, brought the attention of the foreman. "What are you doing driving the fork? Only he" (pointing to me) "can drive it." When he left, I shrugged at my fellow workers. Not wanting any bad feelings to be harbored toward me (especially by a group of white men in a work situation), I shifted my work location. Employees of the factory then began using the machine to finish reassembling the plant.

I saw an ad for a security guard. The company hired me, and gave me a not too-noticeable uniform, but a give-away official hat; I carried this in a bag to the job site. After leaving public transportation, and taking the direct route, I had to walk three blocks. Boston's North End had lots of Italians. If I were not careful, I would encounter some whose dispositions would be an unknown. I glimpsed, on the first trip there, a brightly lit corner filled with a large number of young white men. They were comfortable in that place. Having no desire to test their public accommodation, I circled around that area, sticking to the dark parts of the way. It doubled the distance, but safety first. My job was to monitor a trucking firm's yard from six in the evening until six the next morning. My supervisor, in the home office, told me the simple rule: punch each Watch-clock every hour. The guys, whom I met at the trucking company, were of a good sort. They told me someone had tried to steal from the trucks (which were backed up to the loading docks, and therefore very difficult to access; time and an inert security guard would be required). A short, stocky Italian called Barbuchii gave me a large butcher knife, saying, "Watch out! Don't let those bastards hurt you." "Thanks." The station and the door of the station were brightly lit; outside was tar-thick black. It took at least ten seconds for my eyes to adjust before I could see anything. The Watch-clock stations had bright lights trained on them; otherwise there was no light in the yard. I had not been given a flashlight. Logic entered. Soon I fulfilled the stated task and conserved myself for my main job with Manpower. At ten minutes to the hour, after making sufficient noise (so as to announce my approach to any outside) by knocking twice (not loud, but loud enough) on the door, in a rhythm "bap-bap, - , bap, bap, bap," I opened the door slowly. All stations were punched within four minutes. Then I waited several minutes more, which brought on the new hour. Then all the clocks were re-punched within five minutes. This left me having to be awake for fifteen minutes out of one hundred twenty. After several nights with this regimen, my supervisor called and asked me what I was doing. "What you told me to do: punch the clocks every hour."

The company transferred me to an office building in downtown Boston. Twelve floors needed to be watched. Off the elevator, on each floor, narrow ill-lit halls (all with the same odd odor of unwashed, weary age) were congested by office equipment and stacks of bankers' boxes. Every floor, every hour, every Watch-clock had to be visited. They told me nothing more. In the main lobby, a superb, burgundy leather couch, well made, and comfortable had been placed for customers. Fatigue from the day job finally came one night. The lovely couch took me. In the midst of waking dreams, I heard shouts. Two white men, in uniforms like mine, shotguns at the ready, pistols upon hips, came charging into the lobby. I awoke startled and looked at them. They demanded to know why the stations had not been punched. I told them the truth; I had dozed. They said that I could not. Then I asked who they were and where they had come from. They then explained to me the full scope of the building's scheme. The two men were in an impregnable room, with backup power and ventilation, maybe a TV, fridge, etc. watching a control panel. If the stations were not punched, the panel flashed signals to come out armed, because the canary (they did not use this word) had been prevented from reporting. Something must be afoot. "Oh." Before my next transfer of location, the well-shielded ones had several opportunities to check on the blinkingly reported distress of the weary canary. (All of my immediate, elder kin had worked two jobs, no doubt without napping sessions; my younger kind was soft).

My final job was short lived: one night only, but it was a worthy night. I had been instructed to report to the main office at 6PM. "The Chief" prepped me for my new assignment. In a Cambridge factory, which made industrial rubber products, thefts had been occurring. The old security firm was Fred, a man who had walked the Watch-clock route for forty years. Supposedly, he could not or would not stop the stealing. My firm had been awarded the contract. The chief topped this explanation with the garnish of being the law: the one who made the path straight. "**We** are the new sheriffs in town. **We** are going to show **them**. **They** can't intimidate **us**. **They** may try, but it won't work. **We** will stop **them**." The weighted pronouns sank deeply, but I kept a silent tongue. The man had described a fool's errand. This summary description was immensely more charitable than the reality.

The factory, located in an industrial section, was about a block square, with four stories above ground and at least two below. There were over thirty stations to be punched: non-stop walking. Fred, small, old, and sure of step, showed me the way. Everyone spoke to Fred in the kindly manner of addressing aged kin; this did not augur well for any replacement. The stations were forgotten as soon as Fred punched them. I was digesting the plant's newness, not the incidentals of Watch-clock locations. At night, the factory transformed itself into cubes of dark voids. Housed in gigantic, unlit rooms were machines and products. It would have been impossible to know, from afar, if anything had been stolen or damaged; individual scrutiny of areas would have been required. One corner of the circuit culminated in walking up the fire escape. In the ascent, midnight and noon came and went as the eyes shifted. In the distance, save for several distressed white blots, little of the nearly opaque panorama could be reasoned into shapes. At the zenith, under blinding illumination (that even warmed the face with its hundreds of watts), the fire escape door opened outward and gave access into a vacant, dimly lit hall lined with closed doors. Wind moved in bleating pluses through the open door, the entrance, and the fire-escape structure.

"They roam by night,
Loosed ghosts who moan,
From rooms not bright,
In this, death's home."
(Mannheim's "Quatrains from Castle Belevaux's Dungeon.")

Fred and I descended into the first underground level. Grit&grime (the second-tier atoms of Democritus) had both settled on everything, and in its abundance, impregnated the air. However, the workers moved about in comfort. The low, overhead ceiling, and the three-foot wide square columns supporting it were covered with a dimpled, ash colored coating. The impression was one of being in a hydraulic press, poised for a downward compression. Movement through the underground level mixed several fictions into a stygian pottage: trolls' and *Germinal's* workers mining the earth, and the bureaucratic minions of Lucifer performing their eternal tasks on the damned. On the next level down, the air borne grit had mixed with something. Then the smell of smoke and burning came. Fred let his nose lead him toward the source. Workers were now streaming away from it, and toward us. The smoke, without any place to rise, began piling downward from the ceiling, thickening, congealing from spite. It became difficult to breath, and nearly impossible to see anything except a red glow; Fred moved quickly toward it. Burning electrical smells were overwhelming all. At the source it sat. Hephaestus's forge or the fount of the burning Phlegethon or Satan's flaming brimstone throne? No. A gigantic dynamo, at least ten feet tall, belched fire and sparks and black smoke; *updated* Hyades now had an electric source of fire. Standing next to it, embedded in a smoke shroud, loomed a huge black man (a slave of the new forge?) glaring at all.

Fred hollered, "What the hell is going on?"

The man, while not softening his countenance, spoke with a grudging civility. "They told me not to turn the thing off, so I ain't turning it off!" Other workers heard the declaration and shrugged at Fred, but with distinct indications that implied sympathy with the worker at the switch. The dynamo's whirling rotor kept the air moving, giving somewhat of an ease to sight.

"Turn the goddamn thing off!"

"No! They told me not to turn the fucking thing off, so I ain't turning it off!" The engine, running amok, cackled and threw out sprays of sparks. The motor, truly hell worthy, stood up to its own destruction, sucking in current and changing it to heat, fire, smoke, and noise, burning itself alive with its own fire. The Greeks' river of fire, the Phlegethon, had been made real. Again, Fred demanded. And this time, the scourge of the forge relented. Fred ran to a fire station and pulled an alarm. Fuming himself, Fred saw the episode to its end. This ate up the night. When things were as settled as they could be, morning had arrived. Stinking of smoke and benumbed, I took the short bus ride home.

During the day at the Manpower assignment, my mind roamed about, still lost in the madness I had seen at the rubber factory. Led by an ancient guide, I had entered and spied into a vast nether place filled with darkness, smoke, flames, and danger. I returned morally enlightened: **ACTUAL WORK DONE NEED NOT EQUAL AMOUNT CONTRACTED TO BE DONE *FOR AGREED ON* $ TO BE PAID.** Take the money, and do the work within the limits of sane, personal judgments (which might, unpredictably, by contingencies, be modified). Finally, let both the duty-to-God&Employer work whip, and proper colored behavior sink into the river whose clean waters wash away memory. That evening good fortune, from the gods, fell upon me. I hurt myself while exercising on an old wooden chair. A back spindle broke, with a shear cleavage, and penetrated my hand. It hurt, but I could, of course, walk. Spring-boarding from the gash, I called in saying that I had been injured, and needed to go to the hospital. One day of reported injury, led to two days, then to the third, whereon I returned my uniform. They mailed my summary check to me. When my fellows from LFC finally got together again, I told these work stories as episodes of humor. All laughed; I was pleased at making them laugh. The bond was tight. Dobbs called me within two days. "My father wants to speak to you." I had never met him. When I did, he told me that he worked at MIT in the I Lab and that there were openings. "Please apply." (Dobbs later admitted that he did not like the perils I had been encountering on these types of jobs.)

I went to the I Lab to see a person named Dan.

58

Dan turned out to be very cool for a rocket scientist. We talked. He asked me a question about counting; I gave the answer: an exponential. It was sufficient. Now I would be working on the Apollo Project in the section that constantly verified the software. They gave me a yard-high stack of manuals to read. My English changed. New words became my new language: CSM (Command Service Module), LEM (Lunar Excursion Module), DAP (digital autopilots), hypergolic thrusters, hydrazine, simulator, iterations, alarm codes, torque moments, accumulator, buffers, overflows, perturbations methods, gimbaled engines, thrust vectors, P71, reference matrix-refsmat, and on and on and on. Each term opened outward into scores of others.

The Instrumentation lab or I-lab, at MIT, Mathematics In Truth, was full of brains, metal and flesh. Sending a man to the moon needed, in addition, a rocket, lines of code in its computers, a sharp eyepiece to spot stars to steer by, and a good clock. TIG - time of ignition - was the moment of prayer. TIG minus 10, TIG minus 9, ...TIG: burn sequence initiated. The IMU - Inertial Measurement Unit - was a gimbaled arrangement of three orthogonal gyros, with the necessary electronics, that kept man's place as he climbed the Norse tree: Yggdrasil that held the universe. All who helped could have pride of that place. Gathered in a large room, listening to voices coming from loudspeakers, the engineers beamed and judged with honed ears as the rocket maneuvered. "They had better not IMU cage; it's going at 65 radians per second." On the central table sat the book: the source code of the program in the computers in the spaceship: 1,000 pages thick of line after small line of 1's and 0's (some knew it by memory). Maydean, smiling, opened it to a given page, intimating that those lines of code were relevant. Rubbish, but prideful rubbish. The instructions (in the sections being used) were whizzing about the processes taking place in the ascending rocket, but the good feelings of communal smarts were warm, and sustaining.

Once the ordinary of these people settled: smart, smarter, and smartest, the physicality of them emerged. The fleshy housing of scientists and engineers sat before my eyes. Hollywood was so off kilter in its bias toward the overly attractive as exemplars of good scientists. Casting had been askew in most sci-fi movies, and they were the poorer for it. Rocket scientists were at the I-Lab. These were the people, among many, who were trusted by the three astronauts and the public, to keep the 3,350-ton, 363-foot-high Roman candle acting properly. The only things that mattered were knowledge of and facility with the code. Test it; carve it, test it; shape it; test it; perfect it; test it; test it; test it. Normally, these functions were not all performed by the same individuals. Changes in the code were to be taken seriously; the mission could hang on them. Personal exteriors were, of course, not indicative of professional competence, but oh how interesting to the eye were these architects and the support staff.

Emmy Noether's sisters, stellar luminosities holding the distaff, over time, exuded magnificent, diverse sensuality. Strong in my memory were Franca, Maydean, Mary, Alice, Nita (trying to accommodate conflicting bosses), Strongly-robust Sally, Mrs. Buxom-the ever smiling code carver, huge-racked and mad Lauren, Dollop (I never knew her name, but this moniker was so suggestive of her), Sweet Trolleys, her legs were breath taking, and all the other clothed wonders of faceted-Venus. Shona, her round head, fronted with bangs, surged up and down the halls with decks of punch cards in her hands and a pencil behind her ear. Her feminist polemics (which girded her) were unceasing, not that they weren't necessary for society's education. There would need be contention between the sexes: their aims were of different bodies. But I understood that from the corpus callosum, right and left, to the divine cleft, any assumption of the inferiority of women was a profoundly foolish notion, and it reeked of men's fears. The sound of Shona's shoes gave me notice of catching a fleeting glance of the elastic motion of her superb breasts. Carol, with her short skirts, was looking for a husband; she thought this perfectly reasonable, and it was. Simply smitten by Celia's brilliance, kindness, and grace, I was happy just seeing her. Sara's clothed her fierce intelligence in stylish hippy looks. Her face had the pleasant tension of a blonde she-wolf, but softened, within the vogue, by her glasses. Being lost, yet safe, in bush-dense forests came often to my nighttime dreams.

The men were clothed in the permanent cloth of their personalities. Sam, a manager, every day dressed to the "nines." But his well-made clothes were unsuited to his short muscular frame. Too large shoulders, for the cut of his jackets, made him look unbalanced. Also, he should have practiced walking erect; at times he had a simian slope to his posture. Elegant Battin, (the intellectual father of the section) appeared in a neat jacket and tie, while being fronted and followed by a small entourage; his cigarette in a holder seemed right. Large Sal's clothing always appeared to be just-after ironing's effect has begun to fail. His stomach bounced about as he hustled everywhere in frenzy "I'm not touching P71 (the program for the long road back to earth) unless I ask Barnfeather." Norm, with a temperament of unparalleled "niceness," pencil always behind his ear, ever carved the code. Ram, long armed, like a gibbon in a suit, robotically turned from cubicle to cubicle offering his help on difficult problems. Neat Phillip (who was working on ways to make different kinds of computers "talk" to one another), and his equally neat brother convened, in the hall, over the extraordinary depth of Ram's implicative powers. Dale, frazzled by the thought of returning to the classroom, bit his fingertips raw. Anton, smooth, calm, and elegant in dress, wrote the entire proto program; some say this effort almost did him in. Lepoffski wore his carnal desire as a lapel pin on his rumpled clothes. He was robust, coarse, and he possessed an offensive body odor, to my nose. When he approached, or was seen, all the proximate women quickly realized that they had an important task to perform, or they were just about to set off to keep a date with the keypunch machine. This was an evolved behavior. At first, the hardened ones would eye him with disregard. However, this did not work; Lepoffski bored in upon them. Given this breach, he settled instantly. He then made all things, even to the air within the cubicle, inappropriate; it was almost preternatural. Bob Hasell existed at the other end of this spectrum. His tweed jackets and pipe smoking persona were aloof from all. He did his job, nothing less, nothing more.

The neat and casual dressing Bob Blunt gave me a quick intro into DAP programming (how sine waves are induced in the program to test the damping out of them by the autopilots - these fascinated me). Bearded Lane, with his hearty belly laugh, worked on the simulation program (to write in code, for the huge IBM mainframes, what are the physics of earth and moon that a rocket will encounter). Mayard, balding and quiet, wore suits and thick-soled wingtip shoes. He always seemed to be carrying around decks of punch cards. He had helped develop perturbation matrices: figurations that answered, "Where am I?" from the point of view of: the rocket ship, or the space capsules, or the moon, or the earth, or the vernal equinox, or wherever. Ron (the LEM man), neatly dressed, sweeping his hair back as it fell over his broad forehead, walked with afterburners on, and carried decks of cards to run a simulation on the program "Burn Baby Burn." The LEM had to push the CSM after the explosion on Apollo 13. This configuration was not the norm. The code must be checked for the unusual bending moments resulting from this action. Bernie, in simple dress, carried a giant ego. "They (the powers in the I-Lab) want me to be a resident Norton." This implied that he would learn the entire code by heart. An assumption, seemingly, that was within his intellectual capacity as a given. Short, somewhat-portly Richie told of being kidnapped and robbed while hitchhiking. Hitchhiking was a dumb activity.

HOWEVER: One night, Spider and I, being drunk and a long way from her flat, hitchhiked, and had the same thing happen. It ended differently though. The driver and his pal announced that they were going to "do things" to the two of us. We then noticed that the rear door handles were missing. Extreme fatigue and alcohol humor cum aggression solved the problem. I exploded in laughter (filled with snickering malice) at the idiocy of having threatened someone who is behind you, while you are occupied with a vital task (driving). A sharp fillip, given just to the rear of the driver's right eye, and a hearty laugh taught the two kidnapping, white lads certain realities. "Boy, just drive where you are told, before I rip out both your eyes." We did sober up enough, during the rapid ride home, to instruct the driver to let us out of the car around the block from Spider's house. We had never been intimate, though we had hinted at it. Now was the time; the episode became the push to do it. We kissed, I touched her breasts, and I passed out.

It was glorious working at the I-Lab, and I had money in my pocket, and I lived in Cambridge. A long and probably interesting, but unfulfilling future awaited me. I was not brilliant, not even excessively smart, and years of engineering study (to catch up) would have to be undertaken. Dobbs' father, again, rescued me. "Why don't you go to The Business School?" "Huh? I hate business." Aunt Alice and my youth had set down the principle of adulthood: **GET A GOOD JOB!** To me, business carried the three taints: chicanery, color-control, and greed. "You don't know how valuable the education can be …" The exhortation was lucid. Business school taught the sciences of economic endeavor. This sounded good. I took the test, scored sufficiently, and was admitted.

My New Orleans'snooty's comeuppance from brains.

At my farewell luncheon from the I-Lab, feeling myself to be a New Orleans gourmand, I ordered brains. Would this dish be up to my standards? I was aghast; the damn things looked just like brains. They were not fried or breaded, and no Louisiana hot sauce was on the table. When I cut them (they were soft too) a watery-cloudy fluid ran forth. I managed three mouthfuls. The first went down! The second froze, and then it went down slowly, which brought the constancy of gravity's pull into question. The third overturned that force: the mouthful yo-yoed for at least six seconds. A fourth would have flown out of my mouth. I ate all the capers. Shamefully, the reputed gourmand had been a coward, using his eyes instead of his tongue.

59

Toward the end of the orientation interview, my advisor asked this simple question: "Do you want to make a lot of money?" A quick internal query led me to say, "No, not really, money isn't that important to me." "Then you are at the wrong place." "Oh." I struggled to face this understanding.

"The B school" has a small, beautiful campus. Harvard University somewhat engulfs it, but the sentiments between the two schools are almost antagonistic. Students in one seek to be Chaucer, in the other, Chancellor. Ben Franklin would have frowned on this difference. Thomas Jefferson would have benefited from it: his daughter might not have lost Monticello.

The classrooms have the form of steeply raked, bisected circular amphitheaters, with a wall of blackboards defining the cutting plane. The Business School instructed by examination of actual or manufactured situations. This is called the "case method." Every day, three new cases (one for each of the three daily classes) are pummeled, broken, and laid open in the manner of frenzied anatomy classes, conducted by teachers dressed from the elegant to shop-foreman style. The bloody innards of business situations are held up to view. One could find body analogs in cases: brains, lungs, spleen, etc. The cases are revised, discarded, and novel ones introduced, less over the years they become stale and known, but certain ones had achieved iconic status. The famous case of *Scott Fertilizer* was one; correct analysis of the numerical data indicated that product was not being shipped out, with the attendant joke of warehouses distended by manure. Or the case in Human Behavior in Organizations: HBO (pronounced "hobo") where the entire case was one and half pages (normally they were at least eight pages). Its fame rested in trying to divine and deal with the intractable human quality of ignoring commands from higher up, while being in a hierarchical system.

Every class began with an element of chance. The instructor chose, at random, a student to start the discussion. Being unprepared always could lead to embarrassment. I was spared a monumental humiliation of this sort through the magic of a medallion given to me by Vera. A special class, held in the giant auditorium and attended by the spouses of the section members, would start at 7PM; it was big deal. I was not prepared. Foolishly, I did not think of my odds of being called upon. I went to the gym and played basketball before the class. The medal Vera had given me was sacred; I always wore it. Somehow, for the first time, I feared it being torn off while playing. I took it off and put it in the pocket of my jacket. From there the gods played mute games amongst themselves with it. At the end of my game I could not find it. I searched by walking the exact path I had traversed from the moment of leaving my dorm to arriving at the gym. Back and forth for two hours, meager twilight left; darkness came. Finally giving up, anguished by the lost, I walked slowly to my dorm and changed for the special class. It was midway through by the time I arrived. During it, I sat unmoved, save for the attention I gave to the huge number in the room. The next day, my professor told me: "I was going to call on you to lead the discussion, but you were late."

On Fridays, a special class, Written Analysis of Cases (WAC), was given. The course and the teacher, an ex-military man, were both tedious. At a precise hour, on Sunday, this class's assignment (corrected by young, paid correctors) had to have been turned in. Meeting this validated deadline spawned many legendary stories. Military men abounded as students. From one, I heard an account of the recorded doom of the submarine Thresher. "… 'negative bow angle'… 'still descending'… 'try this!'… 'Oh Jesus!' … 'TRY THIS!'… 'crush depth' … 'h God! Oh Go' … Death's appointment kept; it was not early; it was not late. Joe (a navy man from Texas, and a pious Christian) and I, inexplicably developed the bond of exercise. Daily, together, we went to the Harvard gym. We didn't talk much, but we would have helped one another, even in a difficult situation; we both understood this.

The school had a hereditary dimension: fathers—present leaders, business titans, and other makers and shakers of societies—sent their sons, who then repeated this succession. But the times were changing; business minorities were entering in larger numbers: blacks (both men and women), white women, and less-than-wealthy foreigners. Full dress suits, expensive ones too (Hickey Freemans' as an exemplar) were not the order of the day anymore. Though some students, of lesser means, persisted in this fashion until threadbare patches, on their single suit, showed. Now an intelligent herd (but of questionable pedigrees) walked through the halls. In certain corridors, flanked by portraits of past greats, if one listened closely on hallowed nights, a spectral and piteous lamentation emanated as a comment on these changes.

When nostalgic, I walked into Cambridge by crossing the Charles. Many bridges made this connection. The one at Western Ave was a brown concrete arc, whose sides were embellished with river rock pebbles. It had no drain holes; the curve of the span sent water to Boston or to Cambridge. It was a lovely bridge, strong in its simplicity. The prior June, under a half-moon sky, I had seen a large rat just ahead of me upon the bridge. A sewer rat lent itself to a summer frolic, in the way lions torment and then kill hyenas. Once on the bridge, the rat had nowhere to hide. One way compelled, only the path to Boston offered escape. A race began. I chased the rat completely across the bridge into Boston, stamping at it, trying to crush it against the side of the bridge. My reactions and coordination were still good, as judged from this accidentally met blood sport; I almost got the rodent several times. I didn't think of the creature's terror, its destruction or maiming would have been done within athletic joy. Cruelty-license given by title: "Plague Maker."

One beastly winter night on the bridge, the freezing wind was being as outrageous to me, as I had been to the rat. If Boreas had been truly sentient, and playful in its potency, he might have gusted me over the side, and into the Charles. Walking slanted forward, my head steadily looked at my feet, as I moved them to the New Orleans's speed directive of Baby, Linwood's younger brother. "Hey man, we gotta put sump-um in the pavement." Halfway across, a horn broke through the wind's tune and my ferocious pace. I saw a car stopped on the vacant roadway with the front, passenger's side window rolled down; the driver leaned out, from the warmth, into the cold. A brown face amidst the wind and driving snow-dust: "Saay man, I ain't never see nobody walk like that. You are serious. Yah want ah ride?" "Yeah." Not another word was spoken between us. Near the school, at an intersection where a red light held us: "Right yeh good." "Ah right." "Thank you."

My fond memories of the bridge—both as a playground and a hunting ground had been touched by the ache of the cold. Too many winters sat inside me, and spring break approached. I searched for a place, on the eastern side of the US, with the highest average temperature. Also, it had to be under the US flag, this avoided problems, for I had no passport: **The USVI: The United States Virgin Islands, 82 degrees of average warmth.** I had heard of the Virgin Islands, somewhere below Florida, past Cuba. I bought a ticket to St. Thomas. Others from the section were going there too.

60

The first leg of the trip, via jet, went from Boston to Puerto Rico. When the wheels touched the tarmac, spontaneously, clapping began. To my ear, the initial sound of the applause was unexpected, and odd, but the logic immediately revealed its soundness. Despite modern times, voyages were always uncertain; be grateful upon safe arrival. When I deplaned, the teleportation had been completed; it had put me in a place as alien as the comic book character Adam Strange's Alpha Centari. New suns shone on both. The greeting delegations, for the passengers, were large, and the affections interchanged were almost contagious: I wanted to be happy with family also. The people were different. The translucent pallor that allowed for "putting some roses back in her cheeks" was not the norm. The background staff of clerks, maintenance crews, counter agents, baggage handlers, restaurants workers, etc. looked a great deal like the Creoles I had seen in my youth, though generally shorter in stature. (I had heard that a Creole family in New Orleans had changed its name by shifting the accented syllable. Then they all uprooted and moved to California where they became Spanish and lived passé blanc.)

When Puerto Ricans spoke Spanish to each other, their words burst from them with a rapidity that did not seem possible: language in fifth gear. Diesel fumes, cigarette smoke, and chatter (which came from a crowd that included pregnant women and children) flooded the open-faced terminal building. The latter two groups were odd, in that I came to realize, I had not seen them in Cambridge. Bright colors, in clothes and in women's hair, punched visual holes in the background of liquid heat. Suitcases (some were huge) and boxes were being lugged to airline counters or picked up at the baggage claim area. An inseparable joining of commerce and culture was evident; it spoke to the bubbling, living concoction, brewed on a green-topped hot spot called Puerto Rico. Its huge distance from the tourists' world of frost seemed unbridgeable. The connecting flight, to St. Thomas, was on Prinair. To access its gate required leaving the main terminal and walking a fair distance to a separate, and minor (and left to look so) building. Body accommodations, from the cool airplane to the humid airport, were further extended in walking to the departure counter. The Prinair staff maintained aloof politeness. This turned out to be the best stratagem, given the mercurial nature of the service. While waiting for the flight to St. Thomas, it became apparent that passengers, going to other islands, had been sitting there a long time. The planes were operational pieces being used to suit a calculus of utilization, which did not necessarily involve the published schedules. Impassioned pleas made to agents were answered with an impassive, (and slightly dismissive), "Not yet."

Flying over Puerto Rico was flying over a gigantic emerald cut and mounted on ruddy soil, a rich doorway into an Antillean tale. Galvanized roofs, silvery gray to rusty brown, covered a section near the ocean. They were the tops of shanties; blistered pearls girdled oceanfront real estate. The sea does not exist below a high-flying jet plane, but through the windows of a low-flying aircraft, these do: dark, sopping wet clouds, blue expanse, barges, sail boats, fishing boats, cruise liners, white caps, and a "wrinkled sea" that "crawled beneath." Forty minutes later, "The captain has turned on the fasten-your-seatbelt light. Please fasten your seatbelts." At one one/hundredth the size of Puerto Rico, St. Thomas's length and breadth were entirely visible from the air. Its nuanced aspect, of an articulated shoreline, provided safe moorings. A pirate's haven nestled among St. Ursula's 10,000 virgins, so said the *Prinair Playground* magazine. The airport's short runway required precision in its use.

"Welcome to St. Thomas." The form of the terminal mixed styles: barn-like, or Quonset Hut-like, or a provisional, but sturdy, WWII hanger, and a glorious accommodation to tourists and tourism; the place contrasted so strongly with Puerto Rico. The size and the homogeneity of "PR" made it one place, one people, one country, el pais de la gente de "la isla del encanto." St Thomas looked different, more diverse; it formed part of the darker US root of the Antillean tail.

Jules (a classmate) and I met in PR. Deciding that a communal sharing would be beneficial, we bundled the remainder of the trip. Jules was parsimonious, but not stingy. He had a technical bias toward inflated expenditure, and he felt that the "edge" in all transactions should rest with him. Topping these, and despite his slender build, within a day or two, he exhibited a rapaciousness of want and spirit. His appetites sat on his face and twitched behind his thick glasses. We caught a cab to downtown Charlotte Amalie and had the taxi driver take us to "The Gate" guesthouse. After checking in, we roamed about the town, looking, seeking. But the satiety we each sought had nothing in common: one was heat immersion; the other was carnality.

Open drinking became the first natural accommodation to cultured behavior that I took notice of. Like Mardi Gras, cups, bottles, cans, and whatever were filled with whatever. The need to wash down food, to slake thirst or to cool a heat was human; its assuagement outside of four walls covered by a roof was neither odd nor perverse. Hard inebriation was far more liberal in its origins, and regardless of where one achieved it, one was still drunk, and, as capacity allowed, still able to move about. On St Thomas, confrontation with the law on this matter would have agents of dark complexion deciding one's fate.

Jules wore a handkerchief tied about his neck, with a tropical-ascot spirit to its flair, much as disinherited black sheep of a royal family would. He and I walked. The town's waterfront, which lined the Caribbean, became the food and fruit market. We looked and shopped, in lieu of, for me when a child, the mysterious edge of the Mississippi, where the French Market and unknown wharfs had lain. A tin-ear sensibility hindered recognition of all, but the most blatant resonances induced by the island, but higher order harmonics were setting into motion fundamental parts of me, without the slightest cognition of this on my part.

Sunday, a day of no special import to us, brought the sight of dark people in Christian livery, holding bibles, passing by the rank smells that stood out, on walls and in corners near The Gate. Oozed-down heaps of vomit and, occasionally, runny ordure marked the paths of sick frolicking. Small clumps of people showed where the knots of interest were on the water-front. From the rapid pointing, large gesturing, and loud exclaiming, one gathering topped the rest. We crossed Veterans Drive and walked toward it. Ten faces were looking into the water. Jules and I found a place in the group. Something, something long and powerful and entrapped thrashed near the bulkhead. Both the victors in this battle, and the crowd watching showed extreme diffidence toward the edge. For five feet down in the water, a gray form almost lost in the shifting patterns of light and dark, floated the vanquished: a fifteen or so foot-long hammerhead goring the water with its eye-horns. Pulled parallel with the concrete, gaffed, tail looped, winched, and hauled on land, then gawked at, and feared; its time was done. I nodded to it out of respect and said: "Великий Господин (Great Lord)." Jules and I walked on. Sunday had to warm up. Around lunchtime, it fully awoke itself, and then it took form as the last day of the weekend. From early morning, cruise ships had been emptying themselves of the willing and able. Now, customers haggled for bargains in the open shops, while the churchgoers stepped to Sunday's normal rhythms. The two groups went past one another, each with an altered state of mind from the other.

All the beaches brought pleasure to the eye, but Trunk Bay on Saint John was primal in this exhortation. Its elements had individual beauty: a palette's-worth of subtly colored sand, shades of blue water, coconut palms, small reef fish, a tiny island just offshore. The composite gave each part its just weight, letting nothing overwhelm. A constant refreshment of beauty-to-the-eye was the effect created. The one blot was a redheaded one. A foolish Scot or Irishman or Englishman, normally of pallid-milk hue, had been determined to be "on holiday." He had burned himself to the second degree. The sun also turned its face to the vacation days, and soon consumed them in its fire: time to return to Boston.

The trinity of **What to be? How to be? With whom to be?** had been a questioning in flatland. The trip to St Thomas added a final inquiry, but one remote from the plane: **Where to be?** A part of my mind remained in St. Thomas, the remainder traveled back to Boston, where all that was dissonant made Jacobin tunes while the tumbrels rolled. These carried the sensible dictums and expectations of everyone who had invested in me. The term ended raggedly. A summer job in Worcester, as an analyst for a shoe manufacturer, was exceptionally rewarding though. I encountered an amazing hodgepodge of people: good, bad (more their effects, they twice robbed my apartment), beleaguered, smart, stupid, incompetent: "Hush. Don't make so much noise," from a dental practitioner to a screaming patient in a public clinic, callous, ignorant, and learned. And from a young programmer's rather dense book, I became acquainted with Claude Shannon, a towering intellect in information theory, who enlarged the definition of entropy, thermal energy refusal to fully bend to the will of men, by shifting its base: digital bits now shared the same bed as heat's chaos.

In an October that goaded me in my hesitancy (it became exceptionally warm), I left for St. Thomas. Again, I landed at the Harry S Truman airport, again I caught a cab to The Gate guesthouse, again I checked in, and then I went to The Carousel bar on the waterfront and ordered a large rum and coke. It cost one dollar. I drank it quickly, and ordered another, for I still had thirst. Thus, my Antillean tale continued to unfold.

Part Four

WADADLY

61

For weeks, Boy Blue talks about carnival and Antigua (fondly called LA or Little Antigua or Little Africa or Wadadly - this last name has hints of a persona). "You gonna like it, yah know." We make preparations. The day of departure arrives. The commuter flight to Antigua makes stops (most less than forty-five minutes apart) in different countries. The national similarities are a common geographic area and a preponderance of the inhabitants being black. These two features, to narrow eyes, make for a sameness of location and the oneness of the people. But each island is a country, with all that this fact entails. The languages could be different, too. French need not be understood by those who speak with the Queen's tongue or others who fancy the Dutch guilder or ones who pocket the peso. The LIAT (Leeward Islands Air Transport) cabin is polyglot space. All the links of the like tongues are held in tight pack inside the steerage of the dismissively laden bark: "They all speak the Yankee dollar though!"

We both feel ourselves to be handsome, and we match this by dressing accordingly. We find our stewardess good-looking enough to tag team her during the flight. Now we are good at it. She tells us the location of her dormitory (at the old bottle factory), and agrees to a visit from us, for more chat. We record this fraternal success well before the final landing.

Complete trust in my brother, and sweet ignorance of what to expect lets Antigua suffuse me with itself. The infusion begins immediately upon touching ground. In entering the terminal, the ordinary act of seeing starts overlaying memories, unwittingly dissolving the structures these recollections are supporting. Most people are black. But it isn't the same as St. Thomas. There, a sizeable number of white tourists elongate the spectrum. Here no. In St. Thomas, the custom officials are mixed, here not. Dark-hued men in the livery of officialdom have smiles, and a British crispness of purpose. The immediate feeling is one of being transfixed by novelty, but not by tension. This absence I have never experienced when confronting agents of governmental power who are white. Their intrinsic mission, toward my kind, is to exude an aura of legalized ugliness. Their eyes are always those of the salt-marsh crocodile: calm, and holding boundless malice, mixed with an anticipatory focus of readiness for some kind of a strike.

We stand in a line that leads to a tall officer. When Blue's turn comes, the officer looks and smiles in a friendly, but official way: "Boy Blue." Blue returns the greeting with warmth, and with the slight diffidence that makes sense when dealing with someone who, if not shown the proper respect, can make life difficult. The passage through Customs is so comfortably harmonious, it allows the reverse side of the movement to sound: the scraped dissonance of dislike. (**POLITICS**: political sensibilities, rudimentary in the extreme, peep out in my twenty-sixth year.) A surprising, basal anarchistic feeling has been loosed; I have no love for official power, displayed either by a friendly black face or an unfriendly white face, though the former makes the encounter a good deal more pleasant. But from either, the opportunity for capricious behavior rankles, because it will always be prefaced by "legal authority". **"I AM GOD, AND KING, AND LAW!"** Under the weight of the royal chamber pot, empty or full, we all must bend. But the internal question has ignited within me: Why? "Fuck Em!" lay close to my heart; a revelation. We clear Customs; we are in Antigua Space.

Blue: nature's best light for dark voyages is my guide. I follow with a mind free to watch and be "bathed in the poem of the" land. The taxi carries us to De Souza Road where I meet Ruth, and Jenna (five years old), and the house, a small green dwelling built in the style of a New Orleans' "shotgun." This last introduction sits in a subliminal but structured part of my manners, which rests in mysterious branchings and loci of ganglia. The word "sacred" has been co-opted by religions, but the clay of the body firmly holds the word's force. If felt, it exists; it needs no presumed, higher grounding. Blue's house is a sacred object, as is mine.

We put on lyming clothes and go toward "Carnival City." The hours have begun to slough off the daylight. Cracking open night's door, twilight pushes out its head and grins, with a thin-moon smile, at the Antigua-dark faces it meets shifting, transforming, reflecting the dregs of a draining sun. Diffuse sound and hazy light force their way through the thick trees. Finally, all fall away; an enormity lies before us. Blue near, but unseen lets me (Red-man) form a new birthright sight. A young man approaches. Despite the surrounding din, Red-man hears a burst of audible sounds coming from the boy. They mean nothing to me. Again, perhaps similar to the first, words come from the boy. And again, no meaning; nothing. Then the young man produces something in his hand that looks like a ticket. More mysterious talk comes out of his mouth, while he thrusts forward the ticket. Regardless of the unknown words, the story is bullshit. A small current of Wadadly silently travels from the ground through my body. It first gives rise to the hand gesture of brushing away a buzzing pest, and then it continues to my mouth. Sucking my teeth in annoyance (schuptsing), for the first time in my life, I walk toward the gate. In the background I perceive, without interpretation, bursts of laughter. "I didn't understand anything he said." "In time, you will. Nice going. The little raahss-hole wanted to sell you a ticket. His friends laughed at him when you brushed him off."

It had rained earlier; mud is the ground, and food is in our minds. Around a stage are booths; we go to one and asked for two chicken legs. The large lady, in a print outfit, looks in surprise at me after I open my mouth and say something to Blue. She brings out the chicken legs. I look at them, dumbstruck; they are the size of large frog legs, perfectly formed, but. Each cost three EC dollars; so, six will be the EC total, which comes to a little over $3 US. The Yankee dollars appear. Greed, suspicion, and guile all sit, at the same time, in the woman's face. We know that she will not accept coins. Three US are given; she looks and shakes her head: "Not enough." Blue pulls out fifty cents US. Looking, then turning her gaze inward, "No!" I give her another dollar. She takes it, and almost starts to complain, but Blue has her covered. "What bullshit you trying to pull off? You already got more than you should." She wants to cuss him, and me, her poised face shows it, but Blue's thrust has struck home, and she has given us the food. She stays in her booth scowling. Blue, scowling too, turns his back to her, and we walk away. After a pace or so: "You've got to rough them up, yah know," his face smiling all the while. But the problem exists; we need to change money. The bank will be the place, but we must wait until Monday.

Wait until juve'.

Daily routines enter, they have to, but unlike my accustomed ones, they are neither tedious nor difficult. In the morning, filling up the water drum using water from the communal pipe is not much of a chore. Using the quasi-rural toilet, the outhouse, is fun; I have never used one before. It has no smell and being dumb enough to somehow fall in seems the only danger. It wouldn't kill me, but lord, the experience. In my mind, an outhouse had been "country." Grandly, wind passes through this urban conceit.

Maylock Inn:
(FOOD AND DANCING)

It is close enough to DeSouza Road (a half hour walk) so that a car isn't necessary. **The Law:** Music until dawn & fatigue in the musicians is unacceptable. Fete demands stamina. Stumpy the drummer, arguably the most difficult position to hold (screw up the beat and nobody will forgive you) begins to wobble about 4AM or so. He continues playing, but only by habit; if asked, he might not be able to say his name.

Always and everywhere, day or night, even in chat at Maylock, cricket is a topic. In St. Thomas, groups of West Indian men talk of the game; in Antigua, passion for the game vibrates the very soil. Boys walk down roads with bats in their hands, while others slow mimic that hurling method of throwing used by the bowlers. Conversations, loud or restrained, concerning the game are everywhere. For by the chance of the hour, the West Indies team has the best cricketers in world. The bowlers (I likened them to human trebuchets) in aiming for the wicket are not obliged to take any concern for the well-being of the batter. The ball, flying straight or ricocheting off the ground, hurts. The other side feels pain also. The ball coming off the bat is "hot." Ten feet away from the batsman stands the slip poised, his glove-less hands ready for a catch. To play well requires that both fear and pain be overlooked. Test Matches can last for days; days where a mistake could leave one damaged. The tea and crumpets canard (lodged by some baseball fans) that seeks to dandify the game unseats itself. These are rugged, fit, world-class athletes giving it their all. I will never take to the game, but respect must be given.

Wandering about downtown I run into Mikey, another Antiguan who has come home for carnival from St. Thomas. Mikey seldom smiles, and his face has a masculine serenity to it that impresses. Somehow, he knows about my playing soccer, and tells me of a pickup game the next day. Playing on a field, strewn with rock-stones, the land marks me. It tears my skin and mixes its flesh with my blood. I finish the game with pride; several, on both sides, shake my hand. I took pain and gave the same. Red-man moves through

Antigua as through amniotic fluid: immersed without understanding, bereft of time, womb safe, open to all things. It is late and DeSouza Road is far away. My mind rapidly empties itself of the will to remain awake. Sleep has no more patience; it will have its way. Looking about the deserted street, Red-man sees several openings between buildings; I go to the darkest one, a narrow slit with no doors on either side. At the end of the building nearest to the sea, the cul-de-sac turns and opens onto a tiny space the size of a pallet. Neither bad smells nor refuse fill my sky-lit room. No fear comes into my heart. I lie down, close my eyes, and sleep.

Dawn rises and carries the world with it. The light of morning and a crowing rooster bring me a new day with a clarity that belies the night's inebriation. I walk out of the passageway and start toward Blue's house with my energy replenished. Red-man hardly understands, in words, the accommodation made, but I knew that politeness has been shown to me. Antigua has bad people, but Wadadly, by a sympathy, entered my mind. In the hospitality of this intrusion, he guided me to a place of safe rest, for he has a great deal more to show me. Lee, somewhat concerned, frowns slightly when she hears me tell of my lodgings. Blue laughs and applauds his brother's growing affinity with the land. Red-man, with chores to be done, carries a bucket to the pipe to fetch water for the drum. I wash, and then sit down for breakfast: salt-fish, boiled eggs, pear, coco-tea, and titi bread. The morning is good, a sweet sun shines, a nice head will give a crown to the day. The two of us go out looking for herb and adventure. At West's Gas Station, Blue stops and looks up at the utility pole on the corner.

"Some man too sh-chewpid about woman, yah know."

"Hah yah mean?"

"A woman "knuckle" ah man, so wha he do?"

"Wha?"

"Him climb a light post and drink off a tin of brake fluid."

"Yah lie? He get sick and fall?"

"Sick wha! (H)e dead! And (h)e had lash himself to the pole."

"Wha yah mean? They had to go up and fetch he?"

"Yeah."

"Boy, you too powerful yah know. No "wife" can be that good."

"Good or bad, (h)e dead up there."

"Boy, das sh-chew-pid bad!"

"Me ah tell you."

A grating roar that has been coming on finally breaks in, pulling attention to it. It becomes louder and louder; Blue's face begins to smile. The sound ceases with a screeching of tires and a flinging up of small stones. A white mini-moke sits next to us, and the wickedly smiling face of the driver looks at Blue.

"Brissive Boy, ah-wah goh-on?"
"Boy Blue! Ah when yah get back, man?"
"Me ah come two days ago."
"Ge-tin, man. Leh we goh for a flat, no?"
Rum?

We both seek the radiance of the morning moving quickly toward its source, on the lift of good herb. However, friendship has its ways and its laws. We buy a flat of Caviler, affectionately known as The Clown, and Blue and Red-man each take a single drink. With the car we can scout, more easily, for herb. We find some, smoke it, drive to town, and then go about on foot. The day dissolves without notice. Walking home, I see the streetlights, post sentries for daylight's reign, become lonely in their isolated brightness. And in the old lanes, in futility, they have abandoned their charge. Unclothed darkness sits, heedless of modernity's censure. How black is night, when night wants no light. Jumbie eyes will roll all around nappy-hair heads.

"Blue, you believe that obeah shit?"
"Some man got powers."
"Das bullshit."
"Suit yourself, but you nah want that kind-ah man put weight pon you. Problems."
"Hmmmm, so you say."
"Me nah argue with you. But if your teeth start for rotten, and"
"Hush your rass.".
"Hey, remember the little ting in the blue frock?"
"Boy, she look nice yah know."
"How yah mean! Me ah blaze that."
"She smile at me, not you!"
"Boy, yoh eye too twisted yah know. She nah watch you."
"Yah see, me ah mumble my lickle words, and work roots pon your rass, so you can't see who watching who."
Schupt-sing, "In your pork hole."
"Heh, heh, heh."
When we arrive home, Blue immediately goes to bed and promptly falls

to snoring upon Ruth. I, abed, eyes closed, have glints, of herb-refractions of the day, popping off, like berserk flash bulbs. When consumed, oblivion ties me to my rest.

Wait until juve'.

The next night, movies. The Deluxe Theater brings films to local chaos. A large crowd is gathered around the entrance; some have advanced to the ticket booth. On the flat surface of the projecting marquee are several young men. Others are clambering up. Down into the crowd drop some of the men, who then thrash about, wildly, chaotically and athletically. "Blue, ah wha go on?" "Some man don wan stand in line to get tickets." Near to Blue and Lee and Red-man, well-dressed couples look at the spectacle with condescension. Blue gets balcony seats, which are above "house seats." I, as a child, had been accustomed to this, but here the significance reverses itself. The balcony seats are the classier accommodation. On ground level, in front of "house" is a section known as "pit." Fortunately, though, it differs from Shakespeare's Globe's pit: no "penny stinkards" foul the air. However, there are modes and fashions to be observed; body builders and "hard man" sit on the benches; timid types do not buy a ticket for pit. The first feature has Bud Abbot and Lou Costello slapstick with blacks (producing hair-raising fright in both) in *Africa Screams*. Laughter, deep and hearty, comes from everyone; the stereotypes of blacks, used in making the humor, find no personal identification with the crowd. A spaghetti western (the first Red-man has seen) comes next. The audience loves it, especially the men in pit. With hoops and hollers, and cheers from the crowd, good vanquishes (kills) evil, but in a sanitary way. The finale arrives with the good man, well holding an eighty-pound machine gun, base weight alone, mowing down the enormous number of bad men, who all wear red masks. They drop from the continued fuselage without bloody spurtings; a pantomime of dying plays itself out. Around 1:30AM it finishes; we all walk home. A cool night breeze dries The Deluxe sweat.

That night in Carnival City, Short Shirt performs. He mocks and warns against Buller, the raper man. Warning, warning: outrageous in his actions of lassoing a young girl and dragging her into a building and then raping her. Whether Buller appreciates this song remains unknown. In prison, the rumor has it, the inmates treat him badly; he had said: "God Save the Queen."

Sandra (my girlfriend in St. Thomas) is coming home for carnival. I long to see her, but the libido of the season has infected me. I want to screw, in earnest, Isabella and Joan and, in addition, to test my lure's prowess on others.

Sandra's people live in Villa past the railroad tracks (the now empty road of the old sugarcane trains). I walked the miles to their house, several times. Finally, she arrives, and we meet at Blue's empty house. As soon as I close the door, Sandra's eyes, which are large and brown, narrow, lowering her shades on public modesty. Red-man's big lips part slightly, showing with the creased rigor in my mouth both my un-perjured and perjured lust. Sandra's skin, colored a glowing darken-bronze, is always sweetly pliant. Clinging to it, rejoining my mouth to it, drowning time's reign in the union, I am with her and with the score of others I wish for. My hips move as though through them all. "Ease up no, man, it's not a little bud yah got yah know." Letting all the dream bodies disjoin, I sweat with her and find joy in her flesh. Ruth comes into the room. "Oh! Oh! Sorry!" Embarrassment, always a heavily-mannered social trait, falls from my face.

Cock-cock-ah-do, me ah cock-fowl too!

Carnival approaches: the days and the nights take to the rhythms of fete: both allow sleep to become suspect during their spans. Of course, not all Antiguans abide by this quasi-formal alteration, but it is only that one cannot sustain its rigors that cause transgressions. The iron bands come in early morning. Melodious pinging of iron challenges then breaches the walls of sleep. "Boy Blue! Get tup, man! Ah wha you sleep for?" Outside, dark men in the pre-dawn glisten with sweat under cloud-splashed moonlight. Many wear tatters, showing off their muscles to greater effect. "Fire one, no?" "Boy, me nah got no rum here tahl." "Boy, wha wrong with yor rass." "Me nah got none." "It's carnival, yah know." "Me ah owe you one." The revelers move on, playing on iron. The retreated blasphemer sleep pours forth from the walls and fills the rooms, and once again, it hardens around us all.

Deh man dem soft; dem waun for sleep; iron man in duh road.

Carnival makes for crowns to be worn, and titles to be borne after contests are won. "Kai-so," Calypso, reigns as the sound of carnival. Who will be Calypso Monarch? What will be the Road March?

Michlein, another friend from St Thomas, has come home for carnival. Red-man and she are walking down the road after her group has won a contest, and she is the official person keeping the crown. I ask to wear it while we walk. Someone approaches me: "How did you get that?" Blankly (with a slightly deficient focus) I look at Michelin, then at the young man: "It asked me to wear it yah know, cause it said it needs to be on a big head." The questioner cuts an inquisitive eye at Michelin, and then turns to me and laughs: "Ok, man," and continues down the road. Michelin looks at me, "Boy!" and schupts.

Wait until juve'.

Episodes live as separate books; the chronology between them vaguely presents itself.

Near a corner, on High Street, a man lingers; he is dressed up in black cowboy garb. Two six shooters (toy guns one hoped) are at his side; it is a superb carnival outfit. Never during Mardi Gras had I seen better, and never had I seen one on a black man, of course neither in movies nor on TV had one appeared either. Yet the truth of such people, when thought about, seems obvious. Colored men must have been in the old west; they went everywhere else. They would have had to dress like the other men who lived there. And, my people are a follow-fashion folk. Though transmuted through a circus lens, the man is correct. "Blue, I saw a man in a cowboy outfit." "Star Black. Remember Short Shirt's song: "Star Black the Ranger?" "Iss he?" "The man's bad bad, yah know. He can do tricks 'ah rass' with his guns." Not just a poppyshow, Star Black lives as natural circus.

"The Golden Peanut" sells food; hamburgers are on the menu. *Try one. Why not?* When Red-man opens his mouth, once again, everyone knows that I am a stranger. A clear skin man, with a muscular build, starts making conversation. "Hey Jack, yah got a light?" I give him a book of matches; the man gives a box of matches back in return. It seems odd, but OK. The stranger claims that he is from the states. He uses American slang, especially "yeah, Jack," a good deal of the time, a bit too much. The conversation gets strained on my part because of geography; the man has it all wrong, and I don't know how to respond. New Jersey is in New York, and Connecticut is south of Washington. Chicago is near Philadelphia. "Yeah, boss," is the best answer I can give. When the food comes it is as odd as the talk. The hamburgers are about two inches in diameter, smaller than Grandma Adele's biscuits. Five would have gone down easily.

During the daily question period: "Blue, the hamburgers are tiny." "Yeah man, I don't eat out much, yah nah get your money's worth." "And why the match thing?" "Yah can't find book matches, only box matches. He wanted the pack, so he gave you the box." "Who is the dude?" "Man U. He played pro soccer in England. He wants to be a Yankee so bad." "He ought to learn his geography better."

A Carnival Principle (with extension): two pre-teens, one "thumps" the other; the injured one cries out and looks about for a stone to "chop" his tormenter. A man grabs him and shakes him slightly, shooing the other one off: "You, can't fight, it's carnival." "You cannot kill an ant or pluck a hair" is told to pilgrims on the hajj. The discipline of un-action has wide-flung roots that rests in many types of social earth.

Juve' is coming.

Brissive and I get on well. Brissive, an excellent driver, does not love the lower gears. The moke roars in its tiny fashion, not with the full throat of an adult lion, more like to a hoarse juvenile. In the midst of sound, we ride. Thunder Road becomes Rum Road or, more properly, Grogg Road. On one occasion we three go up to Nelson's Dockyard. It comes up again when we are returning; no one has a bottle opener. "Use your teeth no?" "Boy, me can't do dat deh." My teeth are too soft.

In the road next day, an unmistakable sound comes to me; fifes are playing. A licking kind of snap, the way a whip sounds, counter points the jig. The shifting crowd uncovers what looks like a street performance. The costumed musicians are a small fife and drum corps. "It's John Bull." "Wha?" The remaining performers are body-costumed, and wear masks, and small horns. They move in mock of bulls goring the crowd and each other, but the whip cracks in earnest both on the ground, and on the humped backs of the men in the bull suits. "They pad themselves so they can take blows." Above it all, by height and looks, towers the man with the whip, cracking it as a stern overseer would. The jig's tune sets Red-man on edge. The snare drums beat out a tattoo, which moves between the sounds in the eerie ditty: Tourette-afflicted screech birds marching/stamping in boots. "It's Bilay and the Highlanders." When the repetitive sound slackens in intensity or pace, a menacing look comes from the "severe, bleak-faced old man." A more perfect-looking driver of the damned could not be imagined. Thin, tall, and dark, he is the show in my eyes. His severe outfit, dark and somber as he, becomes him. His gaze, watchful like that of the blood-beaked hawk, takes in all; none of his troupe can rest. "Blue?" "That's Bilay, the butcher, a Monstratten. He sponsors the troop. The man loves cricket, yah know?" "Ah so?" "Yeh, boy. At matches, if someone does something spectacular, he runs out and puts money in their hand."

The image, modified slightly, appeals. A goateed Black Mephisto, lethal with his working hand, takes his leisure with largesse in his heart.

Wait till juve'

MayLock Inn.

"Powerful" talk, John Bunyan sized bragging told by much less heroic men, was not the norm, but it could generate itself in an unpredictable fashion. Everyman has the right to build up his narrative. Blue's wisdom on this is: you must know how to "pick sense from nonsense." Novo, a man in his forties, works as a carpenter on the job in St Thomas. For several nights he has been with a twenty-or-so "biggie." Bragging and confirming his right to boast: "Boy, I threw six water in she last night, yah know." "Wha!" "Humm." Out of earshot, "He too powerful for me, boy." "Huuh, he lie too fucking much."

"Wait till juve'"

By chance Red-man goes into a store on High Street to buy a beer. Behind the counter, the slim, dark-complexioned girl, eyes me with suspicion. For practice, I try my chat on her; her face never softens. Taking to her from her being standoffish, I try again to guile out a smile. Her eyes remain fixed as well as her mouth. Encouraged by the challenge, every four days or so I visit the store. She waits on me, but she keeps her face closed.

Will her eyes ever soften toward me? I long to see her smile.

In the road:

A large man walks in front, it seems, yet the hips have a curvature usually spotted on a woman. The erect carriage ends with a fitted pair of pants enclosing a well-formed backside. At six feet one, man or woman, the person has size. Looking neither to the left nor the right, the face, with a beautiful, unmottled complexion of mahogany brown, perhaps with makeup on, gazes above most people, almost with contempt. A soft jiggle in the chest may or may not indicate breasts. "Blue, das a man or a woman?" "Das Kisha." "Is it a man or a woman?" "Boy, deh got man who love he yah know; deh into dat." "Nobody trouble he?" "He from here, he got people here. Yah trouble he, yah got problems."

"Juve' is coming."

But fundamental Christian rocks lie under all the roads. Roads that have borne clinking iron anklets now freely lead to places of worship where God, Christ, bible, Sabbath, pastor, hell, baptism, salvation, and heaven mix with the soil of the earth, which muddies in the rain. On concrete ground, High Street Cathedral stands, armored "at point cap-a-pie," with spire above and stone bulwark below. The protections of the salvation it offers, most of which come from the squeezings of the dry rag of death, are irrelevant to Red-man. For a blissful sloth, from being gluttoned on life, has firmly gripped me in its sweet languor.

Monday:

"Juve' or J'ouvert: from jour ouvert, or dawn/daybreak."

Blue wakes me. Everyone else is already up and softly about, with sleep still in the air. The wee hours have not gone. Outside, small groups of people are in the road: clusters moving, buzzing within themselves. *Shadows of emboldened memories stoke withered longings that sit just behind my understanding: seeing The Zulus, whose disembarking from the royal barge starts Mardi Gras; hearing the Indians at so fresh an hour.* Through the unbiased air of pre-dawn comes the faint, elastic sounds of bass pans. *BOOMP BOOMP BOOMP:* spectral heartbeats of imperious jumbies come from Dahomey, Congo, Ife, Ghana, and Timbuktu. They command the not-dead to dance as one people. The restless dead need see celebration for that which they still revere: living life with joy. The Dark-Rising-to-Dawn becomes the coquette, teasing by slightly raising, and showing red and azure undergarments, with cock-fowls crowing in delight at the show. Approaching town, the clusters begin to join. It is still dark, but the street is full as a tree, nectar pregnant, swarmed with bees. The higher-tuned pans begin to reach out. Bands are in the road; now one's ears and feet rule: choose a band. Order comes to each throng. In front and back of the trolleys, lines form. Moving, dancing, all feet and ears are in sync. Some hold the person next to them, hand in hand, or body to body; others keep their position without holding anyone. It has started. Dawn rises and leaves in haste, leaving, fully born, the thing called juve': the official time of communal exultation.

Those who enjoy first row seats must pay more: the steel-band trolleys move along by hands pulling them. Red-man, a child of two left feet, finds his place as a red workhorse towing a cart. For the first time in my life, I become part of a carnival parade. Hauling and dancing, at the same time, tax my coordination; too much of my right foot crosses too far to that of my left; a rolling wheel catches the tip of my right shoe. I try to pull my foot out from the shoe; I can't. The wheel moves slowly forward. Curling my big toe gives me a knuckled-up saving space, the wheel rolls. My entire foot will be crushed; jelly smooshed through fingers is my image of the coming ordeal. Blue sees this and runs to me. The big toe now feels the beginnings of a crushing pinch. Both of us try to stop the cart being hauled by a dozen strong men. This is the necessity; the impossibility is its actuality. Men riding on the iron trolley, seeing the struggle, immediately understand the necessity. Jumping down, they seize the railing of the cart. The foot-saviors bring the moving heft of two and a half tons to heel; rusty patinas of iron wheels are left on the road's surface. I get my foot out and then my shoe. A tiny part of the big toe, quite rightly, has been strongly pinched. Gratitude, expressed by Red-man and Blue, is given to all. The cart starts again. The incident lingers, but in an odd way. The near loss of my foot seems the dross in the recollection; its sustaining weight rests in the unbidden help that has been given.

Competing bands are playing road-march candidates. My ears have learned to hear the bass, and thus I find my feet. All bands are open to me now. I leave Blue and Lee and move out into the ten thousand-strong sea. I "bounce up on" an old woman; we sway together. I laugh and she grins in delight with not a tooth in her smile. The oddness of so gummed a mouth loses itself in the hug we give each other, and then our feet go on separate ways. I hail up people with whom the only bond lies in the living joy of the moment. A radio commentator asks me how I like carnival. Like an ass, I revert to a bray. I try to tell of how I know Mardi Gras, and this is great because…. They move the mike to a more suitable mouth. *The old need not be recalled in the midst of a new birth.* The slide and glide of thousands of feet strike sparks in the road: "Antigua on fire." The blind hear the crackling burning; the deaf see the flames; the lame man's foot twitches in heated sync, while I, the stranger, with my clumsy feet made nimble, dance away from my distance. This falls into the pyre and it is immolated. Lee and Blue walk to Carnival City with Sandra and her friends, and me. I, being the odd one out when the talk turns serious, keep silent. "I think the melody is weak," said of one candidate for Road march. "No not really, the first horn is weak." "Uhmm?" These are discussions beyond my understanding.

Carnival!!

Carnival's parades come and go; the road march is chosen. Blue and I sleep through these hours; we each have a huge overflow of youthful carnival memories to lie upon.

Next day in town, we are walking together: "…the red one, the red one, he, for cart, on he foot." I look at a group of young men, somewhat blankly; they are pointing, laughing, and smiling. "They were the ones who stopped the cart." Breaking out into grin upon grin, Red-man hails them up: "Yeah

Man! Yes Man! Yes Boss! Hail up the Man!" They hail me back smiling. My eyes, now widely open in glee, see four girls looking at me and screaming in terror. Then, my green twosome, bugging out even more from the puzzlement, cause the women to take quick steps, distancing themselves from me. "Him got deh'bul eyes!" "Look, look, him got the deh'bel eye!" Crestfallen, Red-man stares; Blue laughs. "Nah study dem tahll. Talk nice and you can blaze all of them. Boy, you should loan me yah face for a day, yah know."

The fete is done; nighttime will need new diversions. Pressed down under strong moonlight, ten men sit on the ground in Pasture. The flatness of the land gives the stars bragging space; they take it all the way to the horizon. The Boy Scout sky of Indian Village, Sturbridge, and Cape Cod are the only comparatives. The talk goes back and forth, while the dense ear of Red-man blocks its entrance to my understanding. No one pays the least attention to me or my deafness. "...dematakme..." A shooting star blazes down toward the west, "...an-demahwipethemahbuttom." Chikeets' gravel-monotone voice (in itself one of the most unusual voices Red-man has ever heard) drones on and on. Men are snickering at his story. It just happens, in stealth; Red-man realizes that his ears have opened. I understand much of what Chikeets is saying, at least enough to get the story: "Dem man com to mah house an take me sheets and tear them and wipe dem bottom with em." Comprehension comes and goes; when the talk finishes, we two leave. "Blue, I understood at least half of what was said." "I told you that in time you would." But the euphoria mixes with the horror of what has been within the lyrical words: the sport torture of a mongoose. Language, the beautiful, changing, amoral vessel can carry all: the known; that which could be known; and that which had no meaning to be known.

Around noon the next day, two men drop by the house to hail up Blue. Ray and Grey have come from Libertas. Looking at, and hearing Red-man speak they turn to Blue:

"Ah who he be? 'Im sound like 'im from Antigua, but"

"He one of Nelson's people."

"Oh."

Defined by sight and sound, I am given place; my temperament puts me at ease. Ray, Gray, and I ride to town. Stopping by Junie's place for beer, we roll spliffs. Then we sit on the floor in a small, unadorned room, leaning on walls or the bed, and talk of man things. Affirming beliefs, and holding onto differences, without rancor, broad-grin laughs are always there. The herb is good in flavor, and sufficient in potency, and all are smokers who know the ways of the head; no novices are here. The Heinekens oil our throats. Seamless chat mounts itself on time's horse and rides the hours with it. Red-man reaches DeSouza Road at dusk. Blue stands outside in the front yard. "Mapson's home." The front door has been left ajar. Walking inside, I see a sheeny, dark bronze-colored man standing with his back to us. He turns around and braces himself with the sway of one who is intoxicated. His face doesn't resemble Blue's or Samwell's; it has more of their mother Davii's contours. Blue introduces Red-man. Mapson looks carefully at me; profound intelligence sits in his gaze. "Well, Sir, do you know..." He begins spitting out facts, in the fashion of a berserker performing his madness in battle, determined to overcome with his cudgels made of words. Pummeling barrages rhythmed in Oxford English. The slight grin tells of him reveling in this prowess, and also of the desperation in displaying it in so vulgar a fashion. The impotent will of a drunk is trying to stitch together, provisionally, a shredded pride. In time his energy fails; he passes out.

"Blue, wha-appen?" nodding toward the sleeping Mapson. "Aah man," shaking his head, "'Im kill 'e best friend, 'im spar, in a car accident." "Me ass hole!" "'E couldn't handle it; 'im start for drink, and 'im nah stop. 'E used to be so good, a teacher, winning awards," Blue breaks off with a hard sigh. The slaughter of all those hours of learning and their promise lies grossly snoring across a bed. Saddened; we walk into the kitchen without speaking. Through the back door comes the spray of a vanishingly light shower sprinkling the darkened earth. Wadadly, too, mourns for one of its lost children.

It is the last Saturday; we go to the market. It has all manner of "things," many are unknown. But my ignorance does not merit a scolding as I had been given on St. Thomas; here, I have a guide. Small black pineapples, like painted miniatures done for a whatnot stand, are in stalls. "Blue, are those real?" "That's Antigua-Black, the sweetest pineapples in the world." "All right." "No bullshit, they don't let you take them out of the country." "Why dey so good?" "Me can't say just why, but that's what they are." The image fits, Antigua Black, nothing can sweet more. But instead we buy cane, strip it, and chew it until it's dry. It too is sweet, like my grandfather's back in New Orleans.

The near-three weeks have ended; we leave tomorrow.

MacManus, O'Rourke, Keggan, Grant, Verret, Berrigan, Coffee, Hall,

Hull, Pavalak, Messina and Hughes: all the black-garbed Irishmen and their brother kind had re-moored my colored barque for the darkness of my own spirit-trek.

Red-man has passed through his minute Antillean tale; it unfolded; it recurves black.

BLACK STAR, RED SON

Boy Blue and Red-man leave Antigua for St. Thomas. LIAT (also, Leave Island Any Time), still consistent, arrives late. We get a drop up to Garden Street and ride the way in silence. The cool night has even turned off Blue's oven-house, but the air rasps, and all the sounds of Long Path are disjointed. We, too, part. Red-man climbs the stairs knowing that the undying beast, called work, is hitching itself again to the rising sun. It rises, and with Biggie and Rose the old days nudge themselves back into dominance. The resurrection ascends on schedule, floor by floor. Blue, the alien, keeps his place. But Red-man's color-qualified vaginal-legitimacy, which gives him Yankee status, has altered; it now encompasses more. Lines of force, generated by brazen blackness dancing ten thousand strong in the street, have led Red-man to turn toward a deeper south. There the heated blue eyes that watch the Negro behave under law have been crossed. The rod of command is less niggardly; it beats, with equal vigor, all who transgress its colorless edicts of: "No one shall..."

Beneficent, smiling Wadadly, the black sun, is shining upon its new red child.

"Am I not black with light?"

"You gave to me a dark sight."

"Will you remember me?"

"Constantly."

In the years that pass: Boy Blue, never liking his nickname, alters it to Darius. He and his family move to another island. After getting his green card, they go to the states. Red-man becomes a teacher, then a father. To feed my family, I change location and become a salesman. But for the next quarter of a century, scores of times during each year, Red-man awakes from sleep confused. In my dreams, my mind has been flung back along a time continuum that intersects with the place of the sweet, black, pineapple.

In my hundreds of visitations, I wander along the trails of my memory. I am just off High Street. Red-man is smoking herb in the country. Star Black is in the road; Short Shirt is singing; Andy Roberts is crippling wickets; Viv Richards is crippling boundaries; I am in Pasture listening to Chek-eets drone on; I hear Brissive's Mini Moke revving; Red-man is watching a movie at the Deluxe; I am in Sandra, sweating with her flesh; Red-man is near Villa's railroad tracks; or in Zachariah's store, trying to get the tall, slim, black girl to like me. Even after twenty-five years, her eyes are wary. I always leave the store sighing, for Red-man longed to swoon, imagining the inky velvet of our dark communion.

Silver Anniversary

HOLY GHOST CHURCH
NEW ORLEANS, LOUISIANA

1916   *1941*

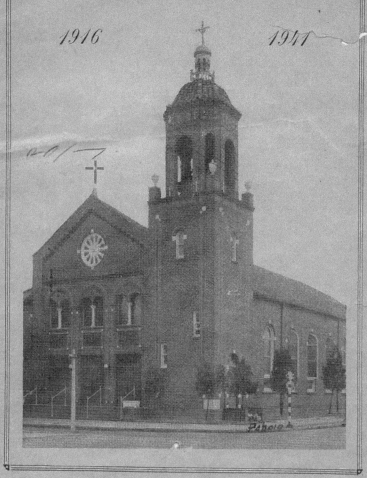

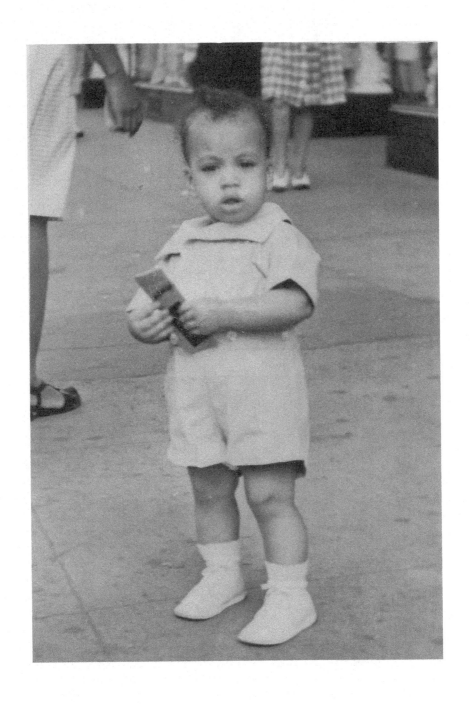

All photos property of the author. Original photos courtesy of C. Brookes; Holy Ghost Parish 25th Anniversary Program 1941; Villard Palladio; and Courtney Gabrielson. Special thanks to: Caroline, Betsy, Myiesha V. Henry, Girard Muton III, Deborah Willis, Nicole, Twin City Coffee House, Diane, Nana, Mia, Jonathan, Twila, Angela, Greasy, Alva, Ted & Sam, Uncle Rodney & Aunt Vonnie, Cha Cha, Big Al, Elaine, Jacinta, A. Jupiter, Analyn, William, Stacy, Bil, Alvin, Patti, Cooch, G. Oliver, Tri Tri, Monica, Carl, Bo, Faye, Heather, Richie, Odile, Lisa, Julie, Gerry, Melvin, and Cop.

Made in USA - Kendallville, IN
1218919_9798574974551
12.30.2020 0810